Student Companion to
Willa
CATHER

Willa Cather. Courtesy of the Library of Congress.

Student Companion to
Willa
CATHER

Linda De Roche

Student Companions to Classic Writers

Greenwood Press
Westport, Connecticut • London

Library of Congress Cataloging-in-Publication Data

De Roche, Linda.
    Student companion to Willa Cather / Linda De Roche.
        p. cm. — (Student companions to classic writers, ISSN 1522-7979)
    Includes bibliographical references (p.   ) and index.
    ISBN 0-313-32842-0 (alk. paper)
    1. Cather, Willa, 1873-1947—Criticism and interpretation. 2. Cather, Willa,
1873-1947—Examinations—Study guides. I. Title. II. Series.
PS3505.A87Z624   2006
813'.54—dc22   2006002441

British Library Cataloguing in Publication Data is available.

Library of Congress Catalog Card Number: 2006002441
ISBN: 0-313-32842-0
ISSN: 1522-7979

First published in 2006

Greenwood Press, 88 Post Road West, Westport, CT 06881
An imprint of Greenwood Publishing Group, Inc.
www.greenwood.com

Printed in the United States of America

The paper used in this book complies with the
Permanent Paper Standard issued by the National
Information Standards Organization (Z39.48-1984).

10 9 8 7 6 5 4 3 2 1

To Stéphane,
Who makes the journey worthwhile

Contents

Series Foreword

This series has been designed to meet the needs of students and general readers for accessible literary criticism on the American and world writers most frequently studied and read in the secondary school, community college, and four-year college classrooms. Unlike other works of literary criticism that are written for the specialist and graduate student, or that feature a variety of reprinted scholarly essays on sometimes obscure aspects of the writer's work, the Student Companions to Classic Writers series is carefully crafted to examine each writer's major works fully and in a systematic way, at the level of the nonspecialist and general reader. The objective is to enable the reader to gain a deeper understanding of the work and to apply critical thinking skills to the act of reading. The proven format for the volumes in this series was developed by an advisory board of teachers and librarians for a successful series published by Greenwood Press, Critical Companions to Popular Contemporary Writers. Responding to their request for easy-to-use and yet challenging literary criticism for students and adult library patrons, Greenwood Press developed a systematic format that is not intimidating but helps the reader to develop the ability to analyze literature.

How does this work? Each volume in the Student Companions to Classic Writers series is written by a subject specialist, an academic who understands students' needs for basic and yet challenging examination of the writer's canon. Each volume begins with a biographical chapter, drawn from published sources, biographies, and autobiographies, that relates the writer's life to his or her work. The next chapter examines the writer's literary heritage, tracing the literary influences of other writers on that writer and explaining and discussing the literary genres into which the writer's work falls. Each of the following chapters examines a major work by the writer, those works most frequently read and studied by high school and college students. Depending on the writer's canon, generally between four and eight major works are examined, each in an individual chapter. The discussion of each work is organized into separate sections on plot development, character development, and major themes. Literary devices and style, narrative point of view, and historical setting are also discussed in turn if pertinent to the work. Each chapter concludes with an alternate critical perspective from which to read the work, such as a psychological or feminist criticism. The critical theory is defined briefly in easy, comprehensible language for the student. Looking at the literature from the point of view of a particular critical approach will help the reader to understand and apply critical theory to the act of reading and analyzing literature.

Of particular value in each volume is the bibliography, which includes a complete bibliography of the writer's works, a selected bibliography of biographical and critical works suitable for students, and lists of reviews of each work examined in the companion, both from the time the literature was originally published and from contemporary sources, all of which will be helpful to readers, teachers, and librarians who would like to consult additional sources.

As a source of literary criticism for the student or for the general reader, this series will help the reader to gain understanding of the writer's work and skill in critical reading.

Acknowledgments

My appreciation for Willa Cather's vision and artistry began in graduate school, when Joseph X. Brennan, Professor of English at the University of Notre Dame, opened her world to me. I extend my thanks to this man of fine intellect and sensitive perceptions.

I also thank Robert Jones, an English major at Wesley College, for research assistance and Deborah Stuck for technical assistance—and so much more.

My husband Stéphane continues to be my strength.

1

A Writer's Life

Willa Cather is so closely identified with the Nebraska prairies of her most famous novels that readers generally assume that she was native born. Like so many of her memorable characters, however, she too was a transplanted midwesterner. Born on 7 December 1873 in Back Creek Valley, near Winchester, Virginia, the nine-year-old child who moved with her family to a farm near Red Cloud, Nebraska, from the Shenandoah Valley in 1883 found the Divide, the high prairie land between the Republican and the Little Blue rivers, as foreign to her as it was to her pioneer heroines Alexandra Bergstrom and Ántonia Shimerda. The first of many subsequent journeys in her life, it was without doubt the most formative, for Nebraska's physical and cultural landscapes were so different from the picturesque wooded hills and the certainty provided by generations of Cathers resting already in the valley's graveyards that she would never again view the world from the same narrow perspective. During the remainder of her life, Cather would make other journeys—to the East Coast and the Southwest of America, to Europe and Canada. In these places, as well as others, she gathered the impressions and imagined the lives that she eventually transmuted into fiction. But always she returned to Red Cloud, the ground in which the writer grew.

Cather's early childhood in Virginia was not unpleasant. It was, however, crowded by family, extended generations of Cathers living in close proximity (Cather had been born on her maternal grand-mother's farm) as well as her own ever-increasing nuclear family (between 1873 and 1892, Cather's parents had seven children). To find her sense of separate self was a struggle. Indeed, as she observed in an appreciation of the British writer Katherine Mansfield's family stories "Prelude" and "At the Bay," every family member, even those in perfectly "harmonious families," lives a "double life: the group life," which everyone observes, and "the real life," which constitutes the singular self. "Always in his mind," Cather continued, "each member of these social units is escaping, running away, trying to break the net which circumstances and his own affections have woven about him" ("Katherine Mansfield," *Stories, Poems, and Other Writings* 877–78). Cather might as well have been speaking about personal experience here, for family history and allegiances were strong influences on her early life.

Cather's paternal ancestors had been colonial settlers from North-ern Ireland who built an "old conservative society" in the Virginia backcountry, she observed in an anonymous biographical sketch she wrote for her publisher Alfred Knopf. Settlers in the area, located near the West Virginia border, were fiercely independent, and because slavery had never really taken root there, the Civil War, which occurred just a few years before Cather's birth, had been particularly divisive. But Cather was born into an "ordered and settled" society. "People in good families were born good," she explained, "and the poor mountain people were not expected to amount to much" (O'Brien 60). Willow Shade, her paternal grandparents' farm, where she and her parents moved the year after her birth, was the sort of place from which to make a good beginning.

Life on Willow Shade was pleasant for Cather. Her father, Charles Fectigue Cather, had studied law, but lacking the drive to practice, the mild-mannered Virginian instead managed the family sheep farm. His daughter remembered the pleasure of accompanying him on his rounds. She also enjoyed listening to the stories of the local women who came to Willow Shade to make quilts or going to Timber Ridge, where a neighbor, Mrs. Anderson, could be counted on for the local gossip. The household was lively, especially with the addition of two brothers, Roscoe, born in 1877; Douglass, born in 1880; and a sister, Jessica, born in 1881. (Cather's other siblings—James, born in 1888; Elsie, born in 1890; and John Esten, called Jack, born in 1892—were Nebraska natives.) To help her mother, Mary Virginia Boak Cather, the family employed Mrs. Anderson's mildly retarded daughter Marjorie, who accompanied them to Nebraska. Perhaps most important for Cather, her maternal grandmother, Rachel Seibert Boak, lived with them. This strong, stoic, and affectionate woman taught her granddaughter to read from the Bible, John Bunyan's *Pilgrim's Progress,* and *Peter Parley's Universal History.* In an early volume of poetry, Cather paid tribute to this woman who helped to mother her by beginning with a poem titled "Grandmither, think not I forget."

In 1883, Cather's life at Willow Shade ended when fire destroyed the sheep barn and her grandfather, who had moved to Nebraska in 1877, refused to rebuild it. Bowing to his father's pressure, Charles Cather moved his wife, four children, mother-in-law, as well as several cousins and household employees to begin a new life halfway across the country on the Nebraska Divide. For a young girl whose life had been "bound up in the woods and hills and meadows around it," Cather was to confess in a 1913 interview published in *The Philadelphia Record,* it was as if she had been "thrown out into a country as bare as a piece of sheet iron" (Woodress, *Willa Cather: Her Life and Art* 31). She suffered initially from a sense of dislocation: "it was a kind of erasure of personality," she remembered. But soon she adapted to prairie life, and it eventually fueled her imagination and inspired her writing.

Until the 1860 Homestead Act, which legitimized settlers' claims to ownership of up to 160 acres of land as long as they farmed it for five years, the Nebraska Territory, which had been created in 1854, was little more than a vast expanse of endless undulating prairie, descriptions of which fill Cather's first Nebraska novel, *O Pioneers!* (1913), and her third, *My Ántonia* (1918). Buffalo roamed freely, and Native Americans were its principal inhabitants. Then Colorado's silver-mining boom drew a steady stream of wagons across the territory, transforming it into a thoroughfare. With the Homestead Act, however, and the extension of the Union Pacific railway between Missouri and the Rocky Mountains, one line of which, the Burlington, made Red Cloud a busy stopping point by 1879, European immigrants and American settlers like the Cathers, in search of new opportunities and beginnings, began to tame the territory. Their task was difficult. Traveling across country on foot or in horse-drawn covered wagons known as "prairie schooners," they built sod houses or dug caves into the rolling red hills, initially more concerned with farming the land that had to sustain them than in erecting proper houses. They fought drought and blizzards and plagues of grasshoppers as well as the Native Americans whose lands they were usurping (Red Cloud had been a Sioux chief). When they arrived in 1883, the Cathers were fortunate not to suffer such hardships, living on the family farm during their first 18 months on the prairie and then moving into a small frame house in Red Cloud, 16 miles away, where Charles Cather first sold livestock and farm equipment and then opened a real estate and loan office. This history, however, was an inescapable fact of life there and the backdrop to the immigrants' stories that Cather delighted in hearing.

Those immigrants opened whole new worlds of culture and experience to the young girl, who visited their homesteads and developed friendships with many of the pioneer women. Indeed, Cather modeled her Ántonia on a Czech immigrant, Annie Pavelka. Waves of immigrants from the European Continent had settled in the Nebraska Territory, bringing with them their Old World customs and beliefs. Germans arrived first, fleeing the political revolutions of 1848. Then came an influx of poorly equipped Czechs, or Bohemians, like *My Ántonia*'s Shimerdas, in search of opportunities such as property ownership denied them in their feudal homeland. In no other state did they settle in such numbers. After the Homestead Act, Scandinavians, learning of the availability of land from their countrymen who had settled in Wisconsin and Minnesota, rushed to stake their claims, and communities of French immigrants also sprang up. By the end of the century, the state's capital, Lincoln, was even home to a large Russo-German population. In a 1923 essay on Nebraska published in *The Nation,* Cather fondly recalled this multicultural landscape, the essence of which she had memorably captured as well in her novels in scenes that revealed its diversity and complexity, from the French Catholic fair in *O Pioneers!* to Mr. Shimerda's Christmas visit to the Burden homestead in *My Ántonia.* Aware of their losses—for she, too, had been wrenched from the only world that she had ever known—Cather admired the immigrants' industry and perseverance as well as their determination to preserve something from their past, some quality of life distinct from any she had encountered in Virginia. She knew the human cost of their bold decisions to journey to the New World, perhaps best epitomized in Mr. Shimerda's suicide, and their difficult struggle to survive. Perhaps for this reason, she invested their lives with such significance in her fiction. Anyone could make a success of a tale of battle or exploration, but for Cather these immigrants were the real adventurers. From her early contact with them, Cather the writer would find her first true subject.

Life in Red Cloud, the bustling prairie town to which her family moved in 1884, provided Cather with another set of experiences from which to fashion a self. For the first time, she engaged in formal schooling and proved to be an eager and industrious student. She also enlarged her education by forming friendships with exceptional people from whom she could learn. A shopkeeper, the Englishman William Ducker, taught her Greek and Latin, and together they read the classics by Virgil, Ovid, Homer, and Anacreon. Her French-German neighbors the Wieners introduced her to European literature (O'Brien 80–81). With the four Miner sisters, whose mother was the daughter of a Norwegian oboe player and all of whom were the inspirations for *My Ántonia*'s Harling family, Cather engaged in amateur theatricals. She also attended her first professional theatrical performances when traveling stock companies stopped at the newly opened Red Cloud Opera House. From the time she moved to Red Cloud until she graduated from high school in 1890, Cather seemed determined to extend her intellectual horizons. Even at night in the constricting household that demanded the cultivation of a "double life," the adolescent, rather like *The Song of the Lark*'s heroine Thea Kronborg, escaped to the attic or her father's office to read everything from Mark Twain's *The Adventures of Huckleberry Finn* and Robert Louis Stevenson's *The Swiss Family Robinson* to Thomas Carlyle's *Sartor Resartus* and Shakespeare's *Antony and Cleopatra*. She also began to build a personal library with a translation of *The Iliad* and other works such as Jacob Abbott's *Histories of Cyrus the Great and Alexander the Great* and George Eliot's *The Spanish Gypsy*. Delivering a speech in defense of scientific inquiry and experimentation, "Superstition versus Investigation," at her high school graduation, Cather was well prepared for a move to Lincoln, where she would begin the next phase of her education.

Cather was certainly eager to begin that phase. While she was extremely fond of her brothers (Roscoe and Douglass were lifelong traveling companions, and she helped Jack enroll in technical college in Pittsburgh), the intelligent and aspiring adolescent had begun early to rebel against familial expectations and social conventions and to define her independent self. Cather's parents had named their daughter Wilella at birth to honor an aunt who had died of diphtheria, and they called her "Willie" as a child. Even before the family move to Nebraska, however, Wilella had begun to claim her identity, naming herself "Willa Love Cather," in honor, she claimed, of an uncle, William Seibert Boak, who had been killed in the Civil War and of the Dr. Love who had attended her birth. Two years after the family moved to Red Cloud, the imaginative 13-year-old, who admitted that she enjoyed becoming "Caesar or Napoleon at will" (*Kingdom of Art* 339), reinvented herself once again. She cropped her hair, began dressing in a boy's suit and cap, and started signing herself "William Cather, M. D." "I was determined then to be a surgeon," she remembered (*Kingdom of Art* 114). Two years later she was conducting experiments with dissection and vivisection in pursuit of that goal. Two years into her college career, however, Cather began to grow her hair once again, abandoning her masculine-identified self, perhaps because it was no longer necessary to rebel against the kind of life that seemed inevitable for a woman from the confines of home and Red Cloud. Indeed, as a member of the first generation of college-educated women to attend public, coeducational institutions such as the University of Nebraska, Cather would become one of the turn of the century's "New Women." These "single, highly educated, economically autonomous" women, according to historian Carroll Smith-Rosenberg, were eager to make their mark in the traditional male professions and to challenge existing gender expectations yet confident of their "rightful place within the genteel world" (245). At university, in other words, Cather could finally become herself.

During her five years at university, Cather began what a biographer, Hermione Lee, calls the "first stage" of her "long apprenticeship" (38), 20 years, in fact, to literature. Because students who attended rural schools were required to complete a two-year preparatory course of study before matriculation to the University of Nebraska, Cather enrolled as a two-year student at the Latin School, but she was so well prepared that officials exempted her from one year. She originally intended to pursue a career in science, but her plans changed when, in the spring of 1891, she learned that an essay she had written on Thomas Carlyle was going to be published in the *Nebraska State Journal* after being submitted by her English instructor (Lewis 31). By the time she began her course work at the University of Nebraska that fall, Cather had settled on a literary career. In preparation, she studied Greek and Latin as well as the classics, French and German literatures and languages, Shakespeare and other Elizabethan dramatists, and nineteenth-century British and American writers including Robert Browning; Alfred, Lord Tennyson; Ralph Waldo Emerson; and Nathaniel Hawthorne. She also became active in literary, debating, and theatrical societies and in student publications, including the university newspaper, the *Hesperian,* of which she eventually became managing editor and to which she contributed short fiction through-out her university career.

Indeed, it was Cather's work on the *Hesperian* that led to her first literary career. Passionate about literature and extremely well read, Cather had little interest in literary scholarship and enjoyed instead the opportunity to publish her poetry, articles, and stories, whatever she felt inspired to write, in the newspaper. When, during her second year at university she studied journalism with Will Owen Jones, the managing editor of the *Nebraska State Journal,* he hired her imme-diately, so impressed was he by her talent, to write a regular column, each one earning her a dollar. Cather quickly became notorious for her strong opinions about the arts and contemporary affairs. In one column, for instance, she attacked the "primal slime" of naturalistic writers Emile Zola and Hamlin Garland; in another, she praised the romantic fiction of Rudyard Kipling, Robert Louis Stevenson, Alexan-der Dumas, and Anthony Hope. Her theatrical reviews, Jones recalled, could be particularly devastating, even to actors of national reputa-tion. They worried, he said, what criticism would flow "from the pen of that meatax young girl" (*Kingdom of Art* 16), whose enjoyment of the theater and lifelong passion for the opera made her unwilling to see compromised her high artistic standards and her native idealism. By the time she graduated from university in 1895, Cather was work-ing as associate editor of the *Lincoln Courier,* for which she wrote a regular column, "The Passing Show."

Until the publication of her first work of fiction, the novella *Alexan-der's Bridge* in 1912, journalism was primarily Cather's principal occu-pation. In June 1896, the ambitious young woman left Red Cloud for Pittsburgh, Pennsylvania, after securing, with the help of friends, a job as editor of the *Home Monthly,* a women's magazine designed to com-pete with the *Ladies' Home Journal.* Its editorial policy was utterly conventional, its pages filled with stories of moral uplift and articles on nursing and gardening. Cather found it "namby-pamby" (O'Brien 227) and chafed under the restrictions, but she was determined to succeed, took pride in her new responsibility, and sometimes, under various pseudonyms, almost single-handedly wrote whole issues. Her escape from such pedestrian journalism was the column she contin-ued to write for the Lincoln paper and the theatrical reviews she began to contribute to the *Pittsburgh Leader.* In these pieces, she could give vent to personal opinion and exercise her intellect.

Cather soldiered on at the *Home Monthly* for a year, until the pub-lication changed ownership, and then she resigned her position.

A few months later, after spending the summer in Red Cloud, Cather returned to Pittsburgh to work on the *Leader*'s telegraph desk, a position that provided a monthly salary but few challenges. (She did, however, earn additional money by writing drama criticism and then added a "Books and Magazines" column as well.) Increasingly frustrated by the mechanical nature of her work and longing for more time to fulfill her literary ambitions, Cather resigned from the *Leader* in the spring of 1900. She had published an incredibly large number of articles as well as some poems and stories and continued to work as a freelance journalist for some time, but she was determined to become a writer.

Cather's move to Pittsburgh provided the opportunity to develop not only professionally but also socially and culturally. Lincoln, Nebraska, despite its "reputation as a complacent, pious, conservative place" (Lee 39), had been settled by European immigrants and transplanted easterners, and the prairie city, according to Lee, "far from being a 'wild west' frontier town" (39), boasted several newspapers as well as two theaters that regularly hosted performances by national touring companies, which Cather frequently attended. The cultural life of Pittsburgh, Pennsylvania, however, made Lincoln seem provincial. Granted, the city may have been built on coal and steel empires, its mines and factories may have made it seem permanently gray and dreary, but the captains of industry who had made their fortunes there—Andrew Carnegie, H. J. Heinz, George Westinghouse, and Andrew Mellon—had also invested in the city's museums, galleries, and educational institutions. In her columns for the *Lincoln Courier,* Cather could express her disdain for "St." Andrew Carnegie's literary pretensions and the absurdity of his providing a French Renaissance library and concert hall for immigrants working 12-hour shifts in the Homestead mines (*The World and the Parish* 857), but it was also difficult to deny herself the pleasure of the paintings and sculpture at the Carnegie Arts Institute, the performances at the Carnegie Opera House, or the sounds of the Pittsburgh Symphony Orchestra. Nor did the rising star of the city's literary societies object to invitations to speak. She also took advantage of the collections at the Carnegie Library to continue her education in European literatures and the classics. In Pittsburgh, as she had done first in Red Cloud and then in Lincoln, Cather again sought congenial friendships among people who could expand her world. She read French literature, for instance, with a German-American couple, George and Helen Seibel, and began a friendship with the actress Lizzie Hudson Collier and the composer

Ethelbert Nevin. Most important, however, she met Isabelle McClung, for whom she developed the deepest emotional feelings of her life.

McClung, the daughter of a wealthy and prominent Pittsburgh judge and his wife, was one in a series of passionate and erotic crushes that Cather had on other girls, actresses, and opera singers during adolescence and young adulthood, but she was, without doubt, the most important. At university, the object of her affection had been Louise Pound, a delicate-looking beauty who was as talented in athletics as she was brilliant in the classroom. (She eventually became a distinguished linguist and folklorist.) But Cather was hurt when she did not return her affection, and their friendship cooled, according to Sharon O'Brien, after Cather lampooned Pound's brother in the *Hesperian* (although they eventually resumed a correspondence [131]). Cather developed other close and lifelong friendships during this time as well, with Mariel Gere and Dorothy Canfield (later the novelist Dorothy Canfield Fisher), but nobody had replaced Pound in her affections. Then, in 1899, Cather met McClung. For the next 17 years, she would draw her chief emotional support and encouragement from her.

Shared interests in theater, music, and literature formed the basis of the friendship between Cather and McClung. When they met, McClung, according to Lee, was "challenging [her father's] orthodoxies by hobnobbing with 'Bohemians'" (58). She and Cather were soon inseparable. Cather visited often at the elegant family home on Murray Hill Avenue, where an attic sewing room would be converted into a private study for her, and eventually made it her primary residence from 1901 to 1906. With McClung, she made her first European journey, visiting the west of England; London, where she met the poet A. E. Housman; Paris, where she paid homage at the tombs of Balzac, Alfred de Musset, Alexander Dumas *fils,* and Heinrich Heine; Marseilles; and Provence. Under McClung's influence, she also began to take a feminine interest in her appearance, indulging her taste in satins, velvets, and bright colors, and finally overcoming the self-consciousness and insecurity that had made social life painful to her. Until 1916, McClung was the emotional center of Cather's life. Even when the author moved to New York in 1906, the women traveled together extensively and maintained a regular correspondence, which the intensely private Cather burned at McClung's death. So the writer was surprised and devastated when the woman she loved suddenly married the violinist Jan Hambourg shortly after her father's death that spring. Despite her hurt, Cather managed to retain their friendship until McClung's death in 1938, testimony to its importance to her life, but McClung's marriage was clearly one of the catastrophes in her life.

During the five years that Cather resided at the McClung home, she was in process of pursuing her literary career. Although she continued publishing as a freelance journalist, she was devoting her creative energy to the production of stories and poems and enjoying the success of publication in periodicals that included *Saturday Evening Post, Harper's Weekly,* and *Scribner's.* She was also teaching school, first Latin, composition, and algebra at Pittsburgh's Central High School for two years, then literature across the river at Allegheny High School for three years. A competent and conscientious teacher, Cather seems to have been well liked by her students, especially those with the ability to appreciate her intellect, but she never intended teaching to be her career. The publication of a volume of 37 poems as *April Twilights* in 1903 and the editor S. S. McClure's promise to publish her stories in *McClure's Magazine* and in book form guaranteed that it was not. In March 1905, Cather published her first collection of stories, *The Troll Garden* (with McClure, Phillips & Company), and by the end of the year she was already being welcomed by the literary establishment. Indeed, on 5 December 1905, Cather was present at a birthday dinner for Mark Twain at Delmonico's in New York City.

Cather's relationship with McClure gave shape to the next seven years of her professional career. In 1906, the writer accepted a job offer at *McClure's,* one of the most influential magazines of the "muckraking" era, and moved to New York City. Within a year, she had been sent on assignment to Boston, Massachusetts, where she verified, researched, and extensively revised Georgine Milmine's *The Life of Mary Baker G. Eddy and the History of Christian Science.* She returned to New York in the fall of 1908 to become managing editor of *McClure's.* A year later, she traveled to London to solicit manuscripts and make contacts with authors for *McClure's,* meeting the British novelists H. G. Wells and Ford Madox Ford and attending performances of the Abbey Theatre with the Irish writer and playwright Lady Gregory. Returning again to New York, Cather assumed sole editorial responsibility for the magazine when S. S. McClure went to Europe.

Cather's tenure at *McClure's* certainly enhanced her professional profile and gave her the opportunity to extend her circle of friends and literary acquaintances, but her schedule and responsibilities were punishing. Cather found it difficult to make time for her own writing, and although she published stories in *McClure's, Century,* and *Harper's* during this period, she was frustrated and discouraged that she was not developing as a writer. With the stress of six years' managerial and editorial work taking their toll on her energy and her confidence, Cather took a leave of absence from *McClure's* in 1911, which she extended in 1912. She never returned, however, after that extended leave, agreeing instead to accept the occasional special editing assignment and ghostwriting S. S. McClure's autobiography, working from his spoken reminiscences, in 1913 (Lewis 59-72). With the publication of that work, Cather's career in journalism (and her long apprenticeship) was behind her.

When she relocated to New York, Cather initially settled in the same Greenwich Village apartment building as Edith Lewis, a friend she had met three years before when she had spent a summer in Nebraska. Lewis, a native of Lincoln and a graduate of Smith College, admired the writer immensely, and Cather eventually helped her secure a position at *McClure's.* Two years later, after traveling again with McClung to Europe, where they spent several weeks in Italy, Cather moved into an apartment with Lewis at 82 Washington Place. In January 1913, they set up housekeeping in another Greenwich Village location, 5 Bank Street, where they would live for the next 14 years with Josephine Bourda, a Frenchwoman who cooked and kept house for them. Cather and Lewis lived together for the remainder of the writer's life at several other New York addresses, Lewis clearly devoted to her friend, Cather clearly reliant on the quiet, self-effacing woman who shared the same tastes, had a talent for making a comfortable home, and lent a critical eye to her manuscripts. (She did not, however, dedicate a novel to Lewis, as she did to McClung, 1915's *The Song of the Lark.*) Lewis was Cather's literary executrix, and she guarded her friend's reputation and privacy throughout her life. Even her memoir of Cather, *Willa Cather Living* (1953), is a model of reticence and likely would have pleased her companion.

The most important friendship that Cather developed during her *McClure's* years was with the New England writer Sarah Orne Jewett. Cather met Jewett during her posting to Boston at what by then had become the literary salon of Annie Adams Fields, the widow of the publisher James T. Fields, at 148 Charles Street. She became close friends with both women, visiting often at Fields's Beacon Hill home and Jewett's South Berwick, Maine, residence, and memorialized Fields in her essay "148 Charles Street" and Jewett in her essay "Miss

Jewett." Jewett's influence, however, was crucially important because the established writer of works including *The Country of the Pointed Firs, A Country Doctor,* and *Deephaven* understood Cather's doubts and frustrations and offered sound advice to the young writer about the concentration and dedication needed to become a writer. Cather admired many qualities of Jewett's work, and much of what she wrote about Jewett in her 1925 preface to a collection of her stories is true of Cather's fiction as well.

The *Pointed Fir* sketches, Cather observed, were "living things caught in the open, with light and freedom and air-spaces about them. They melt into the land and the life of the land until they are not stories at all, but life itself" ("Miss Jewett," *Stories, Poems, and Other Writings* 849). She admired Jewett's ability to render sympathetically and realistically the lives of "everyday people who grew out of the soil" ("Miss Jewett" 851) and her "ear" for "those pithy bits of local speech, of native idiom, which enrich and enliven her pages" ("Miss Jewett" 852). Their literary affinities made Jewett's advice to Cather particularly prescient: in a now-famous letter to the young writer, she urged, "I want you to be sure of your backgrounds ... you don't see them yet quite enough from the outside,—you stand right in the middle of each of them when you write, without having the standpoint of the looker-on who takes them each in their relations to letters, to the world.... You must find your own quiet centre of life, and write from that to the world" ("Miss Jewett" 248). Jewett's advice as well as her example—she was a woman writing outside the tradition of sentimental fiction—came at an important point in Cather's development. Indeed, she took Jewett's death on 24 June 1909 hard, writing to Fields that life without her, according to O'Brien, was "dark and purposeless" (349).

Cather's quest to find her "own quiet centre of life" was not immediately successful. In 1912, following its serial publication as *Alexander's Masquerade* in *McClure's,* Cather published, under its original title, *Alexander's Bridge,* her first novel. (In her preface to the 1922 edition of the work, however, the writer disclaimed it as her first novel because it did not develop the subject matter that she now recognized as her own and argued that she had in fact two first novels.) Indebted in its subject and style to Henry James, the American writer whose work she greatly admired, *Alexander's Bridge* earned Cather some kind and encouraging reviews. Yet even as she was meeting with this success, Cather was writing two stories with midwestern settings, "The Bohemian Girl" and "Alexandra," which she later incorporated into her novel *O Pioneers!* (1913), which were pointing the way toward her true voice and subject.

In the spring of 1912, after attending the seventy-fifth birthday dinner for the American novelist, critic, and editor William Dean Howells, Cather traveled to visit her brother Douglass in Winslow, Arizona, a trip that would liberate forever the best of her fiction from drawing room conventions. She spent the next three months exploring the American Southwest—visiting Native American ruins, negotiating steep canyons and rocky cliff dwellings, attending a Hopi snake dance—and forming a strong attachment with the region that persisted throughout her life. Cather spent the month of June in Nebraska, where she observed the wheat harvest for the first time in several years, and then she spent the remainder of the year in Pittsburgh, where, in her study at the McClungs, she wrote another midwestern story, "The White Mulberry Tree," which also became part of *O Pioneers!*. By June 1913, Cather had published her second first novel, *O Pioneers!*, which she dedicated to Sarah Orne Jewett, to enthusiastic reviews and with a very real sense of her fictional world.

Once she had claimed her territory, Cather published in rapid succession three other novels that drew on her midwestern experience, for, as she told a journalist in 1921, "All my stories have been written with the material that was gathered—no, God save us! not gathered but absorbed—before I was fifteen years old" (Bennett 232n). 1913's *O Pioneers!*, the story of Alexandra Bergson's struggle to tame the prairies and build a life on the Nebraska Divide, was followed in 1915 by *The Song of the Lark,* the tale of opera singer Thea Kronborg's rise to fame in the world beyond Moonstone, Colorado; 1918's *My Ántonia,* the story of a long and complex friendship between transplanted midwesterners Jim Burden and the Bohemian immigrant Ántonia Shimerda; and *One of Ours,* published in 1922, the story of Claude Wheeler's liberation from the American way of life by his service in Europe during World War I. She also published a second collection of stories, titled *Youth and the Bright Medusa,* in 1920, marking the beginning of a long and important professional relationship with Alfred A. Knopf, who would publish the remainder of her life's work. The first three of this group of novels rendered with dignity and sympathy the lives of pioneers on and immigrants to the American heartland at the turn of the twentieth century, and all of them received good to enthusiastic reviews. *One of Ours,* which Cather intended to title *Claude,* was inspired by the life of her cousin, G. P. Cather, who was killed in action at Cantigny, France, in 1918. The author conducted extensive research to lend authenticity to the novel, interviewing soldiers and touring French battlefields, yet critics attacked the work for romanticizing the war. The controversy, rather ironically, fueled sales, and in 1923 Cather received the Pulitzer Prize for fiction for the work.

Cather was now a famous American author, with all that such status accorded. Increasingly in demand for interviews and lectures and honorary degrees, she should have been enjoying her successes, but in the early to mid-1920s, Cather experienced a period of anxiety and depression. Years later, in fact, in an introduction written for her 1936 collection of essays, *Not Under Forty,* she admitted as much, writing, "The world broke in two in 1922 or thereabouts" and identifying herself with "the backward" who belong to "yesterday's seven thousand years." Reasons for her feelings are cause for speculation. It was the time of the "Lost Generation" in America, of disillusion in the aftermath of World War I, and Cather seems to have been affected by it, too. Her essays on Annie Fields and Sarah Orne Jewett, written during the 1920s, are nostalgic in tone; they poignantly recall another era that seemed preferable to her own. Visitors to Annie Fields's home at 148 Charles Street, she reminisced, could escape into "an atmosphere in which one seemed absolutely safe from everything ugly" ("148 Charles Street," *Stories, Poems, and Other Writings* 840); the past not only "lived on" but also "was protected and cherished, had sanctuary from the noisy push of the present" ("148 Charles Street" 842). Jewett's fiction, she tartly observed, with its evocation of "'the old moral certainties'" ("Miss Jewett," *Stories, Poems, and Other Writings* 857), was sadly incomprehensible to a modern generation "violently inoculated with Freud, hurried into journalism" ("Miss Jewett" 856). In the face of rapid change in postwar America, Cather, entering her fifties, was undoubtedly becoming increasingly conservative.

Health trouble may also have played its part in Cather's midlife depression. In January 1922, Cather was hospitalized for a tonsillectomy and spent several weeks recuperating in a Pennsylvania sanatorium; in 1923, she suffered from neuritis in her right arm and shoulder, a condition that made writing painful and for which she took mineral-bath treatments at Aix-en-Provence during a visit to France that summer. One critic, Sharon O'Brien, speculates that the neuritis was a physical sign of her creative paralysis or even the "punishment" she "half expected for venturing into such masculine territory" in *One of Ours* (384), and the condition may indeed have been psychosomatic.

Cather had, after all, been distressed by the controversial response to her novel. She had also had what seems a rather disappointing visit with Isabelle McClung Hambourg and her husband Jan at their villa near Paris that summer (Lewis 120–21). Whatever the reasons, Cather was clearly in emotional distress, and she sought comfort in the certainties of religion, undergoing confirmation with her parents in the Episcopal Church on 27 December 1922.

Cather's fiction of this middle period reflects the sense of frustration and anxiety that she was experiencing. In 1923, she published *A Lost Lady,* the story of Marian Forrester, the "lost lady" of the short novel's title, a woman of immense charm, grace, and sensibility who falls victim to her own attraction to an increasingly vulgar and commercial modern world. Its companion piece was 1926's *My Mortal Enemy,* the tale of another "lady," Myra Henshawe, a brilliant, generous, and charming young woman who sacrifices a fortune to marry the man she loves but, having fallen on hard times, grows jealous and bitter when her husband disappoints her, thereby becoming her "mortal enemy." The best of Cather's middle-period novels was *The Professor's House* (1925), the story of Professor Godfrey St. Peter, a man whose compromises to conventional life have, in middle age, made him increasingly frustrated and dissatisfied with his life choices, especially as he recalls his relationship with a brilliant student, Tom Outland, killed in World War I. The novel clearly reflected Cather's mood, as the other works also did, but it benefited, as the others did not, from her long and deep association with the American Southwest, which evoked in her the same emotion and meaning as her midwestern prairies. Indeed, it may have been a 1925 summer sojourn in the Southwest, during which she discovered a biography of a nineteenth-century French missionary in the territory, that helped her move forward with renewed zest for life.

During that summer, Cather visited Santa Fe, where the French Romanesque cathedral of St. Francis, built in the 1880s by the French Jesuit archbishop Lamy, dominated the landscape. She then made a journey to the Indian pueblo on the great rock mesa of Acoma, west of Albuquerque, driving along a route that took her past the Enchanted Mesa, the rock on which an Indian tribe had once built their village and been destroyed. In this ancient and dramatic landscape, where so many civilizations and so much history overlapped, Cather seemed to recover from the sense of dislocation that had marked her middle period, for *Death Comes for the Archbishop* (1927), the novel that she began to write on her return to the East, offered a vision of the continuous past that asserted the efficacy of beauty and order and heroic action. The story of Father Jean Marie Latour's missionary life in the American Southwest, *Death Comes for the Archbishop* is a work that many consider Cather's best. Its tone is serene and confident; its prose is vivid and precise. Indeed, it is perhaps Cather's most assured expression of her deepest beliefs, and writing it, the author observed, "was like a happy vacation" ("On *Death Comes*," *Stories, Poems, and Other Writings* 961). Cather had a second summer sojourn in the Southwest, visiting in 1926 other locations—the Canyon de Chelly and the ship rock—that feature in the novel, before completing it that fall, and when she had done so, she negotiated a one-time increase in royalties from her publisher, a sign of her belief in the novel's quality and appeal.

This period of relative calm in her personal life and success in her professional life, however, ushered in four years of stress and dislocation for Cather, during which time she found it difficult to concentrate on her writing. During the summer of 1927, Cather cut short a journey through Wyoming's Big Horn Mountains when her father suffered a severe attack of angina. She spent several weeks with her family in Red Cloud and then returned to New York, where she and Edith Lewis were forced to move from their Bank Street apartment to the Grosvenor Hotel on Fifth Avenue because the building was being demolished to permit subway expansion. (Cather intended the move to be temporary, but she and Lewis lived in the hotel for five years before moving to a new apartment at 570 Park Avenue.) In early March 1928, Cather's beloved father died following a heart attack, and she spent several weeks in Red Cloud not only coping with grief but also reconnecting with family and her past. That summer, she traveled to Quebec, Canada, and reread Francis Parkman's history of the province, and gradually, the idea for her next novel, 1931's *Shadows on the Rock,* took shape. She began writing the novel that fall and at Thanksgiving made a second visit to Quebec to conduct research, but except for another trip to Quebec for Christmas in 1929, work on the project effectively ended for more than a year when her mother suffered a paralytic stroke in December 1928.

Because Cather's relationship with her mother had always been a source of some conflict for her, the author struggled during the next two years, until her mother's death in August 1931, to reconcile her feelings for her. Virginia Cather, according to Hermione Lee, was a "well-bred, imperious, handsome Southern belle" who ruled her family by force of her iron will. She was also "subject to prolonged bouts of depression and illness" (28) that "may have made her a difficult mother" (29). Indeed, whereas Cather's grandmother and her father featured prominently in her memories of her early life, Cather's mother rarely surfaced in them. Thus, one of her personal challenges, a biographer, Sharon O'Brien, maintains, was to come to terms with her mother and to acknowledge their similarities. During her mother's final illness, Cather, who visited California annually to help nurse her, found it difficult to watch the frustration of this spirited woman trapped in her unresponsive body, unable even to speak, and following her mother's death, she wrote to her friend, Dorothy Canfield Fisher, "I feel a good deal like a ghost" (*Early Novels and Stories* 1314).

Cather found it difficult as well to concentrate on her writing during the final years of her mother's illness. She traveled not only in the United States but also to France, where she visited Isabelle McClung Hambourg, and twice more to Quebec. But it was not until the late summer of 1930 that she could return to sustained work on *Shadows on the Rock,* which she completed in December 1930. Published to mixed reviews in 1931, the novel, which was a Book-of-the-Month Club selection, nevertheless sold well, but it also marked the end of her best work. In 1935, Cather published *Lucy Gayheart,* the rather sentimental tale of a young Nebraska girl who rejects her midwestern suitor to follow her musical aspirations to Chicago that reworked material and themes that she had used to more effect in *The Song of the Lark.* She set her final novel, *Sapphira and the Slave Girl,* in her native Virginia and took "pleasure," she wrote Dorothy Canfield Fisher, "in listening to those voices which had been nonexistent for me for so many years, when other sounds silenced them" (*Early Novels and Stories* 1316-1317). Published in 1940, *Sapphira and the Slave Girl* is the story of a family for whom slavery becomes the source of an internal civil war, and it was neither a critical nor a popular success.

Throughout this period, Cather also devoted her energies to other projects. In 1932, she published a third collection of short stories, titled *Obscure Destinies.* (A fourth and final collection, *The Old Beauty and Others,* would be published posthumously in 1948.) The following year, she supervised the publication of the "Autograph Edition" of her collected works by the publisher Houghton Mifflin, 12 volumes of which were in print by 1938, proof of her stature as a major American writer.

Cather's final years, however, were plagued by illness and loss and, as nations engaged in a second world war, deep distress about the course of civilization. Within a five-month period in 1938, both Cather's beloved brother Douglass and her dearest friend Isabelle McClung Hambourg died; her brother Roscoe died in 1946. Her recurrent bouts with hand pain, for which she had to wear a brace almost permanently in later years, continued to cripple her efforts at writing, but it was surgery in 1942 from which she never fully recovered. In 1946, she battled influenza. A year later, on 24 April 1947, she died at her New York City home after suffering a cerebral hemorrhage. Willa Cather was buried in Jaffrey, New Hampshire, where for years she had retreated to two attic rooms in the Shattuck Inn, on 28 April 1947. After her death, Edith Lewis destroyed the unfinished draft of a novel, tentatively titled *Hard Punishments,* in which the writer had, perhaps fittingly in her final years, returned to the historical past and to her beloved France, fourteenth-century Avignon, for inspiration.

An intensely private woman, Willa Cather destroyed many of her manuscripts and letters during her lifetime and stipulated in her will that any surviving letters were not to be published. In her will, she also refused permission to adapt her fiction for film or television, so distressed had she been by a film version of *A Lost Lady* produced in 1925. Yet these efforts to conceal the details of her personal life have never prevented public recognition of her literary achievements. In addition to the Pulitzer Prize for *One of Ours* (1923), Cather also received the gold medal of the American Academy of Arts and Letters in 1930 for *Death Comes for the Archbishop* and the Prix Femina Américain in 1933 for *Shadows on the Rock.* In 1940, the National Institute of Arts and Letters awarded Cather its Gold Medal for her career achievements. She also received honorary degrees from the University of Nebraska, Yale University, Princeton University, and Smith College. In recent years, as copyright restrictions have lapsed, *O Pioneers!, The Song of the Lark,* and *My Ántonia* have been adapted as television movies, testimony to Cather's enduring status as well as her place in contemporary popular culture.

Transitions and upheavals shaped Willa Cather's life. Born during the late-Victorian period and in the aftermath of the Civil War, she lived through two world wars, the Great Depression, and the triumph of the modern age and created fiction the best of which reflects these events and the changes they wrought. To the end of her life, however, she never lost sight of the values and habits of mind and being that mattered to her. In the modern age, those values seem antiquated and even a bit reactionary. Yet something about them clearly continues to speak to contemporary readers, some quality that affirms the pioneering spirit that Cather knew from experience had shaped a nation, some abiding faith in the transforming power of heroic action and ideals. Those beliefs sustained Cather through the course of her life, and they remain her legacy to succeeding generations.

2

Within and against Tradition: Willa Cather's Literary Career

From the publication of her first prairie novel, *O Pioneers!*, in 1913, Willa Cather has generally been regarded as the elegist of America's pioneer tradition. Set at the turn of the twentieth century, the trilogy of novels on which she earned this reputation—*O Pioneers!, The Song of the Lark* (1915), and *My Ántonia* (1918)—poignantly records a time when the values and ideals that Americans identify with their national dream of material success and upward social mobility prevailed. In doing so, it offered comforting evidence and reassurance at a time when the changes and problems of modern life seemed to deny it, that the traditional American dream was once—and thus could be again—a reality. While this view of her fiction may have earned Cather acclaim at the beginning of her career, by the 1930s it effectively relegated her to oblivion for being irrelevant to Depression-era concerns and realities. Even F. Scott Fitzgerald, who admired Cather's fiction to "plagiarism," admitting, he wrote the novelist in 1925, "apparent" (Fitzgerald 100) similarities between her novel *A Lost Lady* (1923) and his work *The Great Gatsby* (1925), would eventually joke about her contribution to the "History of the Simple Inarticulate Farmer"—she turned him Swede (Fitzgerald 118).

Today, however, Cather's reputation and her place in American literary history, as well as in the hearts of her large and enduring readership, are secure. Not only has the prestigious Library of America published her collected works in three volumes, but filmmakers have also adapted her novels into television films. Her celebration of traditional American values and heroic human effort still resonates with contemporary readers and critics who have long acknowledged the clarity and supple energy of her poetic prose and have recognized as well the complexity of her vision. No longer is Willa Cather merely Nebraska's first lady of literature, venerated by the members of the Willa Cather Pioneer Memorial and Educational Foundation and the subject each spring of its annual Red Cloud conference. Nor is she simply a writer who celebrates America's pioneering spirit. Indeed, her vision has always been acute, never simplistic. Her best fiction has always documented and responded to the changing social conditions of the world in which she lived. It has also always expressed the sad realities of the human condition. Her characters struggle to attain their goals, and they endure losses and accept compromises that threaten their ideals and their sense of personal integrity. Her worldview shaped not only by her early experience of exile and dislocation but also by her early and continued reading of the Bible and John Bunyan's *The Pilgrim's Progress,* she sought the pattern in life that dignifies the struggle and the losses because it insists on their meaningfulness. Idealistic Cather may have been, but hers was an idealism born of and tempered by tough realities. For its time, Willa Cather's was an original voice. It placed her at odds with literary tradition, especially the fiction of the woman writer, as well as contemporary trends and thus earned her a place among America's great writers.

WILLA CATHER'S LITERARY INHERITANCE

Nearly 20 years after Willa Cather published her first novel, *Alexander's Bridge,* in 1912, the now critically acclaimed writer freely admitted in an essay, "My First Novels," her debt to Henry James and Edith Wharton. They were, after all, America's "most interesting novelists," and thus their fiction provided appropriate models to young writers lacking "their qualifications" (*Stories, Poems, and Other Writings* 964). James and Wharton, however, were not Cather's only literary influences. Indeed, the subjects of her literary reviews as well as her personal reading reveal Cather's grounding in a nineteenth-century novelistic tradition that initially nourished her development but from which she soon turned to pursue her own literary preoccupations in a style more appropriate to them.

Cather grew into adulthood and began her career as a writer during the late-Victorian period in American culture. She was the product of an age that from the 1830s to World War I believed in certainties that produced a sense of stability and clear moral codes. Among the beliefs defining Victorian society, according to the cultural historian Daniel Joseph Singal, were "a predictable universe presided over by a benevolent God and governed by immutable natural laws, a corresponding conviction that humankind was capable of arriving at a unified and fixed set of truths about all aspects of life, and an insistence on preserving absolute standards based on a radical dichotomy between that which was deemed 'human' and that regarded as 'animal.'" To restrain the "instincts and passions that constantly threatened self-control," the mark of the savage, and thereby uplift people into the category of "human" were civilized institutions and virtues such as "education, refinement, manners, the arts, religion, and such domesticated emotions as loyalty and family love" (9). A set of clear and simplifying oppositions formed the "bedrock" of American Victorian culture, according to Singal, including clear racial distinctions between black and white, hierarchical class distinctions between high and low, and clear gender divisions between male and female.

Recording but not necessarily affirming this world of certainties were the writers of the period. During the late nineteenth century, they had responded to trends in European fiction and then formulated a theory of American literary realism that set the standard into the twentieth century. Cather developed into a writer under these influences. She greatly admired the nineteenth-century Russian novelists Leo Tolstoy, Ivan Turgenev, and Nikolai Gogol and reserved special praise for their French counterparts Victor Hugo, Anatole France, and Guy de Maupassant, among others. Indeed, in the 1890s, as she was working out her literary principles in the theatrical and book reviews she wrote chiefly for Nebraska newspapers, Cather observed that, with the exception of the British novelists George Meredith and Thomas Hardy and the American novelist Henry James, "the great living novelists are Frenchmen" ("Mark Twain," *Stories, Poems, and Other Writings* 889).

What Cather admired about these authors, as well as others, including the Americans Sarah Orne Jewett and Frank Norris, was their uncompromising insistence on writing about life as it was lived by real people. Cather's appreciation of Norris's 1899 novel *McTeague*, for instance, stemmed from its verisimilitude. "His art," she affirmed, "strikes deep down into the roots of life and the foundation of Things as They Are—not as we tell each other they are at the tea-table.... [He] is realistic art, not artistic realism" ("Frank Norris," *Stories, Poems, and Other Writings* 929). He drew his characters from among ordinary people and fearlessly depicted aspects of the physical universe, from the "rank smells of crowded alley-ways" ("Frank Norris" 930) to the "delicate perfume exhaled from a woman's skin" ("Frank Norris" 931). His novel, in other words, exhibited the characteristics that defined literary realism—fidelity to life and probability of motive—in both Europe and the United States, and Cather embraced those principles.

CATHER AND THE FEMININE TRADITION

Indeed, while most women writers of the period were deeply entrenched within the tradition of the sentimental novel, a literary form in which the characters have a heightened emotional response to events and that produces a similar reader response, Cather rejected it entirely. She preferred instead vigorous and bold realities to the romanticized version of life depicted in the majority of novels written and read by women. Only a few women writers, among them the French novelist George Sand and the British novelists George Eliot, Charlotte Brontë, and Jane Austen, earned Cather's admiration. Far too many of the others she dismissed in an early review about "Silly Novels by Lady Novelists" for writing false and trivial tales of women's lives. Berating their "sex consciousness" as "abominable" in the essay, Cather confessed that she lacked "faith in women writers" because "they are so limited to one string and they lie so about that." Moreover, she complained, "women are so horribly subjective and they have such scorn for the healthy commonplace" (*The World and the Parish* 276-77). Cather, in contrast, had embraced the tenets of literary realism and effectively defined herself as a writer outside this feminine tradition. She was anything but, to use her patronizing phrase, a "lady novelist," and she had no intention of writing "silly novels."

At this stage in her development, in fact, Cather was intent on assuming the dominant—and therefore masculine—tradition in fiction. She did not wish to be consigned to writing about virtuous young women victimized by unscrupulous male predators, the typical heroine's text of the sentimental novel. She wanted instead to adopt and adapt classical forms and to locate her fictional world outside the drawing room. "The project to take over a male tradition of writing meant, as this stage," observes Hermione Lee, "that she also had to appropriate the dominant male critique of female weakness and emotionalism" (13). Given this need, Cather's terse pronouncement about "Silly Novels by Lady Novelists" that only "when a woman writes a story of adventure, a stout sea tale, a manly battle yarn, anything without wine, women and love … will I begin to hope for something great from them" (*World and the Parish* 276–77) is both a literary declaration of independence from the feminine tradition and a challenge for other women writers to join her.

It explains as well the author's critical attack on Kate Chopin's 1899 novel *The Awakening*. Indeed, Cather could not forgive the talented writer for squandering "so exquisite and sensitive, well-governed a style to so trite and sordid a theme" ("Kate Chopin," *Stories, Poems, and Other Writings* 910). Edna Pontellier, Chopin's heroine, is simply a lesser version of the French novelist Gustave Flaubert's tragic heroine Emma Bovary and a victim of the "over-idealization of love" ("Kate Chopin" 911). For Cather, who launches into a telling diatribe about such victims, "the unfortunate feature of their disease is that it attacks only women of brains, at least of rudimentary brains, but whose development is one-sided; women of strong and fine intuitions, but without the faculty of observation, comparison, reasoning about things" ("Kate Chopin" 911). Cather has nothing but disdain for such women, who, despite their capacity to reason, know their fates:

> These people really expect the passion of love to fill and gratify every need of life, whereas nature only intended that it should meet one of many demands. They insist upon making it stand for all the emotional pleasures of life and art, expecting an individual and self-limited passion to yield infinite variety, pleasure and distraction, to contribute to their lives what the arts and the pleasurable exercise of the intellect gives to less limited and less intense idealists. ("Kate Chopin" 912)

Convinced that women could rise above pure sensibility, Cather rejected passionate heroines such as Chopin's and effectively held women writers who created them in their fiction accountable for perpetrating a stereotype.

Among the few women novelists Cather admired was the New England writer Sarah Orne Jewett, who eventually became the younger woman's literary mentor. The author of, among other works, *The*

Country of the Pointed Firs, a collection of sketches about village and country life and people in rural Maine, and *The Country Doctor,* the story of a woman who aspires to a medical career, Jewett gave Cather, who had not yet begun to write fiction, crucial advice about the writer's life, and she urged her receptive pupil to write from her own experience of the world. As, if not more, important than the advice, however, was the example Jewett's fiction provided the aspiring writer. Her unconventional subjects and their commonplace situations and experiences were proof that writers could make ordinary people engaged in the business of daily life yield as much as the heroic endeavors of exceptional men and women. Writers had only to trust their instincts and respect their subjects to capture life's inherent truths. In an appreciation of Jewett's life and art, Cather praised the simplicity and authenticity of her work, observing (in a prescient statement that could now be applied to her own best work and her own fictional world) that far into the future it would give readers "the characteristic flavour, the spirit, the cadence, of an American writer of the first order,—and of a New England which will then be a thing of the past" ("Miss Jewett" 851). To Cather, Jewett's fiction demonstrated that a woman writer could indeed explore her own terrain and utter the hard, frank truths of real experience. The marriage plot of the sentimental novel did not have to circumscribe her fiction.

CATHER'S LITERARY PRINCIPLES

Cather clearly held strong views about literature, developed during years of reading and study and articulated in the reviews of plays, prose, and poetry that she published in numerous periodicals long before she had written her first novel. In those reviews, written primarily in the 1890s, she clearly articulated a preference for realism, for writing that captures in "accurate and comprehensive description" ("Frank Norris," *Stories, Poems, and Other Writings* 922) the truth of life as it is rather than life as the writer feels it to be. She also expressed her belief that the novelist should write "a true story of the people," as Frank Norris had done in *McTeague,* a novel that presented "people as they are" and was "not afraid of their unloveliness" ("Frank Norris" 922). This preference for proletarian, or working-class, subjects was especially important to Cather, whose fiction makes heroes of rugged pioneers, simple farmers, dedicated priests—indeed, all sorts of ordinary people who face life with courage and dignity and thereby prevail.

Cather's preference for realism, however, did not preclude an equally strong belief in literature as art. She grounded her admiration for Henry James, for instance, a writer whose highly stylized novels of drawing room society were antithetical to her signature tales of the midwestern prairie or the desert Southwest, in his "keen" observation of "human actions and motives" and his perfectly constructed sentences. Indeed, she noted in an appreciation of the writer, even "if his character novels were all wrong one could read him forever for the mere beauty of his sentences" ("Henry James," *Stories, Poems, and Other Writings* 905). Cather, as her praise of James suggests, held high literary standards, and she drew sharp distinctions between literature produced for the marketplace and art. Writers who "manufacture" stories to meet "market demand," she observed in a 1920 essay, "On the Art of Fiction," engage in "a business as safe and commendable as making soap or breakfast foods." True "art," in contrast, "is always a search for something for which there is not market demand," she claimed, "something new and untried, where the values are intrinsic and have nothing to do with standardized values" (*Stories, Poems, and Other Writings* 939-40). While such a view might seem elitist, especially in a writer whose choice of subject was common people engaged in ordinary life, it was instead for Cather a demand for truth and an acknowledgment of its beauty. Subject matter precluded neither.

Cather endeavored from the beginning of her career to write artistic fiction, and she embraced simplicity as her first principle to its attainment. In her essay "On the Art of Fiction," she uses words such as "condense," "suppressed," "cut away," and "discarded" to describe the process of creating art and then asserts, "Any first rate novel or story must have in it the strength of a dozen fairly good stories that have been sacrificed to it." The purpose of art, she declares, is to "simplify" (*Stories, Poems, and Other Writings* 939). Writers must strip the extraneous from their stories. They must develop a form and select details that "preserve the spirit of the whole" and thereby convey the sense that the thing unspoken, the thing unseen, "is there to the reader's consciousness as much as if it were in type on the page" ("On the Art of Fiction" 939). This belief that art is allusive, that it evokes as much as it expresses, is the foundation on which she builds her literary tenets, which she articulated fully two years later in her most famous critical essay, "The Novel Démeublé" (1922).

In this key statement, Cather takes issue with a type of realistic fiction the pages of which are filled with catalogs of material items, explanations of processes and procedures, and minute descriptions of sensory experience and argues that "the novel ... has been over-furnished" (*Stories, Poems, and Other Writings* 834). While such details may serve to fill out a thin story ("The Novel Démueblé" 835) or to satisfy the readers of mass-market fiction, who prefer quantity to quality ("The Novel Démueblé" 834), such "literalness" ("The Novel Démueblé" 836), as far as Cather was concerned, has little to do with realism and nothing to do with art. "But is not realism," she asked rhetorically, "more than anything else, an attitude of mind on the part of the writer toward his material, a vague indication of the sympathy and candour with which he accepts, rather than chooses, his theme?" ("The Novel Démueblé" 834–35). Readers, Cather offered by way of answer, need not learn the intricacies of the banking system and the stock exchange to understand the tale of a banker destroyed by infidelity, greed, and poor judgment. The novel, Cather went on to assert, is not a "form of journalism" ("The Novel Démueblé" 836). Rather, it is an "imaginative art," and thus modern writers, like modern painters, must "break away from mere verisimilitude ... to present their scene by suggestion rather than by enumeration" ("The Novel Démueblé" 836).

What emerges from Cather's reflections on the novel is a literary credo based on subtlety and selection. Indeed, Cather speaks of "whatever is felt upon the page without being specifically named there" as evidence of the writer's imagination and believes this "inexplicable presence of the thing not named" to be the distinguishing characteristic of high literary art ("The Novel Démueblé" 837). As the essay's title indicates, it is the novel *unfurnished* that she advocates. She admires the American writer Nathaniel Hawthorne, for instance, for his "reserved, fastidious hand" ("The Novel Démueblé" 836) and derides the English writer D. H. Lawrence for his exhaustive descriptions of "mere sensory reactions" that dehumanize human emotion ("The Novel Démueblé" 837). To Cather, the writer reveals truth through carefully selected details that create subtle nuances of mood and tone, so she urges writers to "throw all the furniture out of the window" ("The Novel Démueblé" 837). Only by eliminating the meaningless from fiction can the writer become an artist, can the novel be art.

WILLA CATHER AND LITERARY MODERNISM

Her emphasis on subtlety and selection, on the "presence of the thing not named," suggests that Cather was a far more modern writer than critics have traditionally viewed her. Schooled in the tradition of realism, she nevertheless found her literary voice and published many of her most important works during the movement in literary history known as modernism. The movement, which developed and reigned in the period between World Wars I and II, was a reaction to and an expression of the social, political, cultural, and technological changes that were transforming Cather's world. New realities demanded a new mode of expression. They could not be dressed in outmoded fashions, and writers everywhere responded to the poet Ezra Pound's cry to "Make It New." It was a period of experimentation in the arts, and American novelists such as Gertrude Stein, John Dos Passos, Ernest Hemingway, and William Faulkner were challenging traditional forms of narrative structure and point of view. They were seeking, for instance, through montage and repetition and stream of consciousness, to get beneath the surface of life in order to render its moral, intellectual, and psychological realities.

Cather's fiction generally lacks this experimental quality. A social realist, Cather tended to produce chronological narratives and worked within traditional forms. Granted, in *The Professor's House* (1925), she embeds a narrative, Tom Outland's story, within a narrative, Godfrey St. Peter's story, and in *My Ántonia* (1918), she experiments with a first-person narrator and a framing device that lend complexity to the novel. Yet none of these strategies is particularly innovative, and in the case of *My Ántonia,* they coexist with a traditional narrative form. Indeed, most of Cather's major novels fall into the category of the novel of the soil, a special kind of regionalism in the novel, in which the writer portrays the stark lives of people struggling for existence in remote rural areas, or the historical novel, a literary form that reconstructs a past age, usually to emphasize a conflict of cultures. This lack of technical experimentation distanced Cather's fiction from contemporary trends and made her seem far less modern than from other perspectives she was.

"The Novel Démueblé," as previously noted, makes clear that Cather was determined to produce something more than surface realism in the careful selection of physical details that gave body and meaning to her scenes. Indeed, the scholar Phyllis Rose has argued in her essay "Modernism: The Case of Willa Cather" that the formal elements of Cather's fiction, such as her "abstract" conception of character, connect her to the literary movement. Yet formal elements are not the only criteria of modernism. Content and context also characterize modern fiction, and these aspects of her novels place Cather more near the center of literary modernism than some have recognized.

As much as Cather admired the fiction of Henry James and Edith Wharton, for instance, her effort to emulate them in her first novel, *Alexander's Bridge* (1912), was competently conventional but no more. The novel of manners, set in the drawing rooms of polite society, simply did not have the appeal to her that the heroic deeds of ordinary men and women facing new worlds and experiences held for her, and her decision to write about such people placed Cather at odds with such a tradition. Her inclusion, moreover, of characters such as the suicidal tramp in *My Ántonia* or the Mexican migrants in *The Song of the Lark* (1915) as well as her celebration of "primitive" cultures such as those in the Tom Outland section of *The Professor's House* or *Death Comes for the Archbishop* (1927) challenged hierarchical notions of the "proper" subjects of art that belonged to the previous century and the literary establishment. Cather's interest in these others—and especially in these other cultures—was distinctively modern. Indeed, her examination of these other cultures, whose values were so different from her own contemporary world of rampant consumerism, smug provincialism, and anxious disillusionment, offered an alternative to it. Granted, that alternative may have been grounded in traditional values, the effect of which was to lend a nostalgic tone to her work that probably reflected Cather's viewpoint. Yet the fact that cultural comparisons are central to so many of her novels confirms that she participated in the critique of postwar society that was one of the defining characteristics of literary modernism. In her own way, Cather was, in other words, modern.

THE OUTLINE OF A LITERARY CAREER

The mature writer whose major fictional worlds made so much of these cultural comparisons did not immediately know her own subject or even her true genre. Indeed, her first published work was a slim volume of poems titled *April Twilights*. Published in 1903, the volume was reissued in 1923 with 13 additional poems that Cather had previously published in magazines during the intervening 20 years. As a poet, Cather was competent but uninspired. Her poems are bound almost entirely to traditional forms, such as the lyric, and they generally lack the originality of her fiction. Too often, in fact, they are derivative of other poetic masters, especially the British poet A. E. Housman, whose work Cather deeply admired. Several of the poems, such as "Prairie Dawn" and "The Swedish Mother," anticipate the subject and the style that Cather will claim as hers in her fiction.

"Prairie Dawn," for instance, captures in crisp and vivid language the beauty of the midwestern landscape, and "The Swedish Mother" conveys the immigrants' sense of loss and longing. Yet even these poems cannot compare to Cather's prose treatment of similar subjects, a fact that the author herself seems to have acknowledged by concentrating all her skill and talent on fiction.

Even then, however, Cather did not immediately claim her subject. In fact, her first published novel, *Alexander's Bridge* (1912), is so unlike Cather that it might have been written by Henry James. The story of a brilliant but self-destructive engineer, Bartley Alexander, who had built his reputation by designing bridges to connect seemingly unbridgeable distances, *Alexander's Bridge* was Cather's novel of apprenticeship. It is set in the drawing rooms of a staid and conventional Boston and a dynamic and bohemian London, where Bartley, feeling his middle age, must choose between the women who represent both cities, both states of being, and thus two different selves. Cather deftly handles her plot, until the end, when she resolves Bartley's struggle with the artifice of a bridge disaster. She also fails to develop her characters fully. Despite these shortcomings, the novel certainly gives evidence of the writer's early promise. Nevertheless, Cather, who was at the time "intensely" interested in her characters and their situation, was distancing herself from the work within a decade ("Preface," *Stories, Poems, and Other Writings* 941) because it did not represent the fictional world that she had by then made hers.

That fictional world, located primarily in the prairie Midwest and focused almost exclusively on New World immigrants and their descendents, Cather discovered in the work that she considered her first novel, 1913's *O Pioneers!*, and that stands as the first of the four novels that constitute her first artistic phase. *O Pioneers!* is the story of Alexandra Bergson, the daughter of Swedish immigrants, whose firm and abiding identification with the natural world—and especially with the land on which she toils—helps her tame a wilderness and create a satisfying home. Cather's first full-length treatment of her true subject, *O Pioneers!* announced the arrival of an original talent, not only because its setting and subject were unique but also because its heroine was the first of three strong female protagonists who embodied the values and exemplified the spirit of the nation's pioneers.

The second of Cather's pioneer novels, 1915's *The Song of the Lark,* was also her most autobiographical, for it is also a *Künstlerroman,* or a story of the development of an artist. Thea Kronborg, the novel's heroine, is, like Alexandra Bergson, the child of immigrants. Unlike Alexandra, however, who channels her creative spirit into the development of a country and the cultivation of a society, Thea commits herself to her art. In fact, the novel charts her path from obscurity in Moonstone, Colorado, to international fame as an opera singer delivering a triumphant performance at New York City's Carnegie Hall. What is also different here is Cather's "full-blooded" ("My First Novels," *Stories, Poems, and Other Writings* 965) treatment of her subject. The writer may have advocated the "unfurnishing" of the novel, but she fills *The Song of the Lark,* her longest work, with material enough for several novels. Despite these differences, *The Song of the Lark,* like *O Pioneers!,* celebrates habits of mind and being whose origins lie in Old World cultural traditions that have been animated by contact with the New, and thus it extends one of Cather's principle themes.

That theme, in fact, is central to Cather's third novel of the soil and one of her most important works, *My Ántonia* (1918). Set, like *O Pioneers!,* on the Nebraska prairie, the novel explores the complex relationship between its narrator, Jim Burden, and a Bohemian immigrant, Ántonia Shimerda, whose effect on both his identity and his worldview is profound. Ántonia becomes for Jim a touchstone of value by which he measures his fidelity to the ideals of his youth during his progress through life, and thus his responses to her tragedies and triumphs are central to the work. Lyrical in mood, nostalgic in tone, *My Ántonia* evokes a world that is at once elemental and ephemeral, and this contradiction gives the novel depth and keeps it from being naive.

Cather concludes this first phase of her career with a novel that earned her great popular success and a Pulitzer Prize but savage criticism from her contemporaries, 1922's *One of Ours.* Claude Wheeler, the novel's hero, has grown to adulthood on the Nebraska plains, but like Thea Kronborg, he has never felt that he belongs on the land. Sensitive, like Thea, he longs for a life less provincial and materialistic, and he looks to Europe, with its complex history and its cultural traditions, for what America lacks. Frustrated by his possibilities and disappointed by his marriage, Claude seizes the opportunity to escape when the United States enters World War I, quickly enlisting in the army in a spirit of high adventure. In Europe, Claude will experience the reality of war and indeed fall victim to it. But he will also find there everything that has been missing from his life and thus die fulfilled. The novel's critics, including the American writer Ernest Hemingway, who cruelly joked to the critic Edmund Wilson that she had "Catherized" the war (Lynn 222), launched scathing attacks on Cather's romanticizing of war (although her depiction of battle was brutally realistic) and her idealism. In the aftermath of World War I, when the disillusionment of a "Lost Generation" of young men and women set the tone of a decade, *One of Ours* simply lacked authenticity. Yet *One of Ours* was not really a war novel. Rather, it was a further exploration of cross-cultural encounters in which Cather developed one of her recurrent themes, what the scholar David Daiches identifies as "the decline of the pioneering age and the plight of the imaginative hero in an increasingly narrow and self-satisfied civilization" (57). The fact that a majority of readers viewed the novel as a patriotic statement and missed entirely Cather's criticism of her contemporary world makes *One of Ours* a deeply flawed success.

The three novels of Cather's middle period, *A Lost Lady* (1923), *The Professor's House* (1925), and *My Mortal Enemy* (1926), two of which are actually novellas, share a tone of disillusionment rather than simply nostalgic longing, perhaps reflecting Cather's sense that "the world broke in two in 1922 or thereabouts" (*Not Under Forty,* Prefatory Note). Indeed, the tone of these novels of Cather's middle period, especially the best of them, *The Professor's House,* connects them to literary modernism, for they share all the disillusionment and frustration with the twentieth-century characteristic of "Lost Generation" writers such as F. Scott Fitzgerald and Ernest Hemingway.

A Lost Lady, for example, draws a parallel between the decline of the pioneering spirit that had produced America's greatness and the degeneration of a once-grand lady reduced to coarseness by her desire for the bright world of immediate sensation. Marian Forrester, the "lost lady" of the novella's title, had once been the epitome of charm and aristocratic grace during the few months each year that she and her husband lived in Sweet Water, Colorado. When Captain Forrester, the embodiment of the pioneering spirit, falls from a horse, however, the couple must settle permanently in what has now become a backwater town. Bitterly disappointed by the confinement of her life and further impoverished by her principled husband's insistence on paying the depositors when a Denver savings bank in which he has an interest fails, Marian begins an affair with a dashing bachelor, hoping to recapture the romance and excitement of her previous life. When her lover marries, however, she feels only further betrayed and is soon consoling herself with brandy. Eventually, after the series of strokes that her husband suffers reduces her to little more than nurse, she engages in an affair with an unscrupulous lawyer who symbolizes the crass superficiality of the modern generation. Marian Forrester, like her husband, is essentially a remnant of a previous era, and Cather clearly links her downward spiral to the displacement and devaluation of America's foundational ideals. Even the report at the novel's conclusion that Marian has married a "rich, but quarrelsome and rather stingy" Englishman (*Later Novels* 98) and thus recovered her wealth and position does not offer any real triumph of the old, for Cather implies that Marian has paid a high price—the loss of her heroic and romantic spirit—for the cold comforts of materialism. In that loss, she represents the modern generation.

My Mortal Enemy, the second of Cather's novellas of her middle period, dramatizes the bleak and bitter downward spiral of another lost lady, Myra Henshawe. As Myra Driscoll, she had sacrificed the fortune she expected to inherit from her great-uncle, with whom she lived, by eloping with the man she loved, Oswald Henshawe. The couple initially enjoys a comfortable life in New York, where Myra, a brilliant and charming but self-absorbed woman, relishes her social success. When Henshawe loses his job, however (because Myra refuses to allow him to accept an inferior position in the company during a period of economic depression), the couple moves to the West Coast, settling eventually in San Francisco and consigned by finances to life within a cheap lodging house. No longer consoled by the memories of the love and the happy life she had shared with Henshawe in New York, Myra spends the remainder of her days in bitter recrimination for what she now believes was her disastrous decision to marry her husband, blaming him for their bleak and impoverished circumstances. Locked in battle with her "mortal enemy," she dies consumed by resentment and unconsoled. *My Mortal Enemy* shares some of *A Lost Lady*'s plot structure, but it lacks the other work's broad cultural perspective. Because its focus is exclusively Myra's character, it offers little by way of social and cultural critique. As a study of the degeneration of character, moreover, it is not entirely successful. While *My Mortal Enemy* contains some brilliant and memorable scenes that illustrate Cather's artistry, the novella is too "unfurnished" to make convincing Myra's transformation from heroic ingenue to cynical old woman. It remains a curiosity in Cather's literary career, a difficult work that is difficult to place.

Framed by these two novellas is *The Professor's House,* the best and most important novel of Cather's middle period and a work that expresses the sad disillusionment of the age. Professor Godfrey St. Peter, a historian and the novel's central character, is in the midst of a midlife crisis as his tale begins. As a young man, he had had such dreams of adventure and achievement, but he had wanted love and a family as well. So he accepted a teaching position at a mediocre midwestern college, the first offered him, and married the clever woman he desired. Years later, when the fervor of this first romance has cooled and the daily routine of teaching and parenting two daughters has stifled St. Peter's youthful ambition, Tom Outland, a brilliant but mysterious student, walks into his life from the desert Southwest, reviving in the Professor all his submerged desires. His friendship with Outland, his second great romance, fires his intellect and imagination and inspires him to pursue the self that he had intended to be. His travels with Tom to the ruins of an ancient cliff-dwelling civilization that the young man had discovered hidden in the New Mexican canyons provided St. Peter with the understanding to write a critically acclaimed history of *Spanish Adventurers in North America,* and the Professor anticipated additional opportunities to experience life through this sympathetic companion who embodied his own ideal self. Tom Outland's death, however, during World War I and his family's subsequent betrayal of all that he represented cause St. Peter to assess his life and face the unhappy truth that he had compromised his ideals and, indeed, his ideal of self to enjoy the very pleasures that are now so distasteful to him. This realization leads the Professor to personal crisis and its sad but inevitable resolution in stoic acceptance of his fate. *The Professor's House* is a novel about the disappointments of a compromised life, set in a world where compromise is unrecognizable to the majority, who have accepted crass materialism and empty conventions as the epitome of civilization.

The resolution of the Professor's crisis lies partly in the solace St. Peter takes from knowledge that heroic achievement of the sort embodied in the ancient cliff-dweller civilization had once existed. History, in other words, could provide evidence of the beauty and order of civilizations founded by imaginative and selfless individuals devoted to virtue, truth, respect, and other primary values. This perspective is central to *Death Comes for the Archbishop* (1927), the first of two novels in which Cather turns to the historical past to explore alternatives to her contemporary world. In *Death Comes for the Archbishop,* Cather converts into fiction the life and achievements of a French priest who ventured as a missionary into the desert Southwest and forged a civilization among the tribal people, the

Mexican workers, and the American settlers. Father Jean Marie Latour, the archbishop of the novel's title, is a man of sensibility, imagination, and vision who brings utter devotion to his faith and firm dedication to his task. For more than 40 years, he and his faithful companion Father Vaillant toil in the desert to achieve their goal, and by the time of his death, the Romanesque cathedral projecting from the rock cliff above Santa Fe testifies to his success. It testifies as well to the favorable conjunction of Old World traditions and New World vitality that gives the civilization that Father Latour creates its special quality. A deeply felt and beautifully crafted novel, *Death Comes for the Archbishop* is the most important work of Cather's late period. Indeed, it rivals *My Ántonia* as her greatest work.

Cather followed *Death Comes for the Archbishop* with a second historical novel written in the same vein, 1931's *Shadows on the Rock.* She shifts her focus, however, from the desert Southwest in the nineteenth century to the French settlement of Quebec in the early eighteenth century and from the heroic achievement of dedicated missionary priests to the quiet triumph of ordinary people in process of becoming Canadians. The novel traces a year in the lives of these ordinary people, focusing chiefly on the apothecary Euclide Auclair and his 12-year-old daughter Cécile and the quality of the civilization that they are transplanting from the Old World to the New. While great men and historical figures, such as Quebec's governor, the military hero Count de Frontenec, figure in the novel, they are subordinate to the Auclairs. In addition, little of momentous occasion—no great battles, no native attacks—occurs in the novel, yet something momentous happens. These strategies focus attention on Cather's primary subject and give heroic stature to the energy and spirit of the French settlers who created a culture in the wilderness. In its exploration of the conjunction of Old and New Worlds, *Shadows on the Rock* has much in common with early Cather novels, especially *O Pioneers!* and *My Ántonia,* but it lacks the complexity and the edge of those works. The passage of historical time has smoothed the conflicts in *Shadows on the Rock.* Yet the authenticity of the characters and their lives, enhanced by Cather's poetic prose and affirmative tone, gives the novel genuine appeal.

In her two final novels, Cather deviates once again from "her subject" but without great success. *Lucy Gayheart,* for example, published in 1935, shares plot similarities with *The Song of the Lark,* but it lacks that early novel's vigor and passion, its sense of felt experience. Like the early novel's Thea Kronborg, Lucy Gayheart is a musician who longs to escape the provincialism of her midwestern home to pursue a career in the great cities. Where Thea, however, is a singer with a grand talent, Lucy is merely an accompanist. From the beginning, she lacks the possibility for greatness that Thea possessed, and indeed, her story is sad but not tragic. She moves to Chicago to study music and there falls in love with a middle-aged singer to whom she serves as temporary accompanist. Her passion for Clement Sebastian leads Lucy to reject the marriage proposal of her Nebraska suitor, the businessman Harry Gordon. When Sebastian drowns in a boating accident on Italy's Lake Como, she returns, numbed by grief, to her hometown, where she attempts to repair her friendship with Gordon. He had hastily married another woman, however, following Lucy's rejection, and because he still loves the musician, he now rejects her efforts. Not long after, Lucy, too, drowns in a skating accident, her gay heart borne down by the weight of life's realities. *Lucy Gayheart* develops some of Cather's typical themes. Here again she explores the artistic sensibility in conflict with materialism and convention, and she also treats the conflict between romanticism and reality. Yet her treatment of these themes and her subjects in *Lucy Gayheart* lacks the power of her treatment of them in previous novels. Indeed, the novel's melodramatic plot and its sad heroine link it to the sentimental novel that Cather so despised.

Sapphira and the Slave Girl (1940), Cather's final novel, is more complex than *Lucy Gayheart,* yet it too lacks the quality of felt experience that energizes her best work. Equally troubling is its equivocal presentation of its subject, and thus the novel gives evidence of the writer's declining powers. Cather sets her tale of a woman's jealousy and its consequences in her native Virginia at the time of the Civil War, and one of its central characters, Nancy, is the slave of the title. But *Sapphira and the Slave Girl* is not an historical novel. Its focus is neither bitter national conflict nor cruel and unjust institution but rather family conflict. Yet because Cather sets this conflict within a particular historical context, it functions as a political metaphor: the civil war within the Colbert house mirrors the Civil War without.

Cather's central characters embody the warring factions. Sapphira Dodderidge is the daughter of a wealthy and aristocratic family of English descent who surprises her family by marrying Henry Colbert, whose humble Flemish origins and job as her father's miller make him an unlikely husband for a woman of her class. Following their marriage, the Colberts move to property that Sapphira owns in Back Creek, Virginia, a region where northern attitudes toward slavery are as common as southern. The tensions created by these conflicting attitudes are rife in the Colbert household: Sapphira, quite naturally, brings her slaves with her, while Henry, as well as their adult daughter, the widow Rachel Blake, disapproves of the institution on principle. When Sapphira, who is confined by illness to the house, hears gossip linking her husband to her favorite slave, Nancy, she grows bitter and jealous and begins to treat her harshly, even inviting Martin Colbert, Henry's disreputable nephew, to their farm knowing that he will probably seduce Nancy and thereby end the affair. Rachel, however, assists Nancy's escape to freedom in Canada.

Cather handles the complex but chaste relationship between Henry and Nancy with subtlety, yet his passivity tends to undermine his moral position in the novel. Cather's treatment of slavery, moreover, "keeps getting dissolved," observes Hermione Lee, "into picturesque pastoral scenes" (365) that diminish its cruel realities. Further complicating the novel is her characterization of Sapphira, who is at once compelling in her cruelty. Because she resembles both Marian Forrester and Myra Henshawe, Sapphira is at times a sympathetic, at times a hateful character. This contradiction makes it difficult to evaluate her, and Cather's equivocation about her character makes equally difficult resolution of the novel's themes. *Sapphira and the Slave Girl* is thus a rather perplexing novel. Cather, it seems, could no longer find in the past the redemptive truth.

Taken together, Cather's novels form the arc that is her literary career. After several false starts—a volume of poetry and a novel of manners—Cather discovers her true subject, the creative power of the heroic spirit, and her world, the prairie Midwest, and writes in rapid succession four novels (one of which, *My Ántonia*, brings her to the center of the arc) that essentially express her unique vision. During a brief middle period in the early 1920s, when Cather writes three additional novels, including the compelling work *The Professor's House,* her fiction acquires an edge as it assumes a tone of resigned disillusionment reflective of its age. Before the arc begins its downward turn, Cather looks to the distant past and writes two historical novels, including one of her greatest works, *Death Comes for the Archbishop,* that give reason to hope for human civilization again. In her final two novels, however, Cather is unable to sustain her creative powers or even her redemptive vision, and so her literary career ends in decline, in works that merely recall elements of a unique and genuine talent.

CATHER AND THE SHORT STORY

Like other American novelists, Cather learned her craft and worked through her thematic ideas in the short story. During her lifetime, in fact, she published three volumes of stories, *The Troll Garden* (1905), *Youth and the Bright Medusa* (1920), and *Obscure Destinies* (1932), while a final collection, *The Old Beauty and Others,* was published posthumously in 1948. The best and most memorable of the stories in these collections testify to Cather's artistry. They are also connected, usually thematically, to her novels. Although this study focuses on Cather's most representative and significant novels, Chapter 3 includes a detailed analysis of *The Troll Garden* because it was her first published fiction and thus gives evidence of the writer's beginnings. A brief analysis of several of her best stories from her other collections reveals both the range and the depth of her short fiction.

Of the eight stories that constitute *Youth and the Bright Medusa,* four had been published in *The Troll Garden,* so Cather's second collection of short fiction does not represent a significant advancement over her first. It does, however, contain one of her most unique stories, "Coming, Aphrodite!," if only for Cather's frank treatment of sexual passion. Set in bohemian New York, the story focuses on Eden Bower, a singer from the West who had changed her name from Edna to assert her intention to become what Hermione Lee calls the "self-made artist-heroine of the New World" (162), and her relationship with Don Hedger, a painter who refuses to commercialize his ideals. Another exploration of art and the life of the artist, one of Cather's recurrent themes, "Coming, Aphrodite!" essentially opposes two types of artists, two types of art: Eden, the singer, longs for fame and the crowd's applause, so she cheapens her talent to achieve a success that "takes its toll" (*Stories, Poems, and Other Writings* 396) by hardening her spirit, while Don, the painter, despises the "public," who "only wants what has been done over and over" (*Stories, Poems, and Other Writings* 389), and paints to please only himself, thus earning a reputation as an "original" (*Stories, Poems, and Other Writings* 395) and the admiration of other artists. However much these artists are attracted to each other, their different values inevitably cause discord between them, and Cather leaves no doubt that despite Eden's attractive allure, her sympathies lie with Don.

Cather's third collection of stories, *Obscure Destinies,* is also her best, perhaps because the writer was essentially exploring themes and developing material that were familiar to her from her prairie novels. Tales of the Midwest and West, the three stories in the collection, "Neighbour Rosicky," "Old Mrs. Harris," and "Two Friends," are affectionate portrayals of singular characters who, as the collection's title suggests, could have lived unnoticed by the world. Cather, however, rescues them from obscurity by revealing their significance. The stories benefit from Cather's deeply felt engagement with her subjects as well as her beautifully crafted evocation of her American landscapes. Two, in fact, are especially memorable.

"Neighbour Rosicky" revisits the immigrant world of Cather's Nebraska to focus on the conflict between Old World values and New World realities. When Czech immigrant Anton Rosicky, a middle-aged farmer with a household of sons, is diagnosed with a "bad heart" (*Stories, Poems, and Other Writings* 587), he worries that the uncertainties and hardships of farming will drive his boys to the city, where manufacturing jobs promise a steady income and movie theaters and dance halls offer excitement and escape. He is especially worried about the vulnerability to these enticements of his eldest son, Rudy, who has married a modern young American woman, Polly. Determined to save Rudy from such a mean existence, Rosicky uses his final months of life to woo Polly to his worldview, and indeed, at his death, she has grown to love and appreciate this man, who "was like a tree that has not many roots, but one tap-root that goes down deep" (*Stories, Poems, and Other Writings* 600), and, by implication, the traditional values that have given his life meaning. While Cather's obvious affection for Rosicky threatens at times to sentimentalize her subject, the author avoids that weakness by embedding tales of Rosicky's youth and young manhood within the story's contemporary narrative. Set in London and New York, these tales of deprivation, cruelty, and bitter self-betrayal make clear that experience has tested Rosicky's values and his worldview and that he speaks from knowledge rather than naïveté. His death at the story's end is sad, but it also affirms everything that he has represented.

Another, more complicated tale of generational and cultural conflict, "Old Mrs. Harris" is the story of a southern family, the Templetons, who moves from Tennessee to a small town in the West, where they become the subject of their neighbors' misunderstanding and disapproval. Old Mrs. Harris, the title character, is the focus of the conflict. Victoria Templeton's elderly mother, she has accompanied her daughter's rambunctious family to Skyline to ease her load by helping to care for her grandchildren, a duty that she selflessly accepts as right and necessary. After all, Mrs. Harris believes, old women "were tied to the chariot of young life, and had to go where it went, because they were needed" (*Stories, Poems, and Other Writings* 629). Victoria, for her part, accepts her mother's sacrifice without ever seeing it as such, for to her it is merely part of a tradition, woven into the fabric of genteel southern society, the habits of mind and being that she has brought with her to the West. The citizens of Skyline, however—and especially Mrs. Rosen, the Templetons' Jewish neighbor—do not regard it as such. Indeed, they disapprove of Victoria's treatment of her mother and regard her as selfish and self-absorbed. Cather develops her story slowly, only gradually revealing the sad disappointments and social graces that complicate the characterization of Victoria and the genuine love among the members of the household that contradicts the townspeople's judgments. Cather further complicates her tale by focusing on the struggle of Vickie, Victoria's talented eldest daughter, to find sufficient funds to accept a scholarship to the University of Michigan and Old Mrs. Harris's secret effort to assist her. The subplot makes Vickie as oblivious to her grandmother's sacrifice as Victoria is to her mother's, but that similarity lies at the heart of the story's theme. Old Mrs. Harris, Victoria, and Vickie embody the continuity of generations. It is the way of the young to be "heartless" (*Stories, Poems, and Other Writings* 672). It is the way of the aged to be wise. And in the end, the quiet acceptance of life's cycles and patterns in "Old Mrs. Harris" is as right as Rosicky's death in "Neighbour Rosicky."

None of the stories in Cather's posthumously published fourth collection, *The Old Beauty and Others,* represents her best work. Indeed, Cather withdrew the title story from publication when she submitted it to the *Woman's Home Companion* in 1936 because the editor was unenthusiastic about the tale (Woodress, *Willa Cather: Her Life and Art* 256). Thick with uncritical nostalgia and cloying sentimentality, the three stories in the collection could only have confirmed the criticism levied at the end of her life that Cather's fiction was out of touch with modern realities. Her reputation, however, rests with neither these nor her best stories but with a half dozen novels that rightly earned a place in American literary history and their author a place among America's best and most original literary voices. Cather's best stories simply confirm this estimation.

THE ELEMENTS OF THE CATHER
NOVEL: CHARACTER, SETTING, AND THEME

Three elements—character, setting, and theme—contribute to Cather's unique literary voice, and they represent her artistic signature. Her central characters, for instance, are generally bold and imaginative men and women who strive to accomplish a dream. Through their eyes, the world is full of promise, and humans need only the courage of their convictions to make something of it. Alexandra Bergson, for example, can look out on the empty Nebraska prairie in *O Pioneers!*, imagine vast checkerboard fields of wheat and corn, and set about to create them. Similarly, *Death Comes for the Archbishop*'s Father Latour, undeterred by native resistance and even clerical hostility, builds a church in the desert Southwest first by ministering to hungry souls to form a congregation and then by building its symbolic representation on a rock foundation high above a growing city. Because their tasks are never easy, Cather's protagonists frequently meet with hardship and disappointment, so they are not naively optimistic. Yet they refuse to relinquish their dreams. Rather, as the title *O Pioneers!* implies, these are characters who blaze a trail for others to follow, and this characteristic gives them heroic stature.

The names of many of Cather's characters, among them Ántonia Shimerda, Thea Kronborg, Cécile and Euclide Auclair, Lena Lingard, Jean Marie Latour, and Alexandra Bersgon, reveal another significant aspect about them: they are immigrants or the descendants of immigrants from the Old World to the New. Cather's Bohemians, her Swedes, her French, and her Norwegians infuse a raw land with traditions and culture and bring habits of mind and being that add depth and form to crude civilizations. Some, like Anton Shimerda, break under the stress of that rawness, but her heroic characters expand under its influence. In their native countries, they would have been bound by traditions and social patterns, but in America, they have the freedom to use their heritage in bold and innovative ways. Transplanted in new soil, they grow and thrive to become their best selves, as Thea Kronborg does in *The Song of the Lark,* or to create a life commensurate with their intelligence and imagination, as Father Latour does in *Death Comes for the Archbishop.*

Central to these transformations is the land, and indeed, setting is a crucial element of Cather's vision. Like Godfrey St. Peter in *The Professor's House,* who cannot imagine living far from water that recalls to him Lake Michigan, the "inland sea" of his youth (*Later Novels* 114), all of Cather's central characters feel a vital connection to place. For Alexandra Bergson and Ántonia Shimerda, the Nebraska Divide, which extends limitlessly before their eyes, its red grasses undulating ceaselessly in the prevailing winds, is a vision of freedom and movement and possibility that inspires their lives. Thea Kronborg and Father Latour feel the same about the colors and shapes of the desert Southwest. Cather fills her novels with descriptive passages that evoke the beauty of the landscape because place, she recognizes, helps shape a worldview, providing a sense of the relationship between humans and the universe.

This emphasis on place, moreover, grounds Cather's fiction in the pastoral tradition. With roots in classical literature, the pastoral tradition celebrates the values of rural life—the freedom, the simplicity, the naturalness. Living close to nature and following the organic rhythms of time and the seasons, humans feel their connection to the universe and know themselves as part of it. In nature, they have the possibility to grow into their own best selves and to create an ideal civilization. From its beginnings, in fact, the pastoral has had utopian associations and been connected to the perfection of Arcadia and even of Eden. These associations took root in America when the Puritans began their errand into the wilderness, believing that the New World offered a "new heaven, new earth" in which to reclaim a fallen world.

Cather was certainly aware of this tradition, and she made it an element of her fiction through her emphasis on place. Indeed, in a letter to her friend Elizabeth Shepley Sergeant, she referred to her first prairie novel, *O Pioneers!,* as a "two-part pastoral" (Lee 89). Her reference evokes another quality of the tradition of which Cather was certainly aware: its duality. Pastoral, on the one hand, celebrates human connection to and feeling for the land and makes an ideal of rural life. Such a celebration, however, implies the existence of a contrasting reality, one in which struggle and disappointment in a harsh and cruel environment are as probable as growth and fruition. Pastoral, on the other hand, thus mourns a distant and preferable past the characteristics of which have disappeared from the contemporary landscape. This "two-part pastoral" gives the tradition its elegiac tone, its nostalgia for a golden age that probably never truly existed.

Cather's fictional worlds evoke the pastoral's dualities. They are located in places where the promise of that new golden age seems still possible—on the Nebraska Divide or in the Canadian wilderness, in places that provide the raw materials for the creative imagination and the energy of a sympathetic person to tease into being their inherent beauty. Or they are grounded in places where a beautiful civilization once flourished—in the desert Southwest, where the remnants of that lost world of the cliff dwellers testify to the glorious past to inspire other generations. Sometimes, as in *The Song of the Lark,* Cather even evokes both, for Thea Kronborg's Moonstone, Colorado, is simply Red Cloud, Nebraska, relocated to the mountains, and the singer finds both solace and inspiration among Arizona's cliff-dweller ruins. Nevertheless, these idealized worlds clearly remind readers of the distance between the real and the ideal, and that distance provides the novels with their nostalgic tinge, their sense of resigned regret for an irrecoverable loss.

This distance and this tone ultimately arise from Cather's thematic issues. During a period of rapid industrialization and increasing commercialism, Willa Cather had watched with dismay the transformation of American culture and values. The world in which she lived was far different from the Nebraska prairie of her youth, where she had observed the creation of another sort of culture, one produced by heroic action, force of will, and supple imagination. It was in this world that Cather found the inspiration for her true subject. Essentially an idealist, she wrote stories of pioneers (and generally immigrant pioneers), whether in the historical or the recent past, that celebrated the values, the ideals, and the habits of mind and being that created lives worth living and civilizations worth being. Indeed, Cather's best writing is retrospective because the past offers glimpses of ideals still capable of inspiration, and Cather believed in these ideals. As her companion Edith Lewis noted in her memoir of Cather, she had "a great gift for imaginative historical reconstruction," yet "there was nothing of the antiquarian in her; she did not care for old things because they were old or curious or rare—she cared for them only as they expressed the human spirit and the human lot on earth" (119–20).

Cather's pioneers are frequently exiles, and they face an environment hostile to their existence. Their successes are sometimes qualified, and none of them escapes pain. Despite their all-too-human predicaments, however, they refuse to surrender to a conception of themselves or their worlds that gives meaning to their efforts and existence. Alexandra Bergson, for instance, loses her two elder brothers to the commercial spirit of the age and her beloved younger brother to a romantic dream, but the heroine of *O Pioneers!,* inspired by an idea that has become her life, presides over the taming of the land and the creation of a new civilization. Similarly, Tom Outland loses his precious relics and his friendship with Roddy Blake, but he consoles himself with the understanding that these losses have purified his ideal. Indeed, once he loses his "motives" for being there, the mesa, he discovers, is "no longer an adventure, but a religious emotion" (*The Professor's House, Later Novels* 253).

Cather clearly invests her characters' commitment to their ideals with dignity and heroism. She then offers their example to a modern generation for whom progress and materialism have become the engine of life and conformity and conventionality threaten to crush the individual spirit. In this way, she expresses a profound belief in human potential and suggests that the beauty of a civilization derives from those who strive to realize and maintain eternal ideals. Cather's fiction springs from hope, but it is hope tempered by an awareness of the harsh realities and human failings that frequently result in disaster. In fact, according to Joan Acocella, "her idealism, her belief that behind what is essentially the disaster of life there lies some order, some realm of meaning, that explains and dignifies our existence, turns it from a disaster into a tragedy" (81). This transformation gives Cather's best fiction its elegiac quality. It also makes clear that her nostalgia was far from sweet sentimentality, her retrospective vision far from reactionary. Indeed, Cather celebrated not a particular past but exemplary pasts, periods when humans achieved civilizations or even personal goals commensurate with their best selves. Her traditionalism thus springs from her profound belief in life's inherent possibility and significance.

These elements of a literary career confirm Cather's place among the major American writers of the twentieth century. While the quality of her fiction may have declined with age and her disapproval of the modern world solidified, Cather was as much a critic of her era as her contemporaries, including fellow midwesterners Theodore Dreiser, Sinclair Lewis, and Sherwood Anderson. However much she may be identified with the Nebraska prairies, moreover, Willa Cather knew the world beyond her parish, and she expressed her understanding in fiction that continues to resonate a worldview profoundly humane. Indeed, Cather's best fiction has a strength and individuality that promise her a continued place in American literary history.

3

A Writer's Beginnings: *The Troll Garden* (1905) and *Alexander's Bridge* (1912)

Like countless other young writers, Willa Cather struggled to find her subject and her voice, to discover her literary terrain. Thus, her first two published works, 1905's *The Troll Garden,* a collection of seven short stories, and the novella *Alexander's Bridge* (1912), are more Henry James than Willa Cather. Set primarily within the bastions of Anglo-American civilization—Boston, New York, and London—that the elder American novelist had a generation before claimed the most suitable ground for fiction, her stories and novella explored territory that, according to the scholar Hermione Lee, "she felt at the time an American novelist *ought* to use" (83). Tales of the East rather than the West, the literary space that she would soon claim her own, they give evidence of her developing talent but not of her unique vision. Cather herself would eventually dismiss these early works as "youthful vanities and gaudy extravagances" ("Preface," *Stories, Poems, and Other Writings* 942), exercises in imitation by an "inexperienced writer [unable] to distinguish between [her] own material and that which [she] would like to make [her] own" ("Preface" 941). As examples of a writer's beginnings, however, the best of the stories in *The Troll Garden,* such as "Paul's Case" and "'A Death in the Desert,'" and *Alexander's Bridge* are worthy of attention, for in them Cather explores some thematic issues and develops some literary strategies that will prove characteristic of her mature fiction.

THE TROLL GARDEN

Cather prefaces the seven stories that constitute *The Troll Garden* with ominous quotations from the works of two British writers, Charles Kingsley's *The Roman and the Teuton* and Christina Rosetti's "Goblin Market," both of which evoke the principal subject of the collection's best works—the nature of art. Both quotations suggest that art is something "rare and strange," to use Kingsley's words, that, like the goblins' fruit, is dangerously seductive. In this uneven collection of stories, three of which she will later repudiate and four of which she will eventually reprint, with minor revisions, in her 1920 collection of stories *Youth and the Bright Medusa,* Cather explores this subject and theme, as she will do in her 1915 novel *The Song of the Lark.* A literary artist at the beginning of her own career, she certainly had experience of art's seductions. Her stories are perhaps the expression of that experience.

The weakest of *The Troll Garden* stories are those in which Cather tries most self-consciously to demonstrate her talent. Because the influence of other writers, particularly Henry James, is strong in them, the well-structured stories seem rather artificial. Cather had not yet claimed her own authorial voice, so the stories seem too much like exercises in technique. The first of the repudiated stories, for instance, "Flavia and Her Artists," is an ironic tale of a woman who "collects" artists in the self-deceptive belief that she is among the few who possess a true discernment of art. Flavia, however, possesses only the ability to "soak up the very trash and drift" of her artists' "day dreams" (*Early Novels and Stories* 26); she has none of their artistic sensibility. The story's climax comes when Flavia overhears her artists' opinions of her and her husband plays the Philistine, sacrificing himself to permit her to protect her self-image. Cather presents her tale through the eyes of a sensitive young woman who is half in love with Flavia's husband, a strategy that lends it considerable poignancy and demonstrates considerable control of her narrative elements. She demonstrates similar control in "The Garden Lodge," the second of the repudiated stories and one that in its coolly composed heroine, who contains an imaginative and sensitive other self, anticipates the conflict in *Alexander's Bridge.* Its heroine, Caroline Noble, realizes too late in life that she has made herself too "paramountly cool-headed, slow of impulse, and disgustingly practical" (*Early Novels and Stories* 44) to escape her family's bohemian poverty. Awakened again to her own submerged romanticism following the visit of a singer who had once made her long, despite her resolve, for "an hour of life" (*Early Novels and Stories* 58), she spends a long night reviewing "the catalogue of her self-deprivations" (*Early Novels and Stories* 57) in a nightmare that expresses "something she had kept so close a prisoner that she had never seen it herself; it was the wail from the donjon deeps when the watch slept" (*Early Novels and Stories* 60). In the cool light of day, however, Caroline despises her weakness and retreats into the safety of her comfortable but unlived life. "The Garden Lodge" is a competent story, but it lacks the passion of felt experience or deep commitment to an idea. So, to some extent, does the most Jamesian of *The Troll Garden*'s rejected stories, "The Marriage of Phaedra." Like James's "The Author of Beltraffio," the plot of Cather's tale focuses on a philistine wife who misunderstands and mistrusts the artistic creations of her husband, a famous painter. Three years after his death, Lady Ellen Treffinger, bitter still about a quarrel occasioned by a painting that most probably would have been Hugh Treffinger's masterpiece, had he lived to complete it, betrays his final wishes and sells it unfinished to an Australian gallery, entombing it and all it represents to an oblivion she feels it deserves.

The four stories reprinted from *The Troll Garden* in the later collection of stories, *Youth and the Bright Medusa,* share a thematic focus on the artist and the artistic sensibility thwarted by the prosaic, the utterly ordinary. "The Sculptor's Funeral," for instance, brings a distinguished modern sculptor who has died at the young age of 40 home for burial to Sand City, Kansas, where his parents live still. The story's conception provides Cather with an opportunity to expose the petty materialism and narrow conventionality of the sculptor's family and neighbors, all of whom lack the capacity to recognize his genius. His mother's "demonstrative piety and ingenious cruelty" had made her son's life "a hell" (*Early Novels and Stories* 40). The townsfolk, equally hypocritical and censorious, now gloat over what they consider his weaknesses—his lack of practical ability, his preference for an uncommonly fine sunset, even, his sympathetic former Sunday-school teacher and the town's minister recalls, his taste for wine (*Early Novels and Stories* 42–45). Only the town's lawyer, who had hoped for a greatness equal to the sculptor's but had become nothing more than a "shyster" (*Early Novels and Stories* 47) under the influence of his pinched environment and prosaic models, is sensitive to the sculptor's achievement. Cather leaves it to him to chastise his neighbors for their complacent narrow-mindedness and selfish hatred of a man who made them all feel their insignificance (*Early Novels and Stories* 45-47). The lawyer's railing speech is arguably the weakest part of the story because Cather has employed other narrative elements, chiefly irony, or reversals, and tone, the author's attitude toward her subject, to convey her point. It does, nevertheless, provide a dramatic set piece with which to conclude her story of the "yearning of a boy, cast ashore upon a desert of newness and ugliness and sordidness, for all that is chastened and old, and noble with traditions" (*Early Novels and Stories* 42).

Cather returns to this theme, but from a slightly different angle, in "Paul's Case," the last story in *The Troll Garden* and one of her most famous. In it, she offers Paul, as the story's title suggests, as an example of yearning sensitivity destroyed by grim convention. A high school student with nothing but contempt for his drab Pittsburgh home and a dread of the grubby commercial future that seems an inevitability in his life, Paul dreams of escaping to the world of beauty that he imagines just beyond his reach—and far from "the burghers of Cordelia Street" (*Early Novels and Stories* 118) in Pittsburgh. A job ushering at the theater and a friendship with a young actor provide him with a glimpse of that world, opening to him the "portal of Romance" (*Early Novels and Stories* 121), and prompt him to cross its threshold. Removed from school, where he had frustrated his teachers, denied admission to the theater, and forced to take a bank job, Paul plots his escape and then steals a day's receipts and boards a train to New York, where he reinvents himself in his desired image (*Early Novels and Stories* 125). Yet Paul's sense of possibility is narrow, limited by the conventionality of Cordelia Street. Believing that a gaudy artificiality is the essence of beauty (*Early Novels and Stories* 120), he squanders his dreams on a wardrobe befitting a gentleman and a suite at the Waldorf, on the "mere stage properties" (*Early Novels and Stories* 127) of a world that offers so much more, and therein lies Paul's tragedy. He lacks the capacity and the passion to do more than pursue a counterfeit beauty, and he is utterly the product of his world. Nine days after his bold but misguided escape, Paul awakes from his dream when he learns that his father has refunded his theft and is making his way east to bring home his son. Refusing his fate, Paul throws himself beneath a train and "[drops] back into the immense design of things" (*Early Novels and Stories* 131). Paul's has indeed been a "bad case" but not, as Cather makes clear, for the reasons his teachers and father ascribe. They would have had him be satisfied with so much less than life promises. Indeed, they have prepared him for so much less. But at his death, Paul sees "with merciless clearness, the vastness of what he had left undone... the blue of Adriatic water, the yellow of Algerian sands" (*Early Novels and Stories* 131). His epiphany reveals the meaning of Paul's case.

In "'A Death in the Desert,'" yet another tale of the artist, Cather tells the story of Katharine Gaylord, a singer who has come to die of tuberculosis in the cultural desert of Cheyenne, Wyoming. Distinct from the other tales, it offers a cautionary perspective on the seductions of art, suggesting that the artist risks alienation from others in pursuit of an ideal. Although a loving brother and sister, for instance, minister to Katharine's physical needs, Charley, her brother, who would give everything to bring her peace, is acutely aware that a chasm separates them from each other and selflessly sympathizes with her plight. As he tells Everett Hilgarde, the brother of Katharine's teacher and mentor, "She got to Chicago, and then to New York, and then to Europe, where she went up like lightning, and got a taste for it all; and now she's dying here like a rat in a hole, out of her own world, and she can't fall back into ours" (*Early Novels and Stories* 65). The only thing that unites them now is childhood memories of their life in Bird City, Iowa, little consolation the former railway brakeman, who "can't spell straight" (*Early Novels and Stories* 66), forlornly understands.

If the pursuit of art has separated Katharine from her brother and sister, so, too, has it divided Everett from his elder brother Adriance, a famous composer to whom the younger man bears an uncanny resemblance. Brilliant where Everett is merely competent, charismatic where Everett is merely pleasant, Adriance had been secretly and unrequitedly the love of Katharine's life, just as Katharine had been the love of Everett's. Aware that his role in life has been as "stopgap" to his brother's (*Early Novels and Stories* 73), Everett had quietly accepted defeat but walked away from that destiny on the night of Adriance and Katharine's greatest New York triumph, having "[realized] more keenly than ever before how far this glorious world of beautiful creations lay from the paths of men like himself" (*Early Novels and Stories* 73). Now, years later, he finds himself substituting for Adriance to bring comfort to Katharine during the final weeks of her life after she mistakes him for his brother when chance brings him to Cheyenne. Everett's self-sacrificing compassion, like Charley's self-effacing generosity, stands in stark contrast to the essential self-interest, however, unconscious, of both Adriance and Katharine. Their pursuit of art may have elevated them above the mundane, but it has cost them, "'A Death in the Desert'" suggests, a measure of their humanity, isolating them in a moral desert far more troubling than any cultural desert they could possibly inhabit.

In "A Wagner Matinée," Cather continues to develop her contrast between the cultural deserts of the West and the bright world of art in the East but with none of the qualifications of "'A Death in the Desert.'" The first-person narrator of the story, a Nebraska native who made his success in Boston, plans to repay his visiting Aunt Georgiana for "some of the glorious moments" (*Early Novels and Stories* 105) she had given him during his hard and stark youth. Aunt Georgiana, a former music teacher at the Boston Conservatory, had years before rashly eloped with a shiftless country boy with nothing more to recommend him than his good looks. To avoid the criticism of family and friends, the couple settled on the Nebraska frontier, eking out an existence that, 30 years later, has transformed Aunt Georgiana into a wizened old woman seemingly incapable of any thought or feeling beyond worry for a weak calf and a tin of opened mackerel (*Early Novels and Stories* 104–5). Yet the narrator cannot forget the kindness his aunt had shown him in his youth, when, weary from work, she had introduced him to Shakespeare and mythology and taught him Latin and the music scales. To his Aunt Georgiana, the narrator owes all that is fine in him, so when she comes east on business after her long Nebraska "martyrdom," he takes her to hear a programme of music by the German composer Richard Wagner. Under the influence of his *Tannhaüser* and *Tristan and Isolde, The Flying Dutchman*, and Siegfried's funeral march from the *Ring* cycle, Aunt Georgiana's sensibilities reawaken. By the end of the concert, she breaks into tears and pleads not to be exiled again to the barren wilds. Her nephew, who has through her transformation relived his own, understands and sympathizes with her impulse. "For her," he realizes, "just outside the door of the concert hall, lay the black pond with the cattle-tracked bluffs; the tall unpainted house, with weather-curled boards; naked as a tower, the crook-backed ash seedlings where the dish-cloths hung to dry; the gaunt, mounting turkeys picking up refuse about the kitchen door" (*Early Novels and Stories* 110). The pathos in the narrator's own recollections, which Cather substitutes for his aunt's, suggests the irreconcilable differences between rural provincialism and cosmopolitan culture. These differences are the unifying element of the best stories in *The Troll Garden,* and Cather will continue to examine them in novels such as *The Song of the Lark.* At this point in her career, these differences also sound vaguely as a literary manifesto, as Cather the Nebraskan announcing the arrival of Cather the artist. With *The Troll Garden,* Cather had indeed entered the seductive world of art.

ALEXANDER'S BRIDGE

Ten years after the publication of *Alexander's Bridge,* in a preface to a new edition of her first novella, Willa Cather dismissed her early work because it was based on material "external" ("Preface," *Stories, Poems, and Other Writings* 941) to her experience. Critics may have received the work kindly. A critic for the *New York Times Book Review,* for instance, concluded a favorable review of the novel by praising Cather's "faculty ... of catching and describing in terse refined phrase the salient features of personality both mental and physical" (O'Connor 37), and the influential critic H. L. Mencken, writing in *Smart Set,* declared it a "promising piece," praising not only Cather's descriptive ability but also her capacity to invent realistic and purposeful dialogue. The influence of Edith Wharton may have been unmistakable, Mencken conceded, but he found hope in Cather's choice of model and her effort to "aim higher" than the majority of beginning writers. He concluded his evaluation with the observation, "She writes carefully, skillfully, artistically" (O'Connor 41). To Cather, nevertheless, *Alexander's Bridge* did not ring true. It was an exercise in style and technique, written at a time when her chief interest was "discoveries about ... art" ("Preface," *Stories, Poems, and Other Writings* 941), comparable, she wrote nine years later, in another essay, to an artist's "studio picture" ("My First Novels," *Stories, Poems, and Other Writings* 963). Although she had tried to imitate Henry James and Edith Wharton, the "most interesting" (*Stories, Poems, and Other Writings* 964) contemporary American novelists, Cather, in hindsight, judged her effort "shallow" and "conventional" (*Stories, Poems, and Other Writings* 963), too much the product of invention, and was intent on distancing herself from it.

Alexander's Bridge may in fact be an exercise in imitation, but it also contains flashes of the mature Cather in its complicated, self-destructive protagonist, or central character, and in its use of a detached narrator whose presence frames the tale. Published in three installments as *Alexander's Masquerade* in *McClure's* magazine in February 1912, the novella, which was subsequently published as a book (under its original title) in April 1912, tells the story of Bartley Alexander, an engineer who attempts unsuccessfully to bridge conflicting desires. A "tamer of rivers" (*Stories, Poems, and Other Writings* 283), Alexander is one of the most famous and successful bridge builders in the world, his 10 great bridges evidence of his power to shape the future. Raised in the West, the engineer had gone east to build his empire; married a cultured and distinguished woman, Winifred; and settled into comfortable Boston life. But as middle age besets him, Alexander begins to feel the burden of his success and to fear the loss of his youth, with all its promise of possibility. On a business trip to London, he meets again an Irish actress, Hilda Burgoyne, with whom he had been in love in Paris during his youth, and they resume their affair. What follows is a transatlantic struggle, embodied in the two women, between Alexander's conflicting desires, a struggle that the guilt-stricken engineer seems powerless to resolve. An engineered crisis, however, resolves it for him. Just as Alexander seems ready to collapse under the strain, the bridge that he is designing in Canada, the scene of his first triumph, begins to show signs of a fatal flaw. As Alexander inspects the structure, it snaps apart and collapses beneath his feet, plunging him into the river below. Although he survives the fall, he drowns when a gang of French Canadian construction workers, many of whom cannot swim, pulls him to death in their frenzy to survive. His death leaves the women he loved empty and forlorn and prompts Professor Lucius Wilson, one of Alexander's former professors who has remained in the background of his pupil's life, an interested observer of his rise and fall, to sum up the meaning of the engineer's life. "He belonged," Wilson explains to Hilda, "to the people who make the play, and most of us are onlookers at the best" (*Stories, Poems, and Other Writings* 351). Wilson's judgment, however, only hints at the complex contradictions embodied in Cather's protagonist.

PLOT DEVELOPMENT

The plot of *Alexander's Bridge* is tightly structured and economic, qualities that contribute to the tension in Bartley Alexander's story. Chapters 1 to 4 introduce the cast of characters, establish the situation, and initiate the novella's central conflict. On an April afternoon full of all the promise of spring, Professor Lucius Wilson arrives in Boston to visit his former pupil, Alexander. He meets Alexander's wife, Winifred, whose dignity, grandeur, and intelligence impress him favorably, and tries to get beneath the surface of the successful engineer's existence to discover whether Alexander, who had always been rather an enigma to him, has at last reconciled his striving force to life's realities. He concludes that Alexander is a man who "simply wouldn't square" (*Stories, Poems, and Other Writings* 286), a judgment that the events in three subsequent chapters prove most accurate, for when the engineer rekindles his romance with the actress Hilda Burgoyne, he risks all that he has achieved.

Chapters 5 to 9 dramatize Alexander's disastrous struggle to "live out [all] his potentialities" (*Stories, Poems, and Other Writings* 285), a struggle that Cather embodies in the two women he loves. Chapter 5, with its Christmas setting, provides a sympathetic portrait of Alexander's marriage to Winifred and then focuses on a guilt-stricken Alexander's turmoil during a transatlantic ocean crossing to Hilda at the New Year. Cather counters the portrait of Alexander's stately marriage with a glimpse of the joy that the actress and the engineer share in their London life. The remaining chapters in this section of the novella focus on Alexander's increasingly desperate efforts to choose between equally desirable options and his utter inability to do so. The section culminates when Hilda, who has traveled to New York to duplicate her London stage success on Broadway, goes to Alexander's apartment to end their affair, but neither proves capable of self-denial.

Cather resolves Alexander's internal struggle in Chapter 10, when the Moorlock Bridge, which will be on its completion the largest cantilever bridge in the world and the engineer's greatest achievement, collapses under its own weight. The bridge, which has been a "continual anxiety" (*Stories, Poems, and Other Writings* 312) for Alexander, clearly functions in the novella as a symbol, or representation, of the engineer, who has found the weight of his situation equally unbearable. His death in the bridge disaster thus makes clear that the engineer had sought to bridge an untenable gap and, like the structure he had created, had simply self-destructed.

Alexander's death, however, does not end Cather's tale. In an epilogue set six years after the disaster, Professor Wilson, whose perspective had shaped the first chapter and reinforced the affirmative portrayal of his former pupil's marriage in the Christmas scene at the heart of the work, once again delivers his assessment of the meaning of Alexander's life—and to a rather unlikely audience, Hilda Burgoyne. Following a chance meeting at the British Museum, Wilson and Hilda had struck up a fast friendship based only in part on their common friend and have nurtured it in the years since his death. When Wilson returns to London after an extended visit in his homeland, where he had frequently called on Winifred Alexander, he goes straight to Hilda's apartment to confide his reflections to his friend. What he reveals is that Alexander lives still for all of them, that "he left an echo" (*Stories, Poems, and Other Writings* 351), a judgment with which Hilda concurs.

Functioning as a frame about the novel's major events, the scenes in which Professor Wilson figures at both the beginning and the end of *Alexander's Bridge* give evidence of the self-conscious artistry and the seriousness of purpose of Cather's first novel. Its plot is tightly structured, with Cather developing several contrasting scenes to delineate character and dramatize her major themes. In 10 chapters and an epilogue, Cather delivers economically a poignant tale of human temporality and the unlived life.

CHARACTER DEVELOPMENT

The focus of *Alexander's Bridge,* 43-year-old Bartley Alexander is a man of the moment and thus a supreme egoist, a man who cares only about himself. Seemingly untethered from his past or a future, he is the embodiment of now (*Stories, Poems, and Other Writings* 282), of all the possibility and potentiality that life promises. Within his sturdy physique are the power and energy of the machine, and, indeed, Cather likens Alexander to this dynamic force. Professor Wilson, for instance, who has known Alexander from his youth, reflects that "the machinery was always pounding away" (*Stories, Poems, and Other Writings* 285) in his former pupil and that even when he appears to be at rest Alexander has "merely closed the door of the engine-room and come up for an airing." Nothing, it seems, can stop this well-maintained and "powerful machine" (*Stories, Poems, and Other Writings* 299) from functioning.

Yet as he approaches middle age, Alexander begins to feel himself "fading and dying" (*Stories, Poems, and Other Writings* 299). At the beginning of his career, he had intended to use his power to preserve "his personal liberty at all costs," but now this "public man" finds that board memberships and committee obligations, the rewards of his professional achievement and thus in their own way another type of power, are restraining him from his intentions (*Stories, Poems, and Other Writings* 298) and leading to a premature burial. Intimations of mortality combine in Alexander with an innate dissatisfaction with limitation and a fierce determination to possess every potentiality (*Stories, Poems, and Other Writings* 285). He is convinced that "something unconquered" (*Stories, Poems, and Other Writings* 298) still fuels his spirit and is unwilling to accept the "dead calm of middle life" because he fears it (*Stories, Poems, and Other Writings* 298). Consequently, when chance reunites him with Hilda Burgoyne, he seizes the opportunity to experience again his passionate and youthful self, rekindling an affair with his first love for essentially selfish reasons. In her, he can embrace the self he once was and live again in the moment.

Alexander is essentially a divided self, a man who seeks to possess oppositions embodied in the women he loves. Winifred Alexander, for instance, is "the woman who had made his life, gratified his pride, and given direction to his tastes and habits" (*Stories, Poems, and Other Writings* 338). She represents his social self, the person he chooses to be for the world. Dignified and elegant, accomplished and intelligent, she epitomizes for Alexander the "grandeur and beauty of the world" (*Stories, Poems, and Other Writings* 338). In her, he possesses "Romance" (*Stories, Poems, and Other Writings* 338), the awe-inspiring ideal that imparts peace and beauty to his life. A woman who has willingly sacrificed her life to fulfill her husband's needs and desires (*Stories, Poems, and Other Writings* 315-16), Winifred exists only for Alexander, and he loves her with "all the tenderness, all the pride, all the devotion of which he was capable" (*Stories, Poems, and Other Writings* 338). But as the phrase "of which he was capable" suggests, Alexander's love for Winifred is not entirely satisfying. The stately interior spaces that he inhabits with his wife in their elegant townhouse on Boston's historic and refined Charles Street may be redolent with ease and comfort and harmony, yet even at Christmas, when azaleas and holly fill the house with the colors of the season, Alexander feels restless and dissatisfied (*Stories, Poems, and Other Writings* 314-15), trapped by the fine life for which he had once chosen Winifred (*Stories, Poems, and Other Writings* 293). His love for his wife lacks passion, "the energy of youth" (*Stories, Poems, and Other Writings* 338). That he had experienced in Hilda Burgoyne. That he now craves again.

Unlike Winifred, who embodies dignity, elegance, complexity, and maturity, the Irish actress Hilda Burgoyne retains something of the "happy little girl" (*Stories, Poems, and Other Writings* 320) about her when Alexander meets her again more than 12 years after he had ended their affair to marry another. Animated and energetic, Hilda laughs easily and finds joy everywhere, and her love of life is infectious. Simple and unpretentious, she is best suited to playing the role of a "ragged slip of a donkey girl" (*Stories, Poems, and Other Writings* 290) than a fine lady on the London stage. Nor would she ever play a Schumann piano composition with the brilliance and precision with which Winifred performs his "Carnival" for Professor Wilson (*Stories, Poems, and Other Writings* 285–86). Good old Irish songs are Hilda's forte. Indeed, when she plays and sings "The Harp that Once" at Alexander's request, she captivates him as Winifred was unable to do (*Stories, Poems, and Other Writings* 308–9). Everything about Hilda is charming and delightful, including her "jolly" little London flat, as Alexander pronounces it, so full of books and etchings and personal memorabilia that reflect its owner and thus give it an air of homeliness and comfort (*Stories, Poems, and Other Writings* 305). Like Alexander, or at least as Alexander believes himself to be, Hilda also lives in the moment, and she is not afraid to take risks (*Stories, Poems, and Other Writings* 294, 336). In Hilda, Alexander embraces his personal self, his ideal image, and recovers his "old sense of power" (*Stories, Poems, and Other Writings* 341).

If the female characters in *Alexander's Bridge* are important only insofar as they clarify aspects of Bartley's personality, then the only other character in the novel, Professor Lucius Wilson, performs a similar function. Cather presents the elderly man, a philosophy professor at the western university at which Alexander had earned his degree, as an astute judge of human nature. Indeed, he has come to Boston as the novel begins, more than 20 years since he first met Alexander, with whom he will be staying, to attend a "Congress of Psychologists" (*Stories, Poems, and Other Writings* 281). Moreover, he has a great capacity "for looking on at life" (*Stories, Poems, and Other Writings* 315). A man of discernment, of fine impressions and impeccable taste, Wilson has been intrigued by Alexander since his former pupil's school days, convinced that he was destined to "do something extraordinary" (*Stories, Poems, and Other Writings* 281). Alexander's achievements have justified his conviction. His visit with Alexander, moreover, has finally put to rest a nagging fear that his former pupil would someday self-destruct (*Stories, Poems, and Other Writings* 284). After all, any man capable of appreciating the subtle charms of Winifred, as Wilson himself is, and who fits so comfortably into her world must, he feels certain, have determined to accept some limits (*Stories, Poems, and Other Writings* 284–85). A man who has himself accepted limitation, Wilson is a bystander on life and thus stands in sharp contrast to Alexander, a man who shapes the moment by bridging potentialities.

Wilson's role in the novel and the placement of the scenes in which he appears suggest that Cather may have intended the professor to function as well as a point of view character. Yet he spends an insufficient amount of time as a participant in the novel's events, appearing in only three chapters, to carry the weight of an authorial perspective on Alexander's life. His evaluation of Alexander, moreover, as events so obviously make clear, is incomplete and even incorrect. As the omniscient, or all-knowing, third-person narrator observes after Alexander's death, "Even Lucius Wilson did not see in this accident the disaster he had once foretold" (*Stories, Poems, and Other Writings* 347). It is thus as Alexander's opposite that Wilson plays his most important role in *Alexander's Bridge,* and as his opposite he contributes to one of the novel's themes—the unlived life.

THEMATIC ISSUES

In a novel that reflects its Jamesian influences, it seems appropriate that Cather adopts one of Henry James's recurrent themes, or main points, as her own for her first novel, and in the character of Professor Lucius Wilson, she does indeed do so. Wilson is a prime example of the man who lives his life through others, generally, and quite often tragically, to his own regret. By temperament and perhaps even by training, since his education has honed his analytical skills and his discipline encourages a theoretical rather than a practical approach to existence, Wilson prefers to watch rather than to perform in life's drama. The elderly man, for example, has never married, although he had "always [been and continues to be] an interested observer of women" (*Stories, Poems, and Other Writings* 279) and clearly appreciates the charms of both Winifred Alexander and Hilda Burgoyne. Moreover, his only real relationship, if indeed it can be called a relationship, is with Alexander, a former pupil whom he sees infrequently. In fact, more than 20 years have passed since Alexander and Wilson studied together, and as Wilson now admits to Winifred, even those who knew him then probably did not know him (*Stories, Poems, and Other Writings* 281). With his great capacity for observing life, Wilson has clearly led a safe existence. Curious he may be about the world around him, as his interest in Alexander and his pleasure in traveling (*Stories, Poems, and Other Writings* 311) suggest, but he is untouched by tragedy, unscathed by deep emotional trauma, because he lives superficially. He may feel Alexander's loss, but not as those who loved him feel it, and by the novel's end, he has slipped quite happily into a friendship with Hilda Burgoyne, usurping as it were the engineer's place in her life.

As James develops his theme of the unlived life in a story such as "The Jolly Corner" (1909), the protagonist gradually awakens to an understanding that in waiting for his life to happen, he has watched it pass by him and regrets deeply the waste of possibility. He comes, in other words, to a profound self-knowledge too late to change his life, and therein lies his tragedy. As Cather develops the theme, Wilson fails to achieve such an understanding or such stature. These differences, however, do not greatly diminish her treatment of the theme because she uses the example of Bartley Alexander to make clear the pale imitation of life for which Wilson has settled.

Placed against Alexander's passionate efforts to embrace the whole of life and not to leave unexplored any opportunity, Wilson's cautious approach to experience seems pale indeed. As an engineer and a builder of bridges, Alexander has shaped the present and is forging the future. While it may be said that as his teacher Wilson has participated in his pupil's triumphs, Cather makes clear that Alexander's energy and drive are innate characteristics, and Wilson himself confesses that he presented a challenge to his teachers, who were uncertain of the approach to take with such potential (*Stories, Poems, and Other Writings* 282). As a man who has loved well, however unwisely, Alexander has experienced the full range of human emotion from deep content to utter anguish. Wilson, in contrast, inhabits a pleasant world that insulates him from the extremes of human experience, but as Cather suggests, Wilson's is no sort of life. Because she makes Alexander, despite his human flaws and egoistic excesses, the novel's sympathetic character, the character, in fact, whom Wilson appreciates and whose life he vicariously lives, the elderly man effectively exemplifies Alexander's worst fear. Wilson's has been a sort of death-in-life, safe and comfortable but pallid and forlorn. Wilson, unlike James's heroes, never recognizes the emptiness of his life, but he is not, after all, the focus of Cather's novel. Nevertheless, his inclusion in the novel as Alexander's opposite allows Cather to explore the theme of the unlived life and indeed to offer it as a counterpoint to the novel's primary theme, the fact of human mortality and its effect on human psychology.

Alexander's whole life is essentially a flight from death, his determination to pursue and live in the moment merely a manifestation of his fear of mortality. Cather reveals this fear early in the novel, shortly after Alexander discovers that Hilda Burgoyne, the love of his "restless twenties" (*Stories, Poems, and Other Writings* 295), is the toast of the London stage. Uncertain whether to renew their acquaintance, Alexander cannot resist an impulse to find her address in a directory and set off one evening to walk by her lodgings near Bedford Square. His route takes him past the British Museum, whose "sullen gray mass" (*Stories, Poems, and Other Writings* 295) makes him nervous and uncomfortable. To Alexander, the British Museum has always represented the "ultimate repository of mortality, where all the dead things in the world were assembled to make one's hour of youth the more precious" (*Stories, Poems, and Other Writings* 296). He and Hilda had been frequent visitors to the museum during the days of their romance, for it had been Hilda's favorite childhood haunt. Alexander, however, had always been eager and even relieved to escape to the warmth and sunlight beyond its "vaulted cold" (*Stories, Poems, and Other Writings* 296), for he feared that his vital force might somehow be tapped to reanimate the mummies. Twelve years after those previous visits, Alexander cannot shake his lingering impression of the museum's dark significance. Twelve years after those previous visits, firmly in the grasp of middle age and fearing again the specter of his own mortality, he recalls that it was Hilda, so full of youth and energy, who had snatched him back to the world of the living, and now he seeks her out again for the same reasons. In her, he can recover his youthful self.

Alexander conducts his second affair with Hilda in London, a city, he tells her, more than any other that "makes me want to live" (*Stories, Poems, and Other Writings* 328). It may often be sodden and gray, bleak and dull, but it pulses with life. Londoners, moreover, take advantage of the "moment[s] of miracle" (*Stories, Poems, and Other Writings* 327) granted them. On just such a day in mid-January, Alexander delays his departure to Liverpool and drives out to Kew Gardens with Hilda to seize the moment (*Stories, Poems, and Other Writings* 325-28), overcoming in doing so the death of the spirit that frightens him. The excursion is not, readers learn from their conversation, a singular event but rather representative of their relationship. Unlike his marriage to Winifred, which seems a thing surrounded by the stately walls of their Boston townhouse, his affair with Hilda vibrates to the rhythms of a busy city. In London, they dine in Soho, attend the theater, and visit the museums and galleries. Even when they share quiet moments in Hilda's delightful apartments, their conversation is stimulating and full of lively reminiscence. Each moment that Alexander spends with Hilda thereby vanquishes time, his enemy, and thus he is unable to end what he knows is a self-destructive affair (*Stories, Poems, and Other Writings* 331–32). To do so would be to have to accept human limitation, human mortality, and Alexander, as his letter to Hilda shortly before his death makes clear, is too cowardly to do so.

Mortality is, however, humankind's lot, a point that Cather underscores even during Alexander's London idyll by connecting it to the make believe of fairy tale through its dependence on the actress Hilda Burgoyne. Never one to assay challenging dramatic roles, Hilda excels instead at light comedy because she possesses the talent to make probable the improbable. In "Bog Lights," for instance, the play in which she features when Alexander rediscovers her in London, Hilda, who performs the role of a donkey-girl, uses her clear Irish voice, hearty Galway laugh, and lightness of foot to render convincing "what she had seen in the fairy rings at night" (*Stories, Poems, and Other Writings* 291). With her talent for creating illusion, Hilda is, as Alexander's companion on that night observes, the playwright's "poetic motif" (*Stories, Poems, and Other Writings* 291). She plays that role in Alexander's life as well. She re-creates the illusion of his youth and lets him join her on the stage to reenact it. Alexander is satisfied with the illusion, willing, like Hilda's London audience, to suspend his belief in what at some level he knows is truth.

Eventually, like the Moorlock Bridge, which has been "a continual anxiety" (*Stories, Poems, and Other Writings* 312) to him, Alexander also reaches his "strain limit" (*Stories, Poems, and Other Writings* 312) and collapses with his most audacious design. His death, of course, makes clear the obvious, that nobody escapes the grim specter. It also resolves Alexander's dilemma. Yet this resolution seemingly robs the novel of moral weight, denying the engineer the opportunity to make a conscious choice between the women who embody his alternatives. Granted, even as he journeyed north to Canada in a vain attempt to save his creation, Alexander still planned a return to Hilda in London (*Stories, Poems, and Other Writings* 341). He still refused, in other words, to accept his humanity, the effect of which is to diminish his stature, to make him merely pathetic, a sad, self-deceived creature who never really matures into adulthood.

Yet the novel's tone, the author's attitude toward her subject, suggests that Cather did not take this view of Alexander. In fact, in his efforts to defy death is something so human that Alexander is not pathetic but rather sympathetic. Few of us, after all, have not wished to recapture our youth or dreaded our inevitable death. Cather understands this human impulse and explores its consequences in *Alexander's Bridge,* making her true focus psychological rather than moral. What she makes clear in Alexander's story is the profound unease that death imparts to life.

A PSYCHOLOGICAL READING

Because Cather's focus is psychological rather than moral, *Alexander's Bridge* lends itself to a psychological interpretation of its key elements. Critics using this approach apply the methods of the psychoanalyst to the study of literature. They examine the minds of a novel's characters to explain motivation and action and seek in psychology the secrets of the literary work. This perspective is particularly appropriate to a novel that explores states of mind and being through use of the psychological motif of the double, and Cather's characterization of Bartley Alexander certainly indicates that he is such a divided self, a double, a person who contains contradictory desires and impulses. In fact, as the scholar Hermione Lee observes, the "power" of *Alexander's Bridge* resides "not in the relationships, but in the sinister qualities of Bartley's 'second man'" (85). Indeed, that "second man" (*Stories, Poems, and Other Writings* 332), to use Cather's phrase, is beguilingly attractive but dangerously self-destructive.

In his revolutionary study of the human mind, Austrian neurologist Sigmund Freud (1856–1939), founder of the field of psychoanalysis, essentially argued that the psyche is a composite of both conscious perceptions and unconscious urges and that unconscious needs and desires, or instincts, exert a powerful behavioral force on the "self," a force that is as strong as any conscious or physical need. Freud divided the psyche into three parts. The id, he explained, is the primitive part of the unconscious that is dominated by primary urges. It seeks immediate gratification of every desire and impulse, even those that may be self-destructive. Its opposite is the superego, that part of the psyche that creates an ideal self and that also functions as a conscience, registering approval or disapproval of one's thoughts and actions. Mediating between the two is the ego, the "self" that the individual projects to the world and that each person believes to be his or her identity, the conscious "self."

From Freud's explanation of the psyche and his description of what is essentially a composite self come as well the notion of the double. Sometimes called the alter ego or mirror image, the double objectifies a concept of the divided self that developed in the twentieth century and suggests the internal struggle between opposing selves within the individual. In literary terms, the double, which is sometimes known by its German equivalent, *Doppelgänger,* is a device whereby a character is self-duplicated. In other words, two different characters represent the same character. Two famous examples of the use of the double occur in Robert Louis Stevenson's *The Strange Case of Dr. Jekyll and Mr. Hyde* (1886) and Joseph Conrad's *Heart of Darkness* (1899/1902). Stevenson's Jekyll, the respected doctor, and his Hyde, the vicious criminal, are in reality one individual divided against himself. The characters have given rise to the phrase "Jekyll and Hyde personality." Conrad's narrator, Marlowe, discovers his double, Captain Kurtz, during a journey into uncharted territory that symbolically represents the unconscious, and thus the two characters are essentially one. As these examples suggest, use of the double allows writers to give depth to their explorations of their characters' psychology, and Cather puts it, in a less exaggerated form, to good effect in *Alexander's Bridge* to explore Bartley Alexander's divided self. She may not give her protagonist a physical second self, although Professor Wilson, who mirrors aspects of Alexander's public self, does indeed function to some extent in that role. But she does make clear that Alexander carries within himself a "second man" who is every bit as real as the man who bridges chasms.

As its original title, *Alexander's Masquerade,* suggests, performance is a central motif in Cather's novel. That Hilda Burgoyne trods the boards on the London stage is certainly one manifestation of the motif. So, too, is her role as chief illusionist, keeping alive his dream of his powerful youth, in Alexander's drama of self. Yet Alexander also gives a talented performance on life's stage. He is at once the successful professional and the romantic dreamer. His career may have been crowned by prestigious memberships on boards of directors and civic committees and his personal life validated by marriage to a distinguished and cultured woman, but he most desires the power and freedom of his spent youth. Inside the solid pillar of society is what Alexander confesses in a letter to Hilda a "pleasure-loving simpleton" of which he is "rather ashamed" grown "strong and sullen" (*Stories, Poems, and Other Writings* 332) now and vying for control of his life.

Alexander manages to keep his divided self in balance by performing his dual roles on separate stages. With Winifred in Boston, he really appears to be the man whose photograph is sought for the covers of Sunday newspaper supplements because it epitomizes a powerful natural force, as indestructible as the bridges he builds (*Stories, Poems, and Other Writings* 283). With Hilda in London, he believes himself to be that man. But the strain of playing two parts is, like the strain on the Moorlock Bridge, too much for anyone to bear, and Alexander, like his greatest conception, collapses of his own internal defects.

Alexander anticipates his self-destruction in his letter to Hilda, relating to her a memory from his western boyhood of "locoed horses" (*Stories, Poems, and Other Writings* 331) so "cunning" (*Stories, Poems, and Other Writings* 332) that they could escape the corral where wranglers would imprison them by feigning peace and contentment. The wranglers, however, always knew that the horses were merely "scheming" (*Stories, Poems, and Other Writings* 332) to gain their freedom because a diet of loco, which unleashed them from conformity, was preferable to the oats that made them placid. Alexander, too, is like those scheming horses. He lives on "the edge of danger" (*Stories, Poems, and Other Writings* 331) because there he lives. Everywhere else life seems merely counterfeit to him. So he schemes, he dissimulates, he plays his double part, but in the end, he explains to Hilda, "a man is meant to live only one life in this world" (*Stories, Poems, and Other Writings* 332). The impulse toward danger contained in his "second man" obliterates him. For a nature such as Alexander's, divided against itself, obliteration, his example suggests, is the only and inevitable end.

From any critical perspective, *Alexander's Bridge* has a complexity of design and scope that makes Alexander's struggle compelling and sad because it is so very human and even so very contemporary. He strives to achieve all his possibilities and thereby defeat the specter of death that resides in limitation. He responds to the powerful life force that animates every person, even when that force threatens his obliteration. In her debut novel, Willa Cather demonstrated a mature understanding of human nature. She had only to discover her own terrain to achieve her greatness. In her second novel, *O Pioneers!* (1913), she would make that discovery.

4

"The Land beneath Your Feet": *O Pioneers!* (1913)

In 1912, following a six-month leave of absence from her editorial position at *McClure's Magazine* during which she explored the American Southwest, Willa Cather, as she confessed in her 1931 essay "My First Novels (There Were Two)," "began to write a book entirely for myself" (*Stories, Poems, and Other Writings* 963). That book, published in 1913 as *O Pioneers!*, was a tale of immigrants to the Nebraska prairie of her youth. Writing it, according to Cather, was so natural, so spontaneous, that it felt as if she were "taking a ride through a familiar country on a horse that knew the way, on a fine morning when you felt like riding" (*Stories, Poems, and Other Writings* 963). Although it was only her second novel, *O Pioneers!* marked a turning point for Cather. She had discovered, as she later advised, that "fiction [should] grow out of the land beneath your feet." *O Pioneers!* was her first full-length treatment of that land. In it, she laid claim to her true subject and found her authentic voice.

O Pioneers! is the story of Alexandra Bergson, the only daughter of Swedish immigrants to the Nebraska prairie. When her father dies, Alexandra must use all her good sense and her powers of imagination and persuasion to wrest a living for herself, her mother, and her three brothers from the inhospitable land. Sixteen years later, having tamed the prairie and erected a comfortable home-stead, Alexandra now looks with satisfaction on her achievement and in anticipation of her youngest brother Emil's possibilities. Her dreams for his future are dashed, however, when Emil falls in love with a married woman, the lively and lovely Bohemian Marie Tovesky Shabata. When Marie's husband, Frank, murders the lovers, Alexandra must draw on all her resources of hope and faith and her intuitive understanding of the cycles of death and renewal to rise from despair. With her in the end is a childhood friend, Carl Linstrum, whose appreciation of Alexandra's deep capacity to love the land and its inhabitants will help her to heal. A celebration of the human spirit, an exploration of the tensions between the Old World and the New, and an encounter with the land that shaped it all, *O Pioneers!* also announced the arrival of a distinctive literary vision and voice.

GENESIS AND CRITICAL RECEPTION

Even before her journey to the Southwest, Cather had begun to develop some of the material that would eventually constitute *O Pioneers!* in stories of the Nebraskan plains. The plot of her story "The Bohemian Girl," for instance, published in *McClure's* in 1912, anticipates the love triangle of *O Pioneers!* but without its tragic ending. Twelve years after he had escaped the drudgery of the family homestead in Nebraska, Nils Ericson returns from Europe to retrieve the gypsy-spirited Clara Vavrika, the love of his youth. She may be married to his dour and conventional brother Olaf, but Nils and Clara are too much alike to be tamed by the land. Their two dark shadows ride into the midnight sky, and they catch a train that frees them from the weight of obligation that threatens to destroy their spirits, avoiding the tragic destiny of Emil and Marie in *O Pioneers!*. Cather was also composing two other Nebraska sketches, "Alexandra" and "The White Mulberry Tree," that she would eventually incorporate into her novel. Despite the success of *Alexander's Bridge,* she was not inspired by its world and was turning instead to the Nebraska of her youth for inspiration. But until she traveled to Arizona and New Mexico and encountered another alien landscape that needed to be translated into language, she did not know what to do with her vast expanses of sky and earth, her incomparable immigrant intruders. By the time she returned east, however, Cather seemed to have gained perspective on her world and acquired a strategy for writing it into existence. Her prose and her plot should be as natural as her subjects, without the artifice of art. Once she freed herself of conventional expectations about the novel, Cather had begun her fine morning ride, and *O Pioneers!* quickly took shape.

Critical response to the novel, which was published in June 1913, was enthusiastic, a clear validation of Cather's instincts. In review after review, critics responded favorably to the novelty of Cather's subject. Other writers may have treated the West realistically, but Cather, according to Gardner W. Wood in *McClure's,* had given readers "the West in action, a great romantic novel ... in which one sees emerge a new country and a new people" (O'Connor 45). While it did not explore "the large ideas" (O'Connor 47), noted Floyd Dell in the *Chicago Evening Post,* that are by convention the novel's true subject, it was "worthy," nevertheless, "of being recognized as the most vital, subtle and artistic piece of the year's fiction" (O'Connor 47). Critics also praised the style of Cather's work and her treatment of her subject. The novel's "dramatic power," observed the critic for the *Boston Evening Transcript,* was a product of "the simplicity—one might almost say severity," of Cather's touch (O'Connor 45). In "vividly sketched scenes," asserted the critic of the *Sewanee Review,* Cather had "broken new ground" in *O Pioneers!,* and she had achieved her end with "no torturing of words, no forcing of the mood; all is done without conscious effort and with artistic restraint and reserve" (O'Connor 57). Cather had imbued *O Pioneers!,* claimed the critic of the *New York Times Book Review,* with a "deep instinct for the land" and a "vital consciousness of the dignity and value of the life that may be lived upon it" (O'Connor 56). Without doubt, such praise makes clear, Cather's novel had opened new worlds of thought and feeling to her readers, and they had been touched by the experience.

PLOT DEVELOPMENT

The simplicity of treatment that pleased critics of *O Pioneers!* does not mean that the novel lacks artistic control. In fact, the plot of *O Pioneers!,* or the arrangements of its parts, gives evidence of Cather's manipulation of time and event to achieve her effect. She divides the novel into five sections, the first two of which, separated from each other by 16 years, develop character in action and plant the seeds of events that will come to fruition in the last two sections. A brief interlude of mounting tension joins the novel's two parts. None of the sections is packed with event, a strategy that gives weight and meaning to the action that does occur, and always Cather places those events in relation to the land. It is, after all, that relation with which she is most concerned.

Part I of *O Pioneers!*, titled "The Wild Land," establishes the fact of the land and its powerful presence in and effect on the lives of Cather's pioneers, especially its first chapter, wherein she sketches the outlines of the novel's entire plot. On a blustery, bitterly cold January day, 16-year-old Alexandra Bergson and her five-year-old brother Emil have come into what passes for a town on the Nebraska plain—"two uneven rows of wooden buildings" anchored by the "squat red railway station" and grain elevator at one end, the lumberyard and horse pond at the other (*Early Novels and Stories* 139)—to buy provisions for the family farm on the Divide. Everything about the town has a look of impermanence, from the dwelling houses that are "set about haphazard on the tough prairie sod" to the town itself, which is "trying not to be blown away" from the Nebraska tableland to which it is "anchored" (*Early Novels and Stories* 139). The town's human inhabitants, wearing coarse woolens and heavy shawls, scurry briskly from one place of shelter to another. Some fortify themselves with strong liquor. Only the doll-like Marie Tovesky, visiting from Omaha, enlivens the scene, and only Alexandra, a "tall, strong girl" who carries herself with a soldier's bearing (*Early Novels and Stories* 140), seems capable of mastering such a world. When Emil's kitten strands itself on a telegraph pole, she quickly enlists the help of her 15-year-old friend Carl Linstrum to rescue it and thereby proves her mettle. Disaster averted, Emil and Marie are soon playing cheerily together, while Alexandra and Carl resolutely discuss her father's impending death, and then, a long, cold journey ahead of them, Alexandra and Emil, accompanied part of the way by Carl, set off for home, "going deeper and deeper into the dark country" (*Early Novels and Stories* 146) until they disappear into the inhospitable waste.

In this first chapter, Cather introduces Alexandra, her main character, and those who will figure most prominently in her story, foreshadowing their relation to each other and establishing their relation to the land that threatens their existence. She will elaborate this point in the remainder of Part I as she details the circumstances that led the Bergsons to emigrate from Sweden 11 years before the novel's present moment, describes the hardships they and other immigrants struggled to overcome to eke out an existence on the "wild land," and then, by implication, focuses on Alexandra's heroic efforts to preserve the family farm following her father's death. Her success, Cather makes clear, has little to do with the hard, physical labor of her elder brothers, Lou and Oscar, and everything to do with her resourcefulness, her imagination, and her identification with the land itself. Three years after her father's death, when other immigrants, including Carl Linstrum, have given up on their chances of success and returned to the cities of the East, Alexandra makes her own chance as she begins to speculate on land, convinced that the time has come for it to give way to their efforts. Thirteen years later, as Part II begins, readers see that her instincts have been right.

"Neighboring Fields," as the title of Part II of *O Pioneers!* suggests, is not so much about the connection between humans and the land as it is about the relationships between humans themselves. Sixteen years after Mr. Bergson's death, the "wild land" has been tamed into a checkerboard of fertile fields light and dark with corn and wheat, and Alexandra, who owns one of the most prosperous farms on the Divide, has time now to enjoy her success and to cultivate relationships. Her primary companion is Marie Shabata, the little Bohemian girl with whom Emil had played in the novel's opening chapter, a married woman now in her early twenties, having eloped with the handsome but surly Frank Shabata when she was 18, and to whom Alexandra has sold the former Linstrum homestead. She employs three lively Swedish girls, primarily to "hear them giggle" (*Early Novels and Stories* 179) in her kitchen, and has befriended old Ivar, a Norwegian eccentric with a gift for treating animals, who sleeps, at his insistence, in her barn. Having divided the family property among them, Lou and Oscar are as comfortable (but not as satisfied) as their sister, and Emil, who has earned a degree at the state university, has returned to the family homestead to determine his future course.

Homecomings, however, not only Emil's but also Carl Linstrum's, precipitate the crucial developments in this section of the novel and signal the equally treacherous ground that supports human relationships. Emil and the deeply unhappy Marie fall in love, but with no hope of a future together, Emil takes a job in Mexico City to distance himself from his pain. Alexandra, too, must cope with disappointment in love when Lou and Oscar, greedily fearing that she will marry Carl and thereby cause them to lose her share of the family property, confront first Alexandra and then, having failed to bully her into submission, Carl, with the foolishness of their relationship. She is, after all, nearly 40 years old, they remind her, and Carl lacks her material prosperity. Unwilling to flaunt convention, her timid suitor departs for the Klondike to become worthy of Alexandra's love, leaving Cather's heroine lonely and alone within her neighboring fields. Only the loving and happy marriage of French immigrants Amédée and Angélique Chevalier, which occurs early in Part II, serves as counterpoint to the other lovers' pain and as promise of human love.

Part III of *O Pioneers!*, titled "Winter Memories," is a brief interlude, two chapters, in fact, that builds an atmosphere of suspended living and mounting tension. Its tone is melancholic, for, as the narrator observes, "one could easily believe that in that dead [winter] landscape the germs of life and fruitfulness were extinct forever" (*Early Novels and Stories* 229). Indeed, during the long winter months, Alexandra settles back into her routine existence, but without the comfort of Marie Shabata's frank and open confidences or even the irritating interruptions of her brothers' visits. Christmas passes, enlivened only by the traditional visit of old Mrs. Lee, Lou's mother-in-law, whose unregenerate Old World customs are an embarrassment to her Americanized and socially conscious daughter but a great source of empathetic joy to Alexandra. Like the "iron country" outside her door, Alexandra seems frozen, waiting for the promise of spring and new life.

While Part III does not advance the novel's plot by event, it does give psychological depth to Cather's characterization of Alexandra, who has been rendered primarily in descriptive terms such as "resourcefulness" (*Early Novels and Stories* 148) and "strength of will" (*Early Novels and Stories* 149) but whose surface has seldom been scratched. Now Cather offers two "winter memories" that reveal something of the self that Alexandra keeps hidden from others and even that she seldom explores herself. The first memory recalls one of the happiest days in her life (*Early Novels and Stories* 238), when she and Emil had watched a solitary wild duck "swimming and diving and preening her feathers" (*Early Novels and Stories* 237) with such uninhibited joy that in the instant Alexandra had intuited life's beauty. The second recalls Alexandra's "fancy" (*Early Novels and Stories* 238) of a strong man who lifts her in his arms "as easily as if she were a sheaf of wheat" (*Early Novels and Stories* 238), rescuing her from weariness and solitude. These "winter memories" reveal a romantic side to Alexandra's character that may account for her intuitive identification with the land and that also suggests a vulnerability that her physical presence generally belies.

Cather brings the love affair between Emil and Marie to a tragic conclusion in Part IV, titled "The White Mulberry Tree," when death intrudes into this garden. Although they have continued to resist their mutual attraction following his return to the Divide from Mexico City, Emil and Marie, miserable and hopeless, finally turn to each other following the death of Amédée Chevalier, Emil's dear friend, from acute appendicitis only a week after the birth of his first child. They lie in an embrace beneath the white mulberry tree in Marie's orchard when Frank Shabata, who has always been resentful of his wife's ability to enjoy life and suspicious of others' affection for her, returns to an empty house. Armed with his rifle, Frank searches for Marie and, when he finds her in the orchard, fires three shots and then leaves the lovers to die. In this section of *O Pioneers!,* it seems that romantic love and passion are doomed by the forces of man and nature.

In the novel's final section, titled "Alexandra," Cather reintegrates her heroine into the natural life cycle. Gradually emerging from grief, Alexandra travels first to the university at Lincoln to learn something of Emil's life there and then to the state prison to reconcile with Frank Shabata and thereby include him within the human community. Alexandra undertakes these difficult journeys unaccompanied by family or friends, but she returns to the Divide to be comforted by Carl, who had read of the family tragedy in a four-week-old San Francisco newspaper and then made his way by steamer and train to be by her side. All passion spent, all conventions insignificant, the prospect of marriage between best friends Alexandra and Carl seems destined to fit into the larger scheme of life, for they are mature enough to understand that "the land is always here" (*Early Novels and Stories 289*), long after humans have ceased to exist. In its reconciliation of the relation between humans and nature, *O Pioneers!* restores the balance between the transient and the eternal, and Cather celebrates both. It is a resolution toward which every plot element has been tending.

CHARACTER DEVELOPMENT

At the heart of every section of *O Pioneers!* is Alexandra Bergson, Cather's protagonist, or central character, whose strength of being and purpose makes her a human complement to the land. From the moment she appears in the novel, a 16-year-old girl wearing a "man's long ulster" coat and striding "rapidly and resolutely, as if she knew exactly where she was going and what she was going to do next" (*Early Novels and Stories* 140), Alexandra looks capable of facing any challenge. Indeed, Cather describes her in military terms. She has the bearing of a "young soldier" (*Early Novels and Stories* 140), despite her heavy man's coat, and is capable of turning a "glance of Amazonian fierceness" (*Early Novels and Stories* 141) on anyone who affronts her, including the salesman who dares to exclaim at the reddish-yellow mass of hair that she can barely contain in two thick braids. Like the women warriors of Greek mythology who cut off one breast to improve their prowess with the bow, Alexandra is the image of strength and determination. She is primed to stand firm against the vagaries of nature and to tame a wild land.

Alexandra's strength comes at least in part from her innate good sense and native intelligence. Unlike her elder brothers, Lou and Oscar, who are industrious but conventional, "meant to follow in paths already marked out for them, not to break trails in a new country" (*Early Novels and Stories* 161), Alexandra is resourceful and imaginative. She sees, for example, the possibility in the land, even though it resists cultivation, and determines to keep hold of her father's stake when her brothers prefer to sell. She even mortgages her family's future on the acquisition of new land, an act to which her brothers only grudgingly acquiesce but that eventually pays dividends, just as Alexandra had know it would. Before his death, John Bergson had rightly put his faith in his only daughter and entrusted his family's future to her. "A pioneer," observes the narrator, "should have imagination, should be able to enjoy the idea of things more than the things themselves" (*Early Novels and Stories* 161). Alexandra, her father knew, was a pioneer.

As a true pioneer, Alexandra not only understands the land but also develops an intimate relationship with it. During some of her hardest days, she had once returned from a visit to the fertile river farms to experience an epiphany of "love and yearning" (*Early Novels and Stories* 170) for the high Divide. The insects' chirping then had been "the sweetest music" (*Early Novels and Stories* 173) to her ears, and "she had felt as if her hurt were hiding ... with the quail and the plover and all the little wild things that crooned or buzzed in the sun" (*Early Novels and Stories* 173). Sixteen years after her father's death, her prosperity ensured, she seems now almost a part of the land, her house an extension of it (*Early Novels and Stories* 178). Her skin is warm and brown where the sun has kissed it, and the curls that escape from the two thick braids that she still wears coiled about her head transform her into "one of the big double sunflowers that fringe her vegetable garden" (*Early Novels and Stories* 180). A living, growing being who responds to the rhythms of nature, Alexandra has taken root in the land and draws sustenance from it. The land, in response, has "bent lower than it ever bent to a human will before" (*Early Novels and Stories* 170), giving itself like a lover to its beloved.

Alexandra's friendship with the eccentric old Norwegian Ivar confirms her loving and intuitive relationship with the land. A virtual hermit who lives in a clay bank, Crazy Ivar, as everyone calls him, prefers his own company or that of the animals that he instinctively understands to human companionship. His Bible, he tells those who seek his services as a horse doctor or call to purchase one of his handmade hammocks, seems "truer" to him on his "wild homestead" than life in human society (*Early Novels and Stories* 156). Most people scoff at Ivar's peculiar ideas and customs, but not Alexandra. In fact, shortly after her father's death, she seeks and follows his counsel when she fears her hogs may develop the sickness that is killing her neighbors' livestock. Years later, when he has lost his land through mismanagement, Alexandra gives him a home on her farm and even defends him against her brothers' threat to institutionalize the embarrassing old man. He may have retained his Old World habits and failed to learn English, but Alexandra respects his worldview that sees value in all living creatures and understands that his life is a form of worship. Their shared response to the land and its habitants provides a firm foundation for mutual trust and regard.

For all her intuitive understanding of the land, however, Alexandra is surprisingly obtuse about personal relationships and even rather lacking in self-knowledge. Practical in the extreme, she is oblivious to anything unrelated to her goal of taming the land and building her empire, so she fails to notice her brother Emil's infatuation with Marie Shabata and even neglects her own emotional life. In fact, because Alexandra seems perfectly content with her life as a spinster, her brothers meet her announcement of marriage to Carl Linstrum with disbelief. But as Cather reveals in the young woman's winter memories of a strong, supportive man who will share her burdens, Alexandra does indeed desire companionship and love, even if she is only half aware of her need, and will eventually find her life's companion in Carl, a man who may lack her vigor but with whom she shares fundamental values and beliefs.

Cather gives Alexandra's "blind side" (*Early Novels and Stories* 237) about the deep heart's core its opposite in the gypsy-spirited Bohemian Marie Tovesky Shabata. The "carefully nurtured" little girl with the "coaxing" red mouth, dark curls, and tiger eyes who attracts a circle of male admirers in the novel's opening chapter (*Early Novels and Stories* 143) grows into a beautiful but willful young woman who refuses to let life's hardships erase its joys and thus remains admired and loved by others. Whereas Alexandra is "armored in calm" (*Early Novels and Stories* 204), Marie is alert and animated. In her company, others find it hard to be still. She is charming and passionate and breathlessly and infectiously embraces life and its gifts. Sensitive to others' needs and emotions, she suspects Alexandra's feelings for Carl when her own family is oblivious to them (*Early Novels and Stories* 213). She is also sympathetic to her husband Frank's unhappiness not only with life but also with her. Indeed, she understands that the very qualities that define her being and give others pleasure anger her husband and cause him to be resentful and jealous of her resilient happiness. As her marriage disintegrates, she blames herself rather than Frank for its failure, confiding in Alexandra that he should have married a different sort of woman, someone who would have doted on him above every other thing or being in the world (*Early Novels and Stories* 234–35). Marie, however, is not that sort of woman. Her gifts are for laughter and love wherever she finds them, so try as she does to resist her feelings for Emil, she simply cannot do so. She must follow her heart, passionately, even recklessly, no matter where it leads her.

Cather's primary female characters, different though they may be in their response to life, are both strong, capable women who refuse to submit to hardship and unhappiness. It is to Alexandra's care, after all, that John Bergson leaves his family at his death, and one of the irritants in the Shabata marriage is that Frank has been unable to make Marie "[humble] herself" to him (*Early Novels and Stories* 245). Cather's primary male characters, however, are rather weak and ineffectual, not quite capable of the tasks life sets them.

Carl Linstrum, for instance, is a dreamer, Alexandra's counterpart in imagination, but he lacks her practicality and is timid and self-conscious, qualities that undermine his efforts in the world. In the opening chapter, Cather gives the 15-year-old young man the courage to scale a telegraph pole on a blustery winter day to rescue, at Alexandra's request, Emil's wayward kitten and the sensitivity to empathize with Alexandra's stoic confession of her father's impending death. But she also makes it clear that Carl's eyes are fixed on chromium engravings (*Early Novels and Stories* 141) and that, unlike Alexandra, he has far more interest in his magic lantern than in the expense of fattening a steer or the weight of a hog. When the Linstrums abandon farming four years later to return to the city, Carl is only unhappy to be leaving Alexandra. He had never wanted to farm, never felt attached to the land. In fact, he confides to Alexandra 16 years later when he stops to see her as he journeys westward, searching again for success, that he has remained "haunted" by the untamed land of his youth, for it had never felt like home to him (*Early Novels and Stories* 195). Whatever Carl had hoped to achieve in the city, his chance of success had already bypassed him before he arrived (*Early Novels and Stories* 197), for he was old-fashioned even as a teen and remains so still, rooted in the ways of the past and of the Old World (*Early Novels and Stories* 195).

Carl will bend to the will of the community, expressed by Lou and Oscar, and leave Alexandra a second time, venturing into the Klondike to become worthy of her love and her position, but he will achieve no more success on that frontier than he achieved on the Divide or in Chicago. He is too sensitive for the world in which he lives, best suited, in fact, to support Alexandra because he alone truly understands her. His value thus lies not in his achievements but in his being. In a wild land that needs conquered, however, qualities such as his are judged liabilities rather than strengths by everyone except Cather's heroine.

One of the qualities that Alexandra values about Carl is also true of her younger brother Emil: He has "not been tied to the plow ... and ... [has] a personality apart from the soil" (*Early Novels and Stories* 241). It is this destiny that had spurred Alexandra to toil relentlessly on the Divide. Recognizing—and indeed even boasting—that Emil is unlike anyone in the family (*Early Novels and Stories* 194), she has wanted her younger brother to have the freedom to choose his life and sent him to earn a degree at the state university. When he graduates, she will support his course of action, even if he chooses to return to the Divide. What matters to her is that he is free to choose. Yet what Alexandra cannot foresee is that Emil will choose to love.

When he falls in love with Marie Shabata, the little girl who had shared her candy with him in the novel's opening chapter, Emil, restless and brooding, responds to the romantic impulse at his heart's core. The most like his father of all his siblings, Emil is passionate about his feelings (*Early Novels and Stories* 195) and sensitive to his world. In fact, he shares his sister's winter memory of the wild duck's perfection (*Early Novels and Stories* 237-38). So Marie's attraction for him is not surprising. Beautiful, spirited, and independent, she, too, is a wild thing and, like the duck that Emil shoots on an outing with Marie, "too happy to kill" (*Early Novels and Stories* 200). That outing, of course, foreshadows, or anticipates, the tragic outcome of Emil and Marie's relationship, but it also dramatizes the sheer delight and heartfelt sympathy that they take in each other's company and that serve as the basis of their love. Sexual tension is certainly an element of their relationship, but on the day of their deaths, Emil actually determines that he can "love forever without faltering and without sin" (*Early Novels and Stories* 264). Under the influence of Raoul Marcel's haunting rendition of the "Ave Maria" at the Roman Catholic confirmation service, he has an epiphany, or moment of intense insight, that he can be satisfied with the ideal of love, the "rapture" that the feeling instills in him (*Early Novels and Stories* 264). Emil's emotional susceptibility certainly makes him different from most of the settlers on the Divide, and in the end it also makes him unfit for the harsh realities there. His death at the hands of a man who embodies some of those realities is inevitable.

Frank Shabata may be the antithesis of Emil Bergson, brutal where the other man is sensitive, selfish and sulky where he is generous and passionate, but he is no more suited to life on the Divide than Cather's other male characters. The Bohemian immigrant had cut a dashing figure in Omaha, where he had captured the adulation of every young woman in the city, but on the Divide, the only remaining reminders of his young heyday are the little wisp of a yellow cane that he once carried (*Early Novels and Stories* 233) and Marie, the beauty with whom he eloped primarily because her father had refused permission to marry (*Early Novels and Stories* 209). Hard life on the Divide has reduced Frank's stature in the community and annihilated his self-esteem. Trapped in a life that he never wanted, Frank finds his only solace in blaming others—and chiefly Marie—for his situation (*Early Novels and Stories* 267). Because everyone admires and dotes on his wife, he is jealous and resentful and determined to make her as unhappy as he is, but that he cannot do (*Early Novels and Stories* 245). A broken man even before the novel's end, which finds him literally imprisoned in the state penitentiary, Frank Shabata provides evidence of the Divide's destructive power over human destiny. It takes strength, resolve, vision, and a certain amount of stoicism to prevail on the frontier. In *O Pioneers!*, Cather's male characters generally lack such qualities and are thus unfitted for life there.

All of Cather's characters struggle with themselves and others in *O Pioneers!* to forge a productive and satisfying life. They struggle as well with the land itself, for it effectively functions as an independent character in the novel. Cather endows her wild land with human characteristics, using personification to dignify its stature and make it an active participant in life's drama. The "great fact" of *O Pioneers!* is "the land itself," Cather's narrator asserts in the novel's first chapter (*Early Novels and Stories* 144). It wants "to be let alone, to preserve its own fierce strength, its peculiar, savage kind of beauty, its uninterrupted mournfulness" (*Early Novels and Stories* 145). It does not wish to be tamed, and "its Genius [is] unfriendly to man" (*Early Novels and Stories* 147). The land that Cather's pioneers determine to inhabit has a will of its own that makes it a formidable force that they must struggle hard to conquer. Indeed, the struggle between the pioneers and the land is a virtual contest of wills. Drought and wind, blizzards and hail, indeed all the forces of nature, are its weapons against the pioneers' determined encroachment on the Divide, but after years of resistance, it finally awakens to the touch of those, like Alexandra, who have come to acknowledge and respect its being and simply "stretched itself" (*Early Novels and Stories* 194) to them, surrendering its riches at last to the triumphant pioneers.

Cather's use of language clearly invests the land with its own humanity, its own genius, as she calls it, and thus makes it one of the novel's most important characters. In doing so, she makes the contest of wills between the Divide and the pioneers as compelling as that between Marie and Frank Shabata or between Emil's conflicting desires. Her strategy also establishes the ground for her exploration of the relationship between the land and its human inhabitants that is a central theme of *O Pioneers!*. Indeed, she integrates that theme so tightly into her characterizations that it is virtually impossible to separate character from theme in the work.

THEMATIC ISSUES

As the fates of Cather's characters demonstrate, the relationship between humans and the land they inhabit nurtures some and destroys others. Those with the patience and understanding to learn its rhythms and take root in its soil eventually thrive. They are her true pioneers, for, as the narrator asserts, "the history of every country begins in the heart of a man or a woman" (*Early Novels and Stories* 170). Those, in contrast, who cannot accommodate themselves to their world wither on the vine or develop into some sort of tasteless hybrid. Cather's sympathies lie undeniably with the pioneers, and Alexandra Bergson, of course, and even Marie Shabata are the most obvious examples of her bias. She makes her point as well, however, in the example of old Ivar, whose reverence for the land testifies to its spiritual element, but chiefly in the efforts and admonitions of John Bergson and the experience of Carl Linstrum, both of whom speak to the values embodied in the land.

On his deathbed, John Bergson elicits Alexandra's promise to do all she can to preserve their homestead and to prevent her brothers from retreating to the city in discouragement (*Early Novels and Stories* 150) because he believes in the value of the land itself (*Early Novels and Stories* 148). In it lie incomparable possibilities that the city could never hope to offer. Granted, as Carl tells Alexandra, the city provides all sorts of enjoyments, but their price is a shiftless and anonymous existence. Rooted in the land, human beings become individuals; they have unique histories, and others feel their absence or loss (*Early Novels and Stories* 197). In the city, however, humans become part of the mass; they live to pay their rent and leave nothing of significance behind at their deaths, not even someone to mourn them. As Carl reveals to Alexandra, "We live in the streets, in the parks, in the theatres. We sit in restaurants and concert halls and look about at the hundreds of our own kind and shudder" (*Early Novels and Stories* 198). Alexandra may not have entirely understood the reason that her father had extracted his promise from her years before, but her conversation with Carl certainly clarifies his perspective.

Yet Alexandra, like Cather, is not naive enough to ignore the human cost of the land. "We pay a high rent, too," she responds to Carl, "though we pay differently" (*Early Novels and Stories* 198). Life on the Divide offers little to nourish the intellect or to satisfy the artistic sensibility. In the cities, humans may become part of the anonymous mass, but on the land, they risk becoming draft animals, dull and heavy from physical labor. Emil's complaint to Marie, "I get tired of seeing men and horses going up and down, up and down" (*Early Novels and Stories* 213), speaks directly to Alexandra's perspective, and so, too, do the examples of Lou and Oscar Bergson. Neither clever nor ambitious, Alexandra's brothers do not change as they mature; they simply grow "more and more like themselves" (*Early Novels and Stories* 185), becoming conventional and complacent as they prosper. Always mistrustful of their sister's schemes, they now patronize the woman who engineered their success, ridiculing her desire to marry and claiming that her share of the family property is merely hers in trust, that it must one day revert to its true male owners (*Early Novels and Stories* 218–22). Full of others' opinions, they speak authoritatively about matters they barely comprehend. In Lou and Oscar's presence,

Alexandra confronts the effects of the land's limitations, its deadening routine and limited vistas, and knows, as she tells Carl, that "if the world were no wider than my cornfields, ... I wouldn't feel that it was much worth while to work" (*Early Novels and Stories* 198). The land may give humans the opportunity to be and to become, but if it limits their possibilities, then the hardships may be worthless.

Despite these reservations, Cather never loses faith in the land. It is steadfast and eternal, something on which to build. In the aftermath of Emil's murder, Alexandra will falter under her burden of grief and will stumble into uncertainty when she travels to Omaha in an effort to retrieve something of her brother's existence and salvage something of Frank's and thereby redeem her life. But her redemption comes only when she returns to the land. There she knows again the peace and freedom of something substantive and sustaining. There she finds again reason to hope. That is the land's gift to those who understand and accept the transient nature of their hold on it. These are the truths about the relation between the land and its inhabitants that Cather celebrates in *O Pioneers!*.

While Cather may have discovered her true theme in *O Pioneers!*, she did not make it the sole preoccupation of her work. In fact, a secondary theme, the relation between the Old World and the New, continues to link her to her Jamesian origins, even if she gives her international theme its own spin. In doing so, she creates a novel about the immigrant experience that gets beneath the clichés and explores its complexities. As the scholar David Daiches observes, "*O Pioneers!* is the first of a group of novels in which the impact of a young country on the sad sensitivity of uprooted Europeans is presented with a sympathy and an insight rare in American writers" (20). The Old World reflected in Cather's Swedes and Czechs, Germans and French, is not simply a corrupt and decadent place from which they blithely flee to a land of freedom and opportunity. It has values and traditions and a sense of community that had once sustained them, so they transport what they can of those qualities to the New World and labor to transplant them there. But that New World has its own genius, its own demands. Consequently, the new life that takes shape on Cather's prairie arises from the tension between the Old and the New, and the true pioneers are those who can negotiate the space between them, retaining their Old World strengths as they accept the challenges of their New World future.

Cather peoples her frontier with immigrants and their children and conveys some sense of the Old World lives that they left behind in the remnants that they have retained in the New. Lou still plays on his *dragharmonika,* and Alexandra can recite by heart long passages of the "Frithjof Saga," while Marie's talent for baking the dozen different types of Bohemian breads and sweet rolls is a source of delight to many. Religion remains a constant in their lives, with church fairs, weddings, and confirmation services providing a cause for celebration and building as well a sense of community among different ethic peoples. On the prairie, Emil's best friend is the lively Frenchman Amédée Chevalier, and Alexandra employs as her foreman Barney Flinn, a big, redheaded Irishman. Dour and smug Swedes and Norwegians mingle with the freethinking Bohemians and swaggering French.

Those like Alexandra who thrive on the prairie seem to have the ability to adapt Old World customs to the challenges of the New. Indeed, they seem to embrace those challenges as opportunities for growth and development. They, of course, are Cather's true pioneers, forging their destinies in and with the land. Others, however, lack their vision or their resilience. They adapt to their new lives but seem somehow diminished by their experiences. Cather provides two different categories of this second type of immigrant, distinguished by their connection to their European roots.

Alexandra's brothers Lou and Oscar and their families epitomize the first group. Having survived the difficult early days on the prairie and prospered during the intervening years, Alexandra's extended family seems intent on discarding the trappings of their ethnicity and becoming thoroughly Americanized and modern. Lou's wife Annie, for instance, prattles excitedly to a bemused Carl about her new bathtub, her daughter's talent for wood burning, and her plans to relocate her family to the city, awed by the presence of someone who is to her the embodiment of urbanity and oblivious to the superficiality and materialism reflected in her chatter. Carl, of course, knows that less than 20 years ago, Annie had worked barefoot in the fields like her mother. Now, however, the "up and coming" (*Early Novels and Stories* 193) woman draped in jewelry and wearing a hat shaped like a battleship is embarrassed by her mother's provincial habits, insisting that she wear shoes, bathe in that porcelain tub, and sleep without her nightcap (*Early Novels and Stories* 183–84), in other words, that she abandon her Old World ways and habits. For the same reason, Lou and Oscar threaten to send Crazy Ivar to the asylum. Whereas in the Old World, eccentrics like Ivar would have been tolerated, in the New World, they are despised for their difference, their failure to conform a threat to the fledgling social order (*Early Novels and Stories* 182).

For every immigrant eager to divest himself or herself of the taint of the Old World, however, Cather's Nebraska prairie harbors a Crazy Ivar, a Mrs. Lee, and even a Mrs. Bergson, her second group of immigrants. They cling so tightly to their Old World ways that a real future in the New World seems closed to them. Mrs. Bergson, for instance, for whom habit had died hard, had insisted on a log house when the prairie standard was a sod one and sent her boys to the river twice a year because she missed her traditional fish diet. Her chief occupation was preserving and pickling the native fruits and berries and the produce from her garden against want, both physical and emotional, for her every effort once she immigrated to the New World was to "reconstruct her old life" as best she could (*Early Novels and Stories* 152). Habit dies equally hard in Mrs. Lee, who, despite the convenience of her daughter's modern bathtub, only pretends to use it, splashing the water noisily about and then secretly washing in her old wooden tub (*Early Novels and Stories* 184), and who treasures her traditional Christmas visit to Alexandra because her hostess gives her the freedom to indulge her Old World ways. At its best, the unregenerate provincialism of these immigrants is merely comic, at its worst, sad and pathetic. Yet Alexandra's tender indulgence of this group of immigrants, as opposed to her wry accommodation of the other, makes clear Cather's sympathies. Mrs. Bergson's "unremitting efforts to repeat the routine of her old life among new surroundings," notes the narrator, "had done a great deal to keep the family from disintegrating morally and getting careless in their ways" (*Early Novels and Stories* 151). Against the insistent pressure of the raw and the new, the old ways provide a touchstone of value the loss of which would impoverish them all.

In the end, Cather's international theme extends her exploration of the relation between the land and its inhabitants. Her immigrants transported with them the Old World habits and values that had shaped them, and they in turn help shape the New World order that the immigrants are in process of making. The Divide is a physical as well as a psychological frontier, and as Cather's pioneers negotiate their way through both, they gradually lay claim to a place and a self.

A MYTHOLOGICAL INTERPRETATION

Alexandra's intimate connection to the land and Cather's evocation of the Amazons to describe her central character suggest ground for an alternate critical approach to *O Pioneers!,* one that focuses on the mythological elements of the tale. Closely connected to the psychological approach to literature outlined in Chapter 3, mythological criticism seeks to explain the motives underlying human behavior. Unlike psychological criticism, however, it finds its answers not in the biological sciences but in religion, anthropology, and cultural history. To arrive at their conclusions, myth critics thus exa-mine the archetypes and archetypal patterns—the shared images, formulas, and types—on which writers draw to give order and a frame of meaning to their personal perceptions and visions.

Myths, according to scholars of religion and anthropology, make concrete and particular a special perception of human beings or a worldview; they are a symbolic language through which primitive people express themselves and interpret natural events. Found at the beginnings of every culture, myths are part of every literature. They differ from legends because they rely less on historical background and more on the supernatural; they differ from fables because they are less concerned with teaching a moral lesson and because they are the product of a society rather than the creation of an individual. Collective and communal by nature, myths bind a tribe or a nation together in that people's common psychological and spiritual activities.

A dynamic creation, myth transcends both time and place; it unites the past, or traditional modes of belief, to the present's current values and reaches toward the future in its expression of spiritual and cultural aspirations. Furthermore, although every culture has its own distinctive mythology that may be reflected in its legends, folklore, and ideologies, myth is, in the general sense, universal. In fact, the mythology of all groups, as scholars such as Sir James Frazer, Claude Lévi-Strauss, and Joseph Campbell have demonstrated, centers on certain common motifs or themes: they attempt to explain creation, divinity, and religion; to probe the meaning of existence and death; to account for natural events; and to chronicle the exploits of cultural heroes. They also share certain images, called archetypes, that tend to elicit comparable psychological responses and to serve cultural functions. Water, for instance, is universally associated with the mystery of creation; fertility and growth; the cycle of birth, death, and resurrection; and purification and redemption.

Writers, the myth critic believes, draw consciously or unconsciously on these archetypes to express their own unique responses to the world and simultaneously to connect their visions to some universal response that resonates in the minds of readers. The myth critic seeks to discover the universal understanding through analysis of the work's archetypes. As dramatic or narrative embodiments of a people's perception of the deepest truths, myths thus serve as a useful lens through which to examine literature, and mythological critics, who believe that literature is informed by these preliterary constructs, or understandings, find in it traces of primordial ritual and ceremony, collective memory, unconsciously held value systems, and general beliefs.

Cather relies primarily on mythological associations to give depth and meaning to her characterizations of Marie Shabata and Alexandra Bergson. Marie, for instance, is a sort of dryad, or forest nymph, connected to the pre-Christian tree worshippers by her Bohemian heritage and half believing, like them, that the linden tree could "purify" the forest and cast off evil spells that had lasted through the centuries. The comparison certainly suits Marie, whose natural element does indeed seem to be everywhere that growing things thrive and wild things run free, but chiefly her garden and orchard, with its white mulberry trees. Yet, as Marie confesses to Emil, she most identifies with the trees because "they seem more resigned to the way they have to live than other things do" (*Early Novels and Stories* 212), a sad acknowledgment of a spiritual imprisonment that she shares with her mythological counterpart.

Alexandra also has her mythological counterpart. Compared to a sunflower (*Early Novels and Stories* 180), she possesses an intimate connection to the land and the power, it seems, to make things thrive there. During some of his darkest days, for instance, John Bergson draws comfort (and the family an income) from Alexandra's chickens, which continue to lay eggs through a cold winter (*Early Novels and Stories* 145). Years later, the "beauty and fruitfulness" of her far fields, the "order and fine arrangement manifest all over [her] great farm" (*Early Novels and Stories* 178), speak to her capacity to coexist with the land. Indeed, as the narrator observes, "it is in the soil that she expresses herself best" (*Early Novels and Stories* 178). These comparisons connect Alexandra to Demeter, the Earth-Mother or Corn-Mother in Greek mythology, a powerful goddess associated with both life and death.

One of the most important goddesses in ancient Greece, Demeter (or Ceres in Italy) was associated with vegetation and fruitfulness (and especially corn) and worshipped for her life-giving and nurturing qualities. By Zeus, the corn goddess bore a daughter, named Kore, the maiden, sometimes called Persephone (or, in Latin, Proserpina), and through the myth of her daughter's abduction to the underworld by Pluto was connected to the Eleusinian mysteries, a secret religious cult associated with fertility and death. According to the myth, following Kore's abduction, a desolate Demeter wandered over the face of the land in a vain search for her daughter. Disguised as an old woman, she eventually came to Eleusis, outside Athens, where she lived humbly and served as nurse to a young prince. When she eventually revealed herself as the goddess, the queen built her a temple-home, and there she brooded for a year, while the crops shriveled and men and animals died. Eventually Zeus intervened, ordering Pluto to release Kore to her mother. Their joyful reunion, however, was limited because Kore had eaten the sacred pomegranate in Hades and thereby formed a tie that bound her to return for a portion of each year. Yet the myth was generally interpreted to offer a promise of life after death, of eternal regeneration and renewal.

Cather connects Alexandra to Demeter to emphasize her own life-giving and life-sustaining qualities. In addition to her ability to transform the Divide, she nurtures her younger brother Emil, supporting his efforts and encouraging his dreams, and effectively becomes his surrogate mother. Like Demeter's loss of her child, Emil's murder plunges Alexandra into despair, and although she cannot recover her "child," she does find the strength to renew her faith in life. In fact, by the novel's end, Cather has merged Alexandra's identity with the land's in a celebratory vision that foresees her great heart at ease in the "bosom" of the earth, which brings it forth again "in the yellow wheat, in the rustling corn, in the shining eyes of youth!" (*Early Novels and Stories* 290). Like Demeter's, Alexandra's story is a promise of renewal for a new land that has such people in it.

In addition to evoking Demeter in *O Pioneers!,* Cather also draws on the myth of Acis and Galatea as a counterpoint to the tragic tale of Emil and Marie. According to the myth, Polyphemus, the son of Poseidon and a sea nymph, loved the nymph Galatea, but she scorned the one-eyed giant, loving instead the handsome Acis. In a jealous rage, the giant crushed Acis with a heavy rock. He lived eternally, however, when Galatea transformed her beloved into a Sicilian river bearing his name. While both of the lovers die in Cather's version of the myth, the outlines of the original certainly survive in the eternal triangle at the center of her plot and even, to some extent, in the fluttering butterflies that merge and hover above their lifeless bodies (*Early Novels and Stories* 272). That image, like the river Acis, is a promise that their love—and indeed their spirits—will live eternally.

Cather's use of myth in *O Pioneers!,* however, does more than give depth and meaning to its characters and events. It also places the novel within the pastoral tradition, as defined in Chapter 2, and thus enlarges its thematic issues and links it to a recurrent motif in American literature. In broadest terms, the pastoral myth evokes a golden world of perfection embodied in the rural landscape, an Arcadia where gods and humans once comported together in perfect harmony. That golden idyll passes, however. Arcadia becomes Eden under the influence of Christianity, and humans find themselves expelled from paradise, longing for their loss and intent on reclaiming it. This pastoral myth, as the scholar Leo Marx explains, is profoundly linked to the American dream of a new golden age in the New World, providing both a justification of and a plan for possession and expansion of the territory. "Down to the twentieth century the imagination of Americans," he points out, "was dominated by the idea of transform-ing the wild heartland into...a new 'Garden of the World'" (141). *O Pioneers!* is Cather's first exploration of and contribution to that myth in American literature.

Conceived as a "two-part pastoral" (Lee 89), *O Pioneers!* lays claim to its subject on a title page that borrows from the nineteenth-century American poet Walt Whitman for its title and uses an inscription from the exiled Polish poet Adam Mickiewicz's nationalistic epic of his lost land, "Pan Tadeusz." She dedicated the novel to her friend and mentor Sarah Orne Jewett, a nineteenth-century American writer whose stories of vanishing rural life in her fictional world of Dunnet Landing, Maine, Cather admired tremendously. Cather also prefaced her novel with one of her own poems, "Prairie Spring," in which a "somber," "sullen," "unresponsive" natural landscape opposes Youth's "flaming" desire. This various introductory material not only places *O Pioneers!* within the pastoral tradition but also evokes what the scholar Hermione Lee identifies as the "two kinds of pastoral" (91), the romantic, celebratory, but elegiac dream of rural perfection and the tough-minded portrayal of the heroic struggle demanded of humans to tame the land. Cather's "two-part pastoral" is both a celebration of rural potentiality and an acknowledgment of the labor and endurance that creates it.

Cather fills *O Pioneers!* with scenes of beauty and joy on the prairie. The "wild land" certainly has its own terrible beauty to which Alexandra gradually responds (*Early Novels and Stories* 173), but once tamed, the Divide is ripe with vegetation and teeming with set-tlers living in harmony together. As the narrator observes, "Few scenes [are] more gratifying than a spring plowing in that country, where the furrows of a single field often lie a mile in length, and the brown earth, with such a strong, clean smell, and such a power of growth and fertility in it, yields itself eagerly to the plow; rolls away from the shear, not even dimming the brightness of the metal, with a soft, deep sigh of happiness" (*Early Novels and Stories* 174). Neither want nor worry seems possible in such a world, and yet Cather had begun *O Pioneers!* with a harsh depiction of an inhospitable land and includes reminders throughout of the heroic labor and painful sacrifice that went into making it home. Moreover, murder and death intrude into her pastoral idyll, uncompromising reminders of transience. Cather, in other words, accommodates both kinds of pastoral in *O Pioneers!*, acknowledging at once the romantic impulse that animates human desire and the harsh realities that frustrate it.

Cather's mythic evocation of a rural paradise places *O Pioneers!* firmly within an American literary tradition that includes such nineteenth-century works as Nathaniel Hawthorne's *The Blithedale Romance* and Henry David Thoreau's *Walden* and F. Scott Fitzgerald's twentieth-century classic *The Great Gatsby*. Yet tinged with her own view of its limitations, it is also a deeply personal expression of the land beneath her feet. The Divide was Cather's world, and Alexandra Bergson is the embodiment of its ideal tenant. Strong and resolute, with the vision to see into the future and the stoicism to wait for it to happen, Alexandra becomes her best self in relation to the land. Her experience is the fate of all Cather's true pioneers.

5

The Song of the Lark (1915)

Willa Cather may have discovered her literary path in *O Pioneers!* (1913), but her next novel, 1915's *The Song of the Lark,* seems a necessary detour from it. Her story of a young girl's rise from western obscurity to international fame as an opera singer may have some of the features of her newly claimed territory—its western vistas, for instance, its immigrant pioneers, and its evocation of life lived amid hardship and want of every kind—but it is not primarily about them. Rather, *The Song of the Lark* is Cather's artistic manifesto. In it, the novelist examines the forces that shape the artist's vision and considers the meaning and purpose of art itself. In it, she affirms her belief that the artist's life and work do indeed matter. Like other portraits of the artist, *The Song of the Lark* is thus a triumphant tale of vision and voice for both Cather and her heroine and surrogate self, Thea Kronborg.

From her unlikely beginnings in Moonstone, Colorado, to her triumphant performance before the king at Buckingham Palace, Thea Kronborg is an uncommon personality. *The Song of the Lark* brings her to life in all her singularity. One of seven children born to a Swedish Methodist minister and his sensible wife, Thea might have seemed destined to slide into obscurity, but her musical talent distinguishes her from her family and her community. She is, moreover, fortunate in her friends and admirers, one of whom leaves her a six-hundred-dollar bequest to study in Chicago when he is killed in a rail accident. Still in her teens, Thea leaves Moonstone to pursue her muse. Her quest will eventually take her to Germany, but first she must acknowledge that she is not meant to be a pianist but a singer. She must also face personal loss and disappointment to fulfill her vocation. Yet so great is Thea's talent, so determined her soul, that her triumph is inevitable.

GENESIS AND CRITICAL RECEPTION

As several of the stories in *The Troll Garden* (1905) indicate, art and the artist had preoccupied Cather long before she attempted a full-scale treatment of the subjects in *The Song of the Lark*. She also had a great love of music, especially opera, and had written reviews of performances as well as profiles of singers early in her career, so it is not surprising that an opera singer should be the focus of her artistic manifesto. In fact, it may have been her interview and subsequent friendship with the Wagnerian soprano Olive Fremstad for her 1913 *McClure's* article "Three American Singers" that prompted Cather to create Thea Kronborg. At their first meeting, Fremstad was exhausted and too hoarse to give an interview, but later that evening she managed to perform brilliantly as a replacement for a soprano at New York's Metropolitan Opera House, much to Cather's amazement. On another occasion, Cather saw Fremstad just after a performance in Wagner's opera *Parsifal,* utterly depleted by the effort. What fascinated Cather about Fremstad's performance was her ability, according to the scholar Hermione Lee, "to project herself into the *idea* in the music" (121). As Cather wrote in her profile of the singer, "With Madame Fremstad one feels that ... the idea is so intensely experienced that it becomes emotion" (Brown 186–87). This ability to transmute idea into emotion and to transform the self into the vessel that contains it lies at the heart of Cather's artistic credo. Indeed, she will endow Thea Kronborg with the same qualities that she admired in Olive Fremstad and for which she strived with her own literary efforts, exploring the process of that transformation in *The Song of the Lark* perhaps to understand it.

Critics of the novel generally admired Cather's treatment of her subject in their reviews. Writing in *The Nation,* Henry Walcott Boynton observed that Cather "has attempted that most dangerous of feats—to trace the genesis of genius" and succeeded because

"Thea Kronborg we believe in" (O'Connor 63). Indeed, noted Edward E. Hale in the *Deal*, "Cather wants to give the soul of the artist, the sense of art" and manages "a fine realization of the artistic nature" (O'Connor 69). Yet for all their praise of Cather's subject, reviewers were less kind to her method. A long, ranging, densely packed novel, *The Song of the Lark* has little of the lyrical concentration for which she had been praised about *O Pioneers!*, so Frederick Taber Cooper warned in *Bookman* that the reader "who demands action, a strong, well-knit plot carefully worked out with an ever-watchful eye for the greatest economy of means, will feel a growing irritation at the placid, casual manner in which things happen" in the novel (O'Connor 65). James L. Ford, writing in the *New York Herald Tribune,* was more blunt, complaining that the novel had "so much of life, of action, of character study" that it "would have been even more engrossing if [Cather] had condensed it somewhat" (O'Connor 61). Yet it was the influential critic H. L. Mencken who delivered in *Smart Set* the most judicious—and perhaps the most accurate—criticism of the work. "Conventional in its outlines," *The Song of the Lark,* observed Mencken, is also "full of novelty and ingenuity in its details," and it testifies to the fact that Cather "has something to say." Indeed, he recommended the novel for its "intellectual stimulation"—"at least the first half of it" (O'Connor 72–73). Such criticism was certainly not unwarranted.

William Heinemann, Cather's English publisher, had, in fact, rejected *The Song of the Lark,* believing that she had "taken the wrong road" in the novel. "The full-blooded method," he explained, anticipating the novel's critical reception, "which told everything about everybody, was not natural to [her]" ("My First Novels," *Stories, Poems, and Other Writings* 965). Initially resistant to his views, Cather eventually conceded the point in her 1931 essay "My First Novels (There Were Two)," stating that "too much detail is apt, like any other form of extravagance, to become slightly vulgar" (*Stories, Poems, and Other Writings* 965). Yet the history of the novel's composition makes clear that Cather struggled with its form as she was writing and that she continued to work on its weaknesses through its various editions.

Cather's method, according to Hermione Lee, was to compose extravagantly and then to pare her material for publication. She cut *The Song of the Lark* from 200,000 to 163,000 words prior to its initial publication, eliminating "a whole section about Thea's musical education in Germany" (119). In 1932, however, when the novel was reprinted, she was still displeased with her effort, criticizing herself in its new preface for not having "disregarded conventional design and stopped where my first conception [of Thea's 'awakening and struggle'] stopped, telling the latter part of the story by suggestion merely" (Lee 119). The 1937 Autograph Edition of her novels provided Cather another opportunity to revise her work. She made additional cuts to *The Song of the Lark,* abbreviating especially the account of Tillie's activities in the epilogue. Other revisions were largely stylistic. Taken together, they amounted to the elimination of a further tenth of the original. Yet Mencken's criticism of *The Song of the Lark* remains appropriate. The novel still seems too long, too packed with superfluous detail. The "full-blooded method" was not Cather's. Indeed, she would not use it again in her writing career.

PLOT DEVELOPMENT

Perhaps the reason that *The Song of the Lark* seems so long has less to do with unnecessary details and more to do with the plot, or arrangement of its parts, and particularly the portion she allotted to each part of Thea's experience. In her 1932 preface to the novel, Cather admitted that "the chief fault of the book is that it describes a descending curve; the life of a successful artist in the full tide of achievement is not so interesting as the life of a talented young girl 'fighting her way,' as we say!" Cather makes this point as well through the novel's plot. Although she divides the novel into six parts and attaches to it a brief epilogue, part 1, focusing on Thea's life in Moonstone, Colorado, contains more than a quarter of the action, and parts 3 to five combined equal less than another quarter of the work. This disproportionate plot structure certainly accounts for the novel's "descending curve" and makes clear that Cather's interest is indeed the artist's struggle. It is also, as the length and focus of part 1 suggest, in the ground that nurtures Thea's development, in her relation to the landscape that shapes her vision. This interest, so like her exploration of the connection between Alexandra Bergson and the Nebraska prairie in *O Pioneers!,* drives part 1 of the novel so that it effectively eclipses all the other parts.

Part 1, titled "Friends of Childhood," is, as the scholar David Daiches observes, "a complete and satisfying story in itself" (30). In it, Cather traces Thea Kronborg's life from the age of 11, when Dr. Howard Archie, who has come to the Kronborg household to assist Thea's mother in the birth of a seventh child, saves her young daughter from a bout of pneumonia, to just short of the age of 17, when she departs for Chicago to pursue her musical education, having absorbed from Moonstone, Colorado, all that she will ever be but needful still of the experience and teachers to refine her rough beauty and raw talent. Cather explores every element of Thea's environment to convey its impact on her budding sense of self and her difference from them all. In her household, for instance, only her sensible mother recognizes, values, and, most important, gives her the space to develop her special gifts. Her father is far too self-absorbed, her aunt Tillie too much of a girl herself at 35 (*Early Novels and Stories* 309), and her brothers and sister too much involved in their own development to appreciate Thea's uniqueness. But others do. Herr Wunsch, for instance, formerly a German musician but now a drunken ruin, teaches her all he knows about the piano before he disappears from her life, and the unhappily married Dr. Archie draws his only real joy in life from watching and supporting this unexpected little frontier gem. Ray Kennedy, the conductor of a freight train who hopes one day to marry Thea, leaves her a six-hundred-dollar legacy to fund her study in Chicago when a railway accident kills him, so determined is he that she fulfill the promise he senses in her. From Spanish Johnny, who frequently disappears to earn his living as an itinerant musician, returning spent and impoverished to Mexican Town on the unfashionable side of Moonstone east of Main Street, Thea awakens to the sheer joy of music. Beyond these significant others in Thea's life is Moonstone itself, with its social stratification; its complacent ignorance and petty jealousies; its "enemies" (*Early Novels and Stories* 354), the Lily Fishers and Mrs. Johnsons, who want nothing more than to gloat at Thea's failure. Yet as Cather makes clear, Moonstone creates Thea Kronborg, especially the sand hills that lie just beyond the frontier town and connect the young girl to an historical past of human aspiration similar to her own (*Early Novels and Stories* 341). Everything about her life in Moonstone has prepared Thea to leave it, so part 1 ends with her inevitable departure. It could be the end of her story, but Cather now begins to examine the artist in the world. Indeed, the remainder of the novel will focus on Thea and her professional life. Cather's evocation of it, however, will not be nearly so compelling as her rendering of Thea's Moonstone life, for in part 1, she was working with her materials, the world that she knew from her own experience of life.

In part 2 of *The Song of the Lark,* titled "The Song of the Lark," Cather recounts the first year of Thea's musical education in Chicago, a city that is nearly as raw and untutored as she is. It is a tale of material privation, physical exhaustion, and emotional frustration alternating with moments of exhilaration and triumph as Thea finally realizes that her true vocation lies in her voice and not with the piano. Central to this realization is her Hungarian piano teacher, Andor Harsanyi, a demanding but kindly man who unselfishly encourages Thea to follow her voice even though she is his most talented pupil. "She is uncommon, in a common, common world," he explains to his wife (*Early Novels and Stories* 479). To have been her teacher is enough for him. Central as well to her determination to pursue her vocation is what will be Thea's last visit to Moonstone. There she experiences a painful reunion with her family, from whom she feels utterly estranged, especially when she must confront their stern disapproval of her friendship with Spanish Johnny. When Thea departs for Chicago at the end of that summer, she knows that she will not return to Moonstone again.

The sad tone that permeates the end of part 2 hardens into a cold irony at the beginning of part 3, the aptly titled "Stupid Faces." On her return to Chicago, Thea begins voice lessons with the haughty and discontented Madison Bowers, a man who "[likes] her for whatever [is] least admirable in her" (*Early Novels and Stories* 511), working as his accompanist to earn her living. The Chicago music scene that Cather evokes in part 3 is, like Thea, unsophisticated and even rather comic, filled with singers with more money than talent, a voice teacher whose scathing contempt of his pupils renders them pathetic and encourages Thea's tendency to be harshly judgmental, and audiences who prefer the pleasant imitation to the true talent. What saves Thea from developing her instructor's hard veneer is a friendship with Frederick Ottenburg, a wealthy "beer prince" (*Early Novels and Stories* 523) who heads the Chicago branch of the family brewing business. A man who is interested in "talent" (*Early Novels and Stories* 530), Fred becomes another one of Thea's benefactors, introducing her to the Nathanmeyers, German Jews whose own Old World knowledge of musical talent prompts them to support her career (and also provides an alternate view of the Chicago music scene). He also sends her to a family retreat in Arizona to recover her spirits following a bout of tonsillitis. The experience, the subject of part 4, will change the course of Thea's life.

Thea's brief interlude in Arizona among the ruins of "The Ancient People," the title of part 4, connects her once again to a natural landscape that speaks to her internal geography. As she follows the ancient trails in Panther Canyon and explores the ruins of the Navajo

Cliff-Dwellers who had once built a civilization in the arid terrain, Thea recovers her strength of purpose and dedicates herself to her art. By the time Fred joins her at the ranch for a brief holiday prior to her departure, Thea has determined that she cannot return to Chicago but must go instead to Germany if she is to be serious about her art (*Early Novels and Stories* 555). During the three weeks that they clamber together about the ruins, however, Thea and Fred begin a relationship that leads her to escape with him to Mexico and a promise of marriage if so she chooses. Cather's handling of their sexual relationship is subtle, especially given the fact that Fred, she reveals, is married to a woman who will never grant him a divorce. Her treatment of this part of Thea's life, moreover, makes clear that her focus is Thea the artist, not Thea the woman. Romantic love, in fact, seems one of the sacrifices that Thea must make for her art.

Part 5, titled "Dr. Archie's Venture," finds Thea in New York, where she and Fred have come following his confession to her of his marital status, awaiting the arrival of the kindly physician who had once saved her life in Moonstone and who has remained in its background ever since. Disappointed as much with herself as with Fred, Thea has cabled Dr. Archie with the request of a loan to fund her music education in Germany, too much the product of Moonstone to accept money from her lover (*Early Novels and Stories* 594). Dr. Archie, of course, departs immediately from a Denver meeting of stockholders in a silver mine to assist her. He is even willing to sell his shares in the venture, which has yielded nothing more than promise, to help her fulfill her dream.

What gives this part of *The Song of the Lark* its interest, for it essentially functions as a transition between the end of Thea's apprenticeship period and the full flowering of her professional life, is Cather's rehabilitation of Fred Ottenburg. In the conventional melodramatic plot, Fred would be a villain, the evil seducer of innocence. While he may genuinely love Thea and she has freely chosen to ignore the moral standards of the time, he is still more culpable than she because he has deceived her about his marital status from the beginning of their relationship. Yet Thea loves Fred and will eventually marry him, so Cather must redeem him. She does so by securing for him Dr. Archie's approval. Thea's old confidant is fully prepared to dislike Fred, but he cannot. Fred cares too obviously about Thea; he wants too earnestly what she wants. He is undeniably so like Dr. Archie that the physician cannot help but accept him on his terms. So, too, must Cather's readers.

Cather concludes her account of Thea's progress in part 6, titled simply "Kronborg," when, 10 years after her departure to Germany, the singer returns to pursue a career on the New York stage, where now merely her surname is meaningful to opera connoisseurs. She devotes much of this section of the novel to description of operatic performances, which tends to slow the action but leaves no doubt of her heroine's genius. In fact, Cather charts Thea's professional success through a series of increasingly important Wagnerian opera roles—as Elizabeth in *Tannhäuser*, Fricka in *The Rhinegold*, Elsa in *Lohengrin*, and finally Sieglinde in *The Valkyrie*. Isolde from *Tristan and Isolde* and Brünnhilde from *Twilight of the Gods* are clearly in her future (*Early Novels and Stories* 687, 697). In fact, in the novel's brief epilogue, Thea's aunt Tillie reads a favorable review of her niece's performance of Isolde in London (*Early Novels and Stories* 704). Yet this section of the novel builds toward and ends with Thea's triumphant performance as Sieglinde because, as the narrator asserts in what is properly the novel's final paragraph, "from this time on the story of her life is the story of her achievement" (*Early Novels and Stories* 699). With this triumph, struggle—the force that drives narrative—lies behind Thea, so Cather must conclude the singer's story.

Far more compelling is Cather's rendition of Thea's triumph. With her at that performance are the men who love her, Dr. Archie, who is now a director of the San Felipe Mining Company, and Fred Ottenburg, who now heads the Brewers' Trust, and among the honored guests in the audience are Mr. and Mrs. Harsanyi, who recognized and believed in her talent during her first difficult Chicago winter. But high in the concert hall's top gallery, where, unknown to Thea, a graying Spanish Johnny listens rapturously and claps enthusiastically to her performance, is Moonstone at its best. In this stirring triumph lie the meaning of Thea's struggle and the truth in Cather's novel. Nothing else is needed to complete her portrait of the artist.

Cather's tale of Thea Kronborg's emergent voice places *The Song of the Lark* firmly within the tradition of the *Künstlerroman,* a novel form that traces the protagonist's artistic development from childhood to maturity, when he (and traditionally the artist is male) understands his creative mission. Indeed, as Cather's narrator explains at the novel's end, "this story attempts to deal only with the simple and concrete beginnings which color and accent an artist's work, and to give some account of how a Moonstone girl found her way out of a vague, easy-going world into a life of disciplined endeavor" (*Early Novels and Stories* 699).

CHARACTER DEVELOPMENT

The artist who emerges from Moonstone, Colorado, begins as a curiously self-contained little girl who accepts life as it comes to her. Acceptance, however, does not mean indifference, especially in Thea's case. Indeed, Cather's protagonist, or central character, is attune to every detail and incident of her life. Years later, in fact, Thea's memories of dressing beside the cook stove to stave off winter's cold; of pulling her baby brother Thor in his wagon into the low sand hills surrounding Moonstone, where she could experience the closest thing to solitude available to her crowded existence; of encountering human desperation in the form of a tramp who drowns himself in the town's well (*Early Novels and Stories* 413–17); and of listening into Mrs. Tellemantez's seashell to hear the lure of Spanish Johnny's desire (*Early Novels and Stories* 332–33) color her performance. They as well as others are evidence of Cather's belief that every experience, every acquaintance, leaves its impression on the artistic sensibility, to be transmuted into art.

Yet for all her awareness of life, what most distinguishes Thea in her youth is her dogged determination and her powerful will. Indeed, her interest in the "great generals" and in Caesar's Commentaries and Greeley's "Polar Explorations" (*Early Novels and Stories* 344) and her purchase of a photograph of the bust of Julius Caesar (*Early Novels and Stories* 442) suggest that she identifies with strong, powerful conquerors. She may hate "difficult things," as Herr Wunsch, her Moonstone piano teacher, reflects, but she cannot resist their challenge and will have "no peace until she mastered them" (*Early Novels and Stories* 379). Nor will she lower her standards to achieve them. She is, therefore, a rather prickly personality. When she works as Madison Bowers's accompanist in Chicago, for instance, she has nothing but disdain for his mediocre pupils and even less regard for those with professional reputations, whom she is not above correcting because she simply cannot bear their deficiencies (*Early Novels and Stories* 513–14). Nor can she accept their complacency about them. Urged by Bowers to make herself more "agreeable" so that she will be better able to market her talent, Thea asserts her intention to "go without" money that she has "to grin for" (*Early Novels and Stories* 512). She expects people to accept her on her terms. The problem, however, is that Thea is uncertain about her terms. Indeed, for much of the novel, Thea is decidedly unaware about herself, a deficiency, Cather's metaphor of voice makes clear, that will prevent her from becoming a great artist. She may recognize deficiency in others, but as Cather's metaphor indicates, she must find her voice to be a voice.

Language, our primary means of expression, is a signifier of identity. Our "mother tongue" as well as our accent and vocabulary, our grammar and syntax, reveals much about our geographic origins, our social class, our education, our interests, our intellect, indeed, much that constitutes the self. Language, particularly facility with language, also gives some indication of the individual's sense of self. As Thea muses shortly after her arrival in Chicago, "Language was like clothes; it could be a help to one, or it could give one away" (*Early Novels and Stories* 484). The tongue-tied and stammering, for instance, often seem insecure or uncertain, hesitant or cautious, while the glib and quick-witted seem confident and secure, forceful and convincing. Two aspects of Thea's early encounters with language, her inarticulateness and her bilingualism, are significant to her developing personality. In them, Cather reveals the crippling lack of voice that her heroine must overcome to achieve her potential.

Sensitive as a child to language and proud that her father always delivered his sermons in bookish English (*Early Novels and Stories* 305), Thea is, nevertheless, a silent girl who rarely speaks more than monosyllables in her bilingual household until she attends school. Even then she is "inept in speech for a child so intelligent," excelling in written work rather than in recitations (*Early Novels and Stories* 306). Thea's silence, her inability to speak her ideas, certainly offers evidence of her lack of self in *The Song of the Lark,* especially given Cather's emphasis on language and expression in the novel. Thea's life may be full of impressions, but her crowded existence makes it impossible for her to reflect on them and thereby understand their meaning to her. As the narrator observes, "The clamor about her drowned the voice within herself" (*Early Novels and Stories* 344). She may be different, but her difference is as yet undefined because Thea's singular identity is as yet undefined.

Similarly, Thea's bilingualism (actually her multilingualism) indicates a confused identity that also metaphorically signifies her lack of voice. Shortly after she meets him, Thea observes to Fred, "We immigrants never speak any language well" (526). This observation speaks to Thea's need to discover an authentic voice, one that expresses her self. As the child of immigrants, Thea has been raised amid a cacophony of languages and among people who, like her, struggle to express themselves. Both her father and Ray Kennedy, for instance, labor with language, believing that colloquial speech is inadequate to their ideas and depending instead on "bookish phrases" (*Early Novels and Stories* 397) borrowed from others that sound false to their identities. Thea, in fact, "dodged" Ray's "travel-lecture expressions," preferring instead to seek his meaning in "the light in [his] pale-blue eyes and the feeling [in] his voice [that] more than made up for the stiffness of his language" (*Early Novels and Stories* 397). Thea recognizes instinctively the need for an authentic voice that expresses the self, reflecting shortly after she arrives in Chicago that "the most important thing [about using words] was that one should not pretend to be what one was not" (*Early Novels and Stories* 484). Yet because she speaks so many languages (and none of them well), she lacks any voice, any true sense of self that could give her an authentic voice. This quest for a voice, for a self, lies at the heart of Thea's characterization.

Cather charts Thea's journey to her authentic voice in a series of key incidents, the most important of which is her summer sojourn among the ancient ruins of the Cliff-Dwellers in Arizona. Prior to that summer, Thea has experienced moments of self. After she acquires her own room, for instance, and can for the first time converse with her own thoughts, she begins to "live a double life," presenting one self to the world but embracing another self in private (*Early Novels and Stories* 344–45), and when she begins to give piano lessons to the young girls of Moonstone, she revels in the "personal independence … accorded her as a wage-earner" (*Early Novels and Stories* 387). Similarly, Thea's first experience of a concert symphony, Dvorak's "From the New World," does indeed open new worlds to her (*Early Novels and Stories* 467–70), and when Thea sings at the late-night Mexican ball, the appreciative response of these "really musical people" (*Early Novels and Stories* 495) makes her feel for the first time the power of her voice. During that summer in Arizona, however, Thea truly begins to do what Mr. Harsanyi advises: she determines to stop "fighting" her "gift" and to become "the woman [she was] meant to be" (*Early Novels and Stories* 477).

Each morning as Thea bathes with "ceremonial gravity" (*Early Novels and Stories* 551) in the sunny pool at the bottom of Panther Canyon, she feels herself connected ritualistically to a timeless yearning for something that is at once beyond herself and yet part of herself, something that exists in the potsherds that she collects each day. Those fragments of beautifully expressed desire are "like fetters that bound one to a long chain of human endeavor" (*Early Novels and Stories* 553), and they make Thea understand that she has "older and higher obligations" (*Early Novels and Stories* 555). She had had such intuitions as a young girl, when her father had taken her to Wyoming to help him conduct a reunion of old pioneers, and in the deep furrows cut into the land by the wagon wheels of the Forty-niners she had encountered evidence of human striving for the ineffable (*Early Novels and Stories* 340–41). But only when she immerses herself in that feeling, as she does in Panther Canyon, does Thea truly understand its connection to her and her own endeavors. She grows strong that summer and certain of herself. As the narrator observes, "The things that were really hers separated themselves from the rest" (*Early Novels and Stories* 554). With this knowledge, she commits herself to her art, recognizing that her voice is "vitality" (*Early Novels and Stories* 554), life itself to her. In Panther Canyon, Thea begins at last to claim her authentic voice and to move toward her true vocation.

To speak in her authentic voice, Thea must also acknowledge and accept her "second self" (*Early Novels and Stories* 482), "the something [that from her youth] came and went, she never knew how" (*Early Novels and Stories* 363), but that constitutes her true identity. That something, a thing she cannot name, Thea has always felt under "obligation" to conceal, "to protect it even from herself," and thereby to keep it "from being caught up in the meshes of common things" (*Early Novels and Stories* 482). It gives her pleasure and brings her happiness, and it is intimately connected to her voice. In fact, as Thea reflects in a key scene in which she consciously approaches her second self for the first time, "Her voice, more than any other part of her, had to do with [her] confidence, [her] sense of wholeness and inner well-being" (*Early Novels and Stories* 482). But for much of her life, Thea does not own her second self. It is a thing apart, and she is powerless to control it. She knows, however, that she is destined to meet it (*Early Novels and Stories* 483). Indeed, it is toward this meeting that her whole life tends. It is this meeting that Cather describes in Thea's triumphant performance as Sieglinde.

In that performance, which many of those who have responded to her second self attend, Thea comes utterly into herself. Her body becomes "the instrument of her idea" (*Early Novels and Stories* 698); her voice is "equal to any demand." In fact, "its perfect companionship, its entire trustworthiness," are evidence that Thea now owns her authentic voice, and that voice makes her an artist. It is right, therefore, that Thea's story effectively ends at this point, for this achievement of artistic and self-expression is the defining moment of her life. It is right as well that Dr. Archie and Fred Ottenburg, Mr. Harsanyi and even Spanish Johnny are in the audience to experience it, for they have helped her achieve it.

Indeed, the purpose of the significant secondary characters in *The Song of the Lark,* nearly all of whom are male, is to support Thea's development. Cather, of course, gives each a singular background: Dr. Howard Archie, for instance, has married unwisely and thus avoids his home, where his wife's parsimony constitutes an assault on everything he finds pleasurable in life. Raymond Kennedy, the conductor of a freight train, shares Thea's love of the natural world and hopes one day to marry the girl, although he is nearly 20 years older than she. Herr Wunsch, her first piano teacher, has never been able to find or to re-create in the New World the Old World music scene that had once defined his life, so he has dissipated his talent in drink. Spanish Johnny, an itinerant Mexican musician, finds it impossible to settle into ordinary life and flees periodically with his mandolin and high tenor voice to express his own second self. Fred Ottenburg, who is also unwisely married, fulfills his obligations to the family brewing business, but he pursues his passion for music by escaping for months at a time to Bayreuth, the home of Wagner's operas. Despite their differences, however, they share a romantic temperament that finds its fulfillment in Thea's promise. Something about her speaks to their longing for the ineffable, their desire for a reality surpassing materiality, and through her, they dedicate themselves to it. Over and over, they give Thea the means and the opportunity to realize her genius: Ray leaves her a legacy to study in Chicago at his accidental death, Fred gives her a summer in Arizona among the ancient ruins of the Cliff-Dwellers to recover her purpose, and Dr. Archie loans her the money to pursue her vocation in Germany. And because her second self elicits "the most wonderful things" from them (*Early Novels and Stories* 363), her success fulfills their lives.

THEMATIC ISSUES

Thea's gift to her benefactors is evidence of the meaning and purpose of art and the artist, Cather's chief thematic issue in *The Song of the Lark.* Art, as Cather makes clear, is a profound and ennobling expression of human desire, evidence as well as a promise that throughout the whole of history humans have strived and will continue to strive for something beyond their physical and material limitations. As Thea suddenly recognizes one morning at her bath in Panther Canyon, "What was any art but an effort to make a sheath, a mould in which to imprison for a moment the shining, elusive element which is life itself,—life hurrying past us and running away, too strong to stop, too sweet to lose?" (*Early Novels and Stories* 552). That effort to preserve the moment in all its singularity is art. The art object is the vessel that contains the desire.

Herr Wunsch had once intimated this truth to Thea, but she had been too young, too uncertain of herself, fully to understand his meaning (*Early Novels and Stories* 360), but at Panther Canyon, as she studies the remnants of an ancient civilization, she learns what Wunsch had tried to tell her. Those remnants, the shards of clay vessels that the Navajo women had once made to carry water or to store their provisions, are "beautifully decorated" with "patterns in a low relief" or with "graceful geometrical" features. One fragment bears a "crested serpent's head, painted in red on terra-cotta," another a "broad band of white cliff-houses painted on a black ground." What amazes Thea about these fragments is the "care" their makers had taken to produce them. Their decorative features—their art—would not have improved the vessels. They would not, Thea reflects, have held "food or water any better for the additional labor put upon them," and yet the potters had cared enough to make them beautiful as well as functional (*Early Novels and Stories* 553). They had wanted to preserve an emotion, a desire, a something beyond the ordinary that existed for them. Before the remnants of their striving, Thea stands in awe, just as she had done before the "great equestrian statue" and "The Song of the Lark," the painting among all others that speaks to her at the Chicago Art Institute (*Early Novels and Stories* 466). All these art objects, as well as the song that comes from her voice, are expressions of "arrested motion" (*Early Novels and Stories* 552), of some transcendent truth, and they are as vital as life itself. Indeed, as Cather asserts in the novel's concluding paragraph, the art object fulfills a deep human need to know that something exists beyond life's daily routine, for "cut off as they are from the restless currents of the world," the narrator explains, the vast majority of people find their "naked little sandbars ... made habitable and whole" by art (*Early Novels and Stories* 706).

Cather assigns an equally important role to the artist, whose creations affirm human existence, perhaps because she recognizes that art demands ferocious labor. Indeed, it is that labor that distinguishes the talented artist from the great one. As Thea tells Dr. Archie, many singers have good voices, but the true artist reaches into the core of his or her being to produce something so absolutely right that "there's nothing one can say about it" (*Early Novels and Stories* 681). Tapping that core is difficult. It demands "a refining of the sense of truthfulness" (*Early Novels and Stories* 697), which, as Thea's example makes clear, is never easy. It demands that the artist holds to a standard of excellence that only another true artist can appreciate. It demands a hard, muscular energy, a spirit that can soar above "the inevitable hardness of human life" (*Early Novels and Stories* 685). Thea Kronborg, of course, who is like the eagle in Panther Canyon (*Early Novels and Stories* 567) and the lark of the title, embodies these qualities in *The Song of the Lark*. She indeed is proof that such greatness exists.

Fiction itself—Cather's own art objects, in fact—also fulfills this purpose. Certainly the emphasis throughout the novel on the difficulty and the importance of language is pertinent not only to Thea's quest for an authentic voice but also to Cather's (or any writer's) struggle to make words pay. It is not chance, moreover, that finds Tillie, Thea's adoring aunt, the focus of *The Song of the Lark*'s final paragraphs. Late in life, she has become the preserver of her niece's life story. She reads about her achievements in the newspapers, collects memorabilia of her life in a scrapbook, and has even attended one of her concerts, the high point of her life. Another of Cather's "romancers" (*Early Novels and Stories* 705), Tillie, too, has dreamed of a life beyond helping to care for her brother's family or running a millinery shop in Moonstone. She has lived by stories and lives now on her niece's. But Thea's story is enough for Tillie, terrifying proof, in fact, that our "wildest conceits" (*Early Novels and Stories* 705) can come true. Moreover, Thea's story has transformed Tillie into a sort of artist. As she recounts her niece's triumphs to the upright citizens who live on Moonstone's fashionable Sylvester Street and then, when they tire of listening, to those on the east side of town, "where her legends are always welcome" (*Early Novels and Stories* 705), Tillie becomes like Cather, whose stories, like Thea's songs and the Navajo potsherds, are evidence of the eternal striving that is art. Her stories, like Cather's, give them "something to talk about and to conjecture about." Tillie thus does what every artist does: she brings them "tidings of what their boys and girls are doing in the world" and thereby offers "to the old, memories, and to the young, dreams" (*Early*

Novels and Stories 706). In Tillie, Cather claims for herself and her art their meaning and significance.

A FEMINIST INTERPRETATION

Because the *Künstlerroman* is by tradition a narrative form that focuses on the development of the male artist, Cather's female example offers evidence of an effort to revise tradition and to claim for the female artist an equivalent role in society. To the feminist critic, who looks at literature through the lens of gender roles and gender expectations, such an effort deserves attention, especially given the fact that Cather had in her early journalistic career written reviews critical of women writers, including Kate Chopin's 1899 feminist classic *The Awakening*. In her review of Chopin's novel, Cather had criticized its heroine, Edna Pontellier, for being too much like the French novelist Gustave Flaubert's Madame Bovary. "Studies in the same feminine type," she complained, they were "victims of the over-idealization of love" ("Kate Chopin," *Stories, Poems, and Other Writings* 911). In another review about "Silly Novels by Lady Novelists," Cather complained about the tendency of the "lady novelist," a term that implies a genteel, civilized writer as opposed to a tough, realistic professional, to present limited and distorted views of female experience. "When a woman writes a story of adventure, a stout sea tale, a manly battle yarn, anything without wine, women and love," she asserted in response, "then I will begin to hope for something great from them, not before" (*The World and the Parish* 276-77). Within this context and from a feminist perspective, Cather's female *Künstlerroman* certainly seems an effort to challenge the tradition of the lady novelist.

To understand the perspective of the feminist critic, we need first to have a basic understanding of the theory that grounds it. Histories of feminist criticism generally divide it into three broad phases and stances. The first phase involves analysis of patriarchal culture, a term for the institutions, attitudes, and beliefs of a society dominated by men. Feminist critics thus analyze literary interpretations of male-dominated society to expose what Elaine Showalter calls "the misogyny of literary practice," the stereotypical images of women in literature, "the literary abuse of textual harassment of women in classics and popular male literature, and [the] exclusion of women from literary history" ("The Feminist Critical Revolution" 5). In the second phase, feminist critics set out to map the territory of the female imagination. Concerned with women as writers giving expression to the female experience through their work, feminist critics seek to define the distinctive means of communication and the subjects and concerns that distinguish women's texts from men's. These critics generally share the idea that gender difference determines much about a person's life experience and hence about one's means of communicating, reading, or writing. Feminist criticism of the third phase focuses on the shared experience of all people rather than the fundamental differences between men and women, emphasizing the humanity of all people regardless of gender as the foundation of real equality and understanding among people.

Whatever their stance, feminist critics do seem to share one important idea about literary criticism: the impossibility of achieving objectivity. For years, critics believed that the author's personal history, the social expectations of his or her time, and the historical events that occurred during the author's life had no bearing on understanding literary works. Instead, literature was a world of its own, complete in itself, and thus could be evaluated without reference to personal, social, and historical contexts. Feminist critics believe that such objectivity is impossible. Instead, they acknowledge and promote subjectivity—responses based on experience and belief. They recognize that every reader brings both elements to the literary work and thus understands literature from a personal perspective.

Thea Kronborg, of course, embodies Cather's challenge to the tradition of the lady novelist and thus to patriarchal culture, for she is unlike the typical female heroine of the time. Certainly she is no Edna Pontellier or Emma Bovary, sacrificing herself for love. Utterly without sentiment but attuned instead to an intellectual and emotional construct that she translates into her art, Thea possesses the will and determination to succeed. Indeed, her identification with powerful male figures such as Julius Caesar (*Early Novels and Stories* 442) indicates that she favors the active, adventurous life generally accorded to men rather than the passive, domestic world that is traditionally the domain of women. Unlike the typical woman of the time, she dreams not of marriage but of a career, and she pursues her vocation at the cost of her personal life. When her mother lay dying, for instance, Thea could not come to her bedside because she would have missed her opportunity to launch her career by singing the role of Elizabeth with the Dresden Opera (*Early Novels and Stories* 628), and although Thea eventually marries Fred Ottenburg, Cather makes clear that her heroine has not had to choose between marriage and her career because Fred supports her dream. (Cather also conveniently makes that marriage impossible during the period of their early passion by giving Fred a wife he cannot divorce, a plot device that does not, nevertheless, deny the significance of Thea's intentions.) Like the strong Wagner heroines that she portrays on stage, including Fricka, who she redeems from the traditional scolding housewife to her original wise goddess (*Early Novels and Stories* 671), Thea possesses something of the elemental, a savageness that connects her to the Valkyrie, the fierce daughters of Wotan who carry dead heroes to Valhalla. Mr. Harsanyi was one of the first persons to remark on this quality of his pupil (*Early Novels and Stories* 449), but Fred is one of the few truly to understand it. As Thea stands on the edge of a crag in Panther Canyon, her figure projects "muscular energy and audacity…, a personality that carried across big spaces and expanded among big things." He compares her to the creatures "that used to run wild in Germany dressed in their hair and a piece of skin" (*Early Novels and Stories* 566). Thea's savageness and muscularity are typically masculine attributes. No soft femininity for her. But she combines them with the female sensibility that she perceives in the potsherds crafted by the Navajo women and that is also part of her essential self, and from that combination come her singularity and her greatness. She does not demand, as Cather says of *The Awakening*'s Edna Pontellier, "more romance out of life than God put into it" ("Kate Chopin," *Stories, Poems, and Other Writings* 911), and thus she is realistic enough to make her success.

Although Thea's romance with and eventual marriage to Fred is one of *The Song of the Lark*'s plot elements, it is not the novel's primary focus, and here again Cather deviates from what critics have identified as the marriage plot typical of women writers. Exemplifying this plot are the opening lines of the English novelist Jane Austen's *Pride and Prejudice* (1813), "It is a truth universally acknowledged, that a single man in possession of a good fortune, must be in want of a wife," and Jane Eyre's triumphant assertion, "Reader, I married him," at the conclusion of the English novelist Charlotte Brontë's 1847 classic. The marriage plot, as these quotations indicate, typically focuses on a young woman's quest to find true love or a suitable match and to marry him. Her story ends with her marriage and the assumption, of course, that, the adventure of her life now concluded, she will live "happily ever after." Nothing of greater significance to her life than marriage could possibly happen to her again. The "lady novelists" of the nineteenth and early twentieth centuries endlessly reproduced the marriage plot, but Cather deviates from it almost entirely, choosing instead the traditionally masculine *Künstlerroman* as a structure for her novel's plot. Thea does eventually marry, but on her terms and only after she has achieved her success.

Cather's treatment of several of the novel's other marriages, moreover, raises qualifications about the institution itself. Both Dr. Archie and Fred Ottenburg suffer unhappy and unfulfilling marriages that neither can or will escape, victims, on the one hand, of their own romantic notions about women and, on the other, of manipulative and duplicitous women who conceal their real selves during courtship only to reveal them after marriage. Their wives care less about the quality of their marriages than the fact of them, and having attained the ideal female role, they live for the material and social advantages that marriage to professional men brings to them. The examples of these marriages suggest that the institution is a trap, imprisoning both men and women in unsatisfying conventional roles and, in the case of women, for whom marriage is the only sanctioned option for their lives, distorting their personalities. Although the Harsanyi marriage as well as the Kronborg marriage modifies this bleak perspective to some extent, presenting examples of working partnerships and happy unions, the predominant perspective on marriage in *The Song of the Lark* undermines traditional romantic notions about the institution and the relationships that it enforces " 'til death do us part."

Cather also challenges traditional gender expectations by characterizing the men rather than the women as the primary romantics in *The Song of the Lark*. Dr. Archie, Ray Kennedy, and Fred Ottenburg all possess a yearning for the ideal and a belief in the possible. Dr. Archie, for example, the physician, still holds a "romantic feeling about the human body; a sense that finer things dwelt in it than could be explained by anatomy" (*Early Novels and Stories* 371), while the chivalrous Ray, with his "sentimental veneration for all women" (*Early Novels and Stories* 338), nurses a hope that Thea will one day marry him and shares with her an intuitive appreciation for the courage and desire, the passion and forbearance in ancient civilizations (*Early Novels and Stories* 399). Fred Ottenburg, who has seldom experienced boredom because he takes a profound interest in life in all its forms (*Early Novels and Stories* 537), values "talent" (*Early Novels and Stories* 530). He places his faith, in other words, in potential, in the promise of possibility. In a conventional novel, any one of these male characters would be the hero; any one of them would drive the plot and be the focus of thematic issues. In *The Song of the Lark,* however, Cather's male characters all play subordinate roles. Indeed, their function is to support Thea's efforts to achieve her goals, perhaps because their rather dreamy romanticism smoothes their hard, aggressive edges and makes them contemplative instead of active. They are content to fulfill their lives through Thea, a reversal of traditional gender roles and expectations that enhances Cather's own challenge to the tradition of the lady novelist.

In dispensing in *The Song of the Lark* with the literary conventions of lady novelists and seizing the *Künstlerroman* for a female protagonist, Willa Cather did indeed claim for herself an alternative literary voice. In Thea Kronborg, she also created a memorable heroine whose artistic principles and dedication to her craft mirrored Cather's own. Perhaps the most autobiographical of Cather's novels, *The Song of the Lark* is like the "piece-picture" of Napoleon's retreat into Moscow (another powerful masculine figure, by the way) that Thea had admired as a young girl when she went to the Kohler home for her piano lessons with Herr Wunsch. An apprentice piece that demonstrated the tailor Fritz Kohler's skill at his craft, the piece-picture is actually a work of art, reproducing in glorious color, texture, and pattern the original painting of the subject, but on his own terms. In fact, Kohler had worked with difficult woolens rather than the more pliant and various silks to achieve his effect, a reflection of the seriousness with which he fulfilled what was clearly to him more than an assignment (*Early Novels and Stories* 317–18). *The Song of the Lark* is Cather's piece-picture. Born of her experience and produced with reverence for her craft, it exposes the passion that lies behind artistic creation and the forces that give it shape. It is the work of a writer who knew that the novel should be more than an exercise and set about to fulfill her own demands. The result, however flawed, is indeed a work of art.

6

My Ántonia (1918)

My Ántonia is Willa Cather's masterpiece, the novel on which her literary reputation continues to flourish. Working again with her own materials, Cather tells the story of the friendship between Jim Burden, a 10-year-old orphan who journeys from his native Virginia to his grandparents' home on the Nebraska prairie, and Ántonia Shimerda, a 14-year-old Bohemian immigrant whose arrival at that untamed landscape corresponds with his own. In the novel, she recaptures the strengths of subject and style that had made *O Pioneers!* (1913) such a success and abandons the "full-blooded method" ("My First Novels," *Stories, Poems, and Other Writings* 965) that had threatened to overwhelm *The Song of the Lark* (1915). She also experiments with point of view, or the perspective from which the events are told, and that experiment transforms *My Ántonia* into a moving meditation on memory and memorializing, a recognition, as the novel's epigraph from the Latin poet Virgil makes clear, that "the best days are the first to flee" and a reclamation of them. Written during the turmoil of World War I as well as a period of rapid change in the United States, *My Ántonia* is elegiac in tone, celebrating human values worth retaining and remind-ing readers to appreciate the best of the past. Indeed, in the novel's title character, Cather offers the embodiment of the best of those values.

Central to *My Ántonia* is a deep and abiding friendship that persists for more than 30 years between an impoverished immigrant girl and a comfortable American boy both of whom find themselves strangers on the Nebraska prairie. As they explore their new world and discover its beauty as well as its terrors, Jim Burden and Ántonia Shimerda build the foundation of their friendship. He teaches her English; she shares her Bohemian tales. He offers appreciative acceptance; she provides sympathetic support. During their youth, in other words, each comes to value the other's presence in his or her life. Their friendship will be tested, however, when they move from the prairie to Black Hawk, Jim to follow his grandparents, who have prospered enough to enjoy some ease, and Ántonia to take a position as a hired girl in the home of Jim's neighbors, the Harlings. Teenagers now, Jim falls half in love with Ántonia and so disapproves of her attempts to find some enjoyment from life. When a chivalrous gesture results in a beating that leaves him bruised and embarrassed, Jim blames Ántonia for placing him in the humiliating situation and departs for college without bidding her farewell. At university in Lincoln, he engages in an innocent flirtation with Lena Lingard, one of the hired girls with whom Ántonia had cavorted in Black Hawk, and then, to get back on track, transfers all his attention to completing his degree at Harvard. During this time, he learns that Ántonia has been betrayed by a man who promised marriage and has returned to the family home to give birth to a child. When Jim visits a disgraced Ántonia nearly two years after the birth of her daughter, he begins to reestablish their friendship, but they will not reach true accord until Jim returns to Black Hawk 20 years later and discovers that his Ántonia has remained true to her essential self and thereby fulfilled her destiny. Their friendship is thus a journey back to their beginnings, a return to a past made whole and good by shared memories and common values. It is a journey, Cather makes clear, well worth the effort.

GENESIS AND CRITICAL RECEPTION

Cather fills *My Ántonia,* as she did *O Pioneers!* and *The Song of the Lark,* with autobiographical elements. Like Jim, she had spent her early childhood in Virginia, moving to Nebraska—but with her family—when she was 10 years old. Initially distressed and disoriented by the unfamiliar landscape, she soon adapted to her new world, making friendships with pioneer farm women, many of whom were European immigrants who shared with her stories of their homelands. Indeed, the immigrant experience of one of those women, the Bohemian Annie Pavelka, gives shape to the tale of the Shimerda family that is the focus of Book I of the novel (Lee 34-35). What may have prompted Cather's use of these elements was a return to her past that she made during the summer of 1914 and again in 1916, when she journeyed to her former home in Red Cloud, Nebraska, the novel's model for Black Hawk. There, she became reacquainted with the lives of her friends, including Annie Pavelka and the Miners, a family with three lively girls who served as models for the Harlings. (Cather, in fact, dedicated her novel to two of the girls, all of whom were lifelong friends.) By the end of the summer of 1916, during which she nursed her sick mother, Cather returned to her New York home with several chapters of *My Ántonia* complete (Lee 35-36). She clearly had found the way to reclaim her past for her fiction.

Familiarity with her subject may have eased the novel's composition, yet Cather struggled some, but not to the degree she had with *The Song of the Lark,* with form, most notably with the novel's brief introduction. In fact, in 1926, she rewrote that section of *My Ántonia,* which provides a frame for the story, eliminating some details about Jim's disappointing marriage and his "big Western dreams" (*Early Novels and Stories* 712). She also omitted the idea of rival narratives that Jim and his unnamed traveling companion agree in the original 1918 version to write (Lee 134-35), the effect of which was to strengthen Jim's authorial stance. These revisions, however, were relatively minor, indicating a degree of satisfaction with her tale. *My Ántonia,* she later observed, "came along, quite of itself and with no direction from me," and "it took the road of *O Pioneers!,* not the road of *The Song of the Lark*" ("My First Novels," *Stories, Poems, and Other Writings* 965). Her method was subtle and nuanced, not an accumulation of every detail but a series of carefully selected scenes and images that implied their meaning and significance.

Critics of *My Ántonia* certainly appreciated what Cather had made of her autobiographical material on the novel's publication in 1918. A reviewer in the *New York Sun* praised Cather's "great gift" for "[recapturing] the past and [rekindling] the ancient fires" (O'Connor 79), while another reviewer admired the novel's "vivid" descriptive passages because they "are poetic and excite the imagination" (O'Connor 86). The influential critic H. L. Mencken, who had championed Cather's work since *O Pioneers!,* actually praised *My Ántonia* in two separate reviews for *Smart Set,* claiming in February 1919 that the novel "shows an earnest striving toward ... free and dignified self-expression, ... high artistic conscience, ... [and a] civilized point of view" (O'Connor 87) and a month later that it was not only Cather's best work but also "one of the best that any American has ever done" (O'Connor 88–89). Yet despite its uniformly good reviews, *My Ántonia* did not sell well, a disappointment to Cather, who faulted her publisher Houghton Mifflin's approach to book design and marketing for its failure to reach an audience (Lee 160).

PLOT DEVELOPMENT

Like *The Song of the Lark, My Ántonia* is a tale of maturation, both Jim's and the title character's, so its action spans an extended period, more than 30 years, in fact, thereby complicating its plot structure. Jim Burden, Cather's surrogate voice in the novel, will actually apologize for his story's lack of "form" (*Early Novels and Stories* 714) when he submits it to his unnamed traveling companion some months after their first accidental encounter on a train speeding through the Iowa plains. But, in fact, the manuscript has a great deal of form. To control her material, Cather divides the novel into five sections and uses her thematic issues—memory and the value of the past—to determine the length of each. Books I and II, covering the period of Jim's boyhood to his late teens, constitute more than half the novel's length and together are twice as long as Books III to V combined because their subject matter—the development and nature of the friendship between Jim and Ántonia—is crucial, to quote the scholar Hermione Lee, "to the process of memory-making" (139). These sections are full of closely observed events and sharp details, the evidence of a shared history and the stuff of which memories are made. In fact, Jim begins sentence after sentence with the phrases "I can remember" (*Early Novels and Stories* 723) or "I can see them now" (*Early Novels and Stories* 766), injecting the present tense so seamlessly into the past that time differences collapse. When he asserts, "All the years that have passed have not dimmed my memory" (*Early Novels and Stories* 730), he clearly speaks the truth, so real are the people and places, the events and experiences that fill these sections of the novel.

Books III to V do not require the same volume of detail because their purpose is to reveal the effect of this accumulated life on the adult who retains their impressions and has through the years come to understand them. Because such understanding frequently requires separation and distance, recollection in tranquillity, Jim will leave Black Hawk in Book III to acquire some experience of the world beyond his sheltered borders. He will in effect leave his past behind to move into the future. In Book IV, he returns to it but finds it changed almost beyond comprehension because Ántonia, its embodiment, is changed. Jim will spend another 20 years making sense of those changes and of his past, but its meaning will come vividly clear to him in Book V, when he visits Ántonia once again. *My Ántonia* is not, therefore, without form. Rather, it has a tightly woven plot structure that is central to its thematic issues as well as its characterizations.

The novel begins with a brief introduction that functions as a frame for Cather's story. A common narrative device with which the well- and widely read Cather would have been familiar, the frame creates a complex and rather ambiguous relationship between Cather, her narrator, and her subject. Traveling across the Iowa plains, the unnamed narrator of this section, presumably the author, and Jim Burden, who had grown up together in the same Nebraska town, share memories of their youth and particularly of a Bohemian girl, Ántonia Shimerda, who had been a "central figure" (*Early Novels and Stories* 712) in their lives. Jim expresses surprise that his companion has never written about Ántonia (*Early Novels and Stories* 713), implying that the narrator is an author, and they subsequently agree to compose separate versions of their memories of her. Some months later, Jim presents his untitled manuscript to the narrator, who confesses her failure to do more than jot a "few straggling notes" (*Early Novels and Stories* 713) about their subject. Surprised again, Jim reveals that he had not needed notes to "arrange" (*Early Novels and Stories* 713) his memories. He had simply recorded them as he recalled them. They were, after all, his reflections, and thus he titles his manuscript "My Ántonia." What follows, the narrator then explains, after admitting that she had never written her memories of Ántonia, is Jim's manuscript, without any substantial revisions (*Early Novels and Stories* 714).

Because the unnamed narrator of this introduction presumably represents the author, her failure to write her story of Ántonia implies that she is appropriating Jim's, that his truth is hers as well. In the narrative that constitutes the remainder of the novel, in other words, Jim functions as Cather's surrogate. He also serves as a mediator between her and her subject. Jim, after all, cannot know her biography, but he can know her Ántonia. The strategy provides Cather some necessary distance from her autobiographical material, making it possible for her to avoid the excesses of *The Song of the Lark* and to be far more selective with her material than she had been in the previous novel. It also permits her to make Ántonia a more symbolic character than Thea Kronborg, one who embodies an idea of the western past as opposed to one who voices Cather's artistic creed. Given its various functions, not least of which is providing a motive for telling the story, *My Ántonia*'s introductory frame is clearly essential to Cather's design. From the novel's present, she is now able to dive into its past.

That past begins near the end of the nineteenth century, when 10-year-old orphan Jim Burden arrives in Nebraska to begin life with his grandparents after what seems an "interminable journey" (*Early Novels and Stories* 715) by train from his native Virginia. Making a similar journey in the train's "immigrant car" (*Early Novels and Stories* 715) is a family among which only one member, a girl entering her teens, speaks English. Book I of *My Ántonia*, titled "The Shimerdas," charts the intersection of these disparate lives as they all struggle to adjust to a new world. Differing backgrounds and circumstances might have been a source of division between the new arrivals: Jim settles into life in a comfortable farmhouse, complete with his own pony and the companionship of two hired men who are as much a part of the family as he is, while the Shimerdas, who have virtually been swindled by one of their countrymen in the purchase of land, farm animals, and farming equipment, take shelter in a dark and dank sod house "no better than a badger hole" (*Early Novels and Stories* 726) and survive their first bitter winter on the Nebraska plain with the Burdens' assistance. Yet Jim and Ántonia develop a deep and enduring friendship rooted in that same Nebraska plain. He teaches her English, she opens his eyes to the Old World through her tales of home, and together they explore the countryside and grow to know and love it.

Cather fills Book I with haunting descriptions of the Nebraska landscape as well as episodes and events, such as Jim's encounter with a snake and a winter blizzard that prompts an old-fashioned Christmas celebration. Some, such as the tale of Peter and Pavel and their encounter with the Russian wolves, seem unrelated to the story of Jim's Ántonia. All contribute to a sense of the fullness of life on the prairie, its hardships as well as its glorious moments of pure joy, and to an understanding of the immigrant experience in both the Old and New Worlds that lies in its background. The central event of this section of the novel, however, is Mr. Shimerda's suicide. His shocking and tragic reaction to his overwhelming new circumstances shatters Ántonia's life, and from this point, she and Jim begin to move away from each other. Forced now to work in the fields to help support her family, Ántonia can no longer attend school, and a feud develops between Jim and the Shimerdas that requires the subtle intervention of Jim's grandfather to resolve. By the end of Book I, Jim and Ántonia are friends again, but her final words to Jim, "Things will be easy for you. But they will be hard for us" (*Early Novels and Stories* 802), foreshadow the different paths that their lives will take.

In Book II, titled "The Hired Girls," Jim and Ántonia continue their progress down their individual paths even as they accumulate additional shared experiences with which to cement their friendship. This section of *My Ántonia* finds Jim and his grandparents settled in the "clean, well-planted little prairie town" (*Early Novels and Stories* 805) of Black Hawk, where they have moved so that 13-year-old Jim can receive proper schooling and the Burdens can escape the hard physical labor their farm demands. Worried that such work is spoiling Ántonia, Mrs. Burden secures a job for the teenager as hired girl to her neighbors, the Harlings. There, amid their lively household and under the influence of its strong, competent, and independent mistress, Ántonia begins to flourish again. Jim, the Harling children, and Ántonia enjoy games of charades and taffy making; they hold costume balls in the parlor or sit in the kitchen listening to Ántonia's stories while she bakes cookies or pops corn for them. Yet Ántonia is not the only immigrant girl to work in Black Hawk. Indeed, as the book's title indicates, she and a group of "hired girls," including the Norwegians Lena Lingard and Tiny Soderball and the three Bohemian Marys, are soon cavorting about town and dancing away their evenings at Vanni's tent. When her activities draw Mr. Harling's ire, Ántonia takes a position at the Cutter home rather than sacrifice her freedom and independence, even though Wick Cutter has a reputation for seducing his hired girls. When he does, in fact, attempt to assault Ántonia, Jim feels vindicated about his disapproval of her changes and choices. Yet Jim, too, has also been changing as a result of his relocation to Black Hawk. Chafing under the prairie town's conventional morality and insipid entertainments, Jim has been slipping out of his bedroom window at night to join the hired girls at the dance hall. When his grandparents discover his deception, however, he turns all his attention to his studies and prepares to take his place at university. Book II thus finds Jim and Ántonia facing the challenges of Black Hawk's "curious social situation" (*Early Novels and Stories* 838) as they also negotiate their entry into adulthood. Both leave an imprint on their relationship.

Ántonia disappears entirely as an active presence in Book III, titled "Lena Lingard," as Jim begins his university studies in Lincoln, yet her influence shadows the events throughout. A serious student intent on making up any deficiencies of his prairie education, Jim finds a mentor in the Latin scholar Gaston Cleric, yet he quickly realizes that the scholar's life is not for him. Far too often the new ideas to which he is being introduced send him back in memory to "the places and people of my own infinitesimal past" (*Early Novels and Stories* 875). Soon, in fact, that past comes to him in the shape not of Ántonia but of Lena Lingard, who has opened a dressmaking shop in Lincoln and is on her way to becoming a successful entrepreneur. She and Jim enjoy an innocent flirtation, the highlight of which is a touchingly comic scene where they attend a performance of the opera *Camille.* Although the lead actress is well beyond her prime and lacks any subtlety of expression, the production moves both Lena and Jim to tears, confirming the untutored romanticism that directs his response to life. Jim's dalliance with Lena ends, however, when Cleric, who has seen the couple at the theater, suggests that Jim should continue his studies at Harvard because he will never recover his purpose as long as Lena is in his life (*Early Novels and Stories* 891). When his grandfather gives his permission to move east, the "Lincoln chapter" (*Early Novels and Stories* 893) of 19-year-old Jim's life abruptly ends.

Book III's chief importance lies in its depiction of the way in which Jim begins immediately on his departure from Black Hawk to make sense of memory. In Black Hawk, for instance, he had always preferred the lively immigrant girls to the placid American girls. Their enthusiasm for life was far more attractive to him than the restraint and decorum that stifled any natural response in the majority of Black Hawk's young belles (*Early Novels and Stories* 838–39). Jim's university studies provide a context for this preference. Reflecting on the poetry of Virgil, with its celebration of the pastoral in the Georgics, he suddenly connects his hired girls to that rural dream of perfection to realize that "if there were no girls like them in the world, there would be no poetry" (*Early Novels and Stories* 880). Jim's introduction to the world beyond Black Hawk, as Book III reveals, is crucial to understanding his past.

Two years later, having completed his undergraduate degree, Jim returns to Black Hawk for a summer holiday prior to entering law school. This direct confrontation with his past—and particularly with his relationship to Ántonia—is the focus of Book IV, "The Pioneer Woman's Story." Jim initially tries to avoid this section's chief subject, the sad tale of Ántonia's betrayal by the passenger conductor Larry Donovan, but it is a subject difficult to escape in a town where Ántonia, rather than hide the evidence of her shame, allows a photograph of her baby daughter to be displayed at the photographer's shop (*Early Novels and Stories* 898). Seeing the picture, Jim acknowledges that he must learn the truth about Ántonia's predicament, so he calls first on the Widow Steavens, who lives still in his grandparents' old homestead and had supported the young woman through her days of hope and disappointment, to hear her account of the tale and then on Ántonia to reconcile with her. By the end of Book IV, Jim and Ántonia have found again the ground of their friendship. Indeed, as this section's final image of a boy and girl shadowing Jim's solitary departure along the "familiar road" (*Early Novels and Stories* 911) of his past suggests, it has always been there.

In Book V, titled "Cuzack's Boys," Jim pays another brief visit to Ántonia and his former life because, having parted with "many illusions" during the intervening 20 years, he does not "wish to lose the early ones," which are realities "better than anything that can ever happen to one again" (*Early Novels and Stories* 912). In other words, he comes to redeem memory so that its meaning can live in his life. At the center of all his memories is, of course, Ántonia, and this visit to her will lead to his full understanding of her meaning and significance. Twenty years after their last reunion, Jim finds Ántonia happily married to another Bohemian immigrant, Anton Cuzack, and the adored mother of 10 or 11 lively children. What she lacks in material comforts is more than surpassed by the happiness, contentment, and love that fill her home, and Jim spends two days as a member of her family, enveloped in its warm reality, before he departs, having promised to take two of Ántonia's boys hunting the following summer (*Early Novels and Stories* 935). Jim's visit with Ántonia in Book V is, as he realizes, "a coming home to myself" (*Early Novels and Stories* 937), so here Cather's tale ends.

Although Book V gives *My Ántonia* a conventional happy ending that essentially erases the tragic note on which Jim and Ántonia had parted 20 years before, when he had promised to return and her answering smile had implied that he would not, it seems necessary to Ántonia's story. Without it, in fact, Ántonia's destiny would not have been resolved, and Cather could not have conveyed her full significance. Ántonia has found fulfillment by returning to the elemental. Certainly her resumption of her native language, which she speaks exclusively with her family, is evidence of this point. So, too, is her marriage to Cuzack. Like Jim, she has come home to herself. This is the destiny that she deserves and that Cather's themes demand.

POINT OF VIEW

As its title implies, *My Ántonia* focuses on the development and self-discovery of its heroine, but Cather's choice of point of view, or the perspective from which she relates the events, makes its first-person, or "I" narrator, Jim Burden, equally important to the tale. In fact, because readers know the thoughts and feelings of the narrator but not of its title character, Jim is effectively the novel's main character, or protagonist. Everything that readers learn of Ántonia filters through his consciousness, and he selects the events and incidents that reveal her to them. In one section of the novel, Book III, Ántonia even disappears as a physical presence; in another, Book IV, a third person, the Widow Steavens, relates the tale of her betrayal to Jim, who then includes it in his narrative.

One of the effects of this choice of point of view is to raise questions about the narrator's credibility. Because Ántonia is essentially an objectification of Jim's emotions, readers must consider the degree to which they can trust his version of her life. Cather handles this problem at least in part in the novel's brief introduction, that frame, as previously explained, that connects the authorial voice to the narrator's voice and thereby invests Jim's tale with credibility. The author, after all, is the source of the novel's truth. If the narrator speaks for him or her, he or she must speak the truth. This strategy also diminishes the gender issues inherent in having a male narrator relate the story of a woman. Because the traveling companion is presumably the author and therefore presumably a woman, collapsing authorial voice and narrator's voice into one implies that Jim's temperament and sensibility are sympathetic to Ántonia. His masculinity, in other words, is not a barrier to understanding the woman at the heart of his story because she is the same woman at the center of another woman's.

Cather handles the problem of narrative credibility as well with her title. When Jim prefaces Ántonia's tale with the word "my," he makes it clear that what follows is his understanding of the heroine, and he offers no apologies for his subjectivity. In fact, as he explains to his traveling companion, he can only ever hope to write about Ántonia by relating his history as well, for their stories are intimately combined. "It's through myself that I knew her and felt her," he reveals (*Early Novels and Stories* 713), a disclaimer that establishes Jim as an honest and a forthright narrative voice. He does not pretend to speak for her but intends, rather, to explain her influence on him. Readers cannot, therefore, fault him for his truth. It is all he has ever offered to present. Jim's credibility as narrator is thus never significantly challenged in *My Ántonia*. Like any first-person narrative, it is subjective and even incomplete, but Cather's introductory frame and her characterization of her narrator make it clear that she trusts him with the truth.

One other aspect of *My Ántonia*'s point of view is significant to the novel, its retrospective nature. Jim Burden relates his story from the perspective of adult wisdom. In consequence, the novel acquires an elegiac tone. Sadness and a sense of loss pervade the novel because the adult narrator is ever aware of the difference between the self that he was and the self that he is. His memories of his childhood and adolescence lack the innocence and inscrutability that typically accompany that stage of human development and are always colored by knowledge of their meaning and significance. Jim's boyhood encounters with the Nebraska prairie illustrate the point.

The 10-year-old orphan who finds himself transplanted to the Midwest may not entirely understand his experiences, but the adult who recalls them does. From the back of the wagon that transports him from the rail station to his grandparents' farmstead on the day of his arrival, Jim peers out into what appears to a boy from the forested hills of Virginia a landscape of "nos"—"no fences, no creeks or trees, no hills or fields . . . , nothing but land," he observes, and then, his adult self reflects, "not a country at all, but the material out of which countries are made" (*Early Novels and Stories* 718). In a land without boundaries, with nothing but "the complete dome of heaven" above him, the narrator remembers encountering his own insignificance and feeling "erased, blotted out" (*Early Novels and Stories* 718). The next day, however, the boy Jim begins to develop his relationship to this nothingness. Looking into the distance at the long, red prairie grasses, he has a sense of motion; "the whole country seemed, somehow, to be running" (*Early Novels and Stories* 722). Later, after his grandmother has taken him to her garden, pointed out the badger hole, and cautioned him about the snakes in this edenic landscape, he sits with his back against a warm pumpkin in utter contentment that the adult narrator recalls as a feeling of having been "dissolved into something complete and great" (*Early Novels and Stories* 724).

As these encounters with the Nebraska prairie demonstrate, Jim is both an inquisitive child and a perceptive adult, and this dual perspective clearly arises from Cather's use of the retrospective first-person narrator. It was a narrative strategy that certainly suited her purpose, creating *My Ántonia*'s elegiac tone and conveying, as further analysis will reveal, elements of characterization and thematic issues.

CHARACTER DEVELOPMENT

Indeed, the Jim Burden who emerges from these early scenes in *My Ántonia* is sensitive and serious, inquisitive and imaginative, attune to the people he encounters and perceptive of his surroundings. About the land he is especially so. Indeed, Jim's midwestern Eden is not a fearsome place, although its extremes of heat and cold, when crops can wilt in a day or a blizzard of thick-falling snow can obliterate the human attempts to create boundaries and mark paths, can be fearsome. It is instead a place that gives him scope and substance on which to grow. Here, for instance, he first knows male pride when he kills a snake (*Early Novels and Stories* 742) and earns Ántonia's praise. Here, too, he roams free on his pony (when he is not running errands or collecting the post, jobs that fill him with pride), becoming intimate with the rhythms of nature and every form of prairie life. Soon he is rooted in the soil.

Jim is equally responsive to the people in his life. His grandparents he loves and respects, and he relies for companionship and approval on the warm, human core of the rough and untutored hired hands, the immigrant Otto Fuchs and the mountain boy Jake Marpole, who become his elder brothers. The Shimerdas, however, especially Mr. Shimerda and Ántonia, most elicit his curiosity and fellowship. While Ambrosch, the eldest son, is cunning and sullen and Mrs. Shimerda is coarse and complaining, a bullying woman determined to advance her son's prospects no matter the cost, Mr. Shimerda is far too cultured and sensitive for the new world in which he finds himself living. Unable to speak English, he cannot communicate well with those like the Burdens who appreciate his efforts to maintain his dignity in the face of grinding poverty and finds his only solace in the Russian immigrants Peter and Pavel and his favorite child, Ántonia, a character, the scholar David Daiches observes, with "a personality rich enough to make up for all deficiencies in other members of her family" (38). Jim is sensitive to Mr. Shimerda's Old World gentility and to the "far-away look" in his eyes, the "sadness" of his smile (*Early Novels and Stories* 738). One of his sharpest memories, in fact, is of Mr. Shimerda's Christmas visit to the Burdens, when the soul-weary man comes to thank them for their gifts to his family and stays long into the night, having found a temporary haven of "peace and order" from the "crowded clutter" (*Early Novels and Stories* 768) of his own cave. Jim receives a lesson in religious tolerance on this occasion from his generally dogmatic grandfather, who tells his grandson after Mr. Shimerda makes the sign of the cross over him that "the prayers of all good people are good" (*Early Novels and Stories* 770), but Jim really has no need of it. He judges people on their words and deeds, and Mr. Shimerda is to him a gentleman. From their first meeting, when Mr. Shimerda looks "searchingly" in his face, the young boy, who has grown accustomed "to being taken for granted by [his] elders" (*Early Novels and Stories* 729), feels the connection between them, so his sense of loss when Mr. Shimerda commits suicide is genuine. Indeed, it is one of the bonds between him and Ántonia.

Jim's formative years on the Nebraska prairie shape his temperament and his worldview. He is an independent thinker, genuine and sincere, who enjoys simple, honest pleasures and values authenticity and tolerance in himself and others. He is also another of Cather's romantics (*Early Novels and Stories* 856). He believes in the goodness of others and their potential for doing good. These qualities account for his disdain of Black Hawk's prejudice against the immigrant girls, who are good enough to cook their meals, care for their children, and tidy their houses but not to marry their sons. Although adolescent rebellion certainly lies behind his feeling, Jim genuinely prefers the hired girls to Black Hawk's American belles. Among them all, however, he prefers Ántonia. For Jim, she is the embodiment of every fine thing in life, of all that matters to him, his memories of her as potent as her reality, and thus she is part of his being.

Ántonia Shimerda is clearly a symbolic character in the novel, and yet Cather endows her with a reality that gives her life. As inquisitive and imaginative as Jim, Ántonia, among all her family, has her father's sensitivity to life and his generous, sympathetic nature. Indeed, when Ántonia attempts to give him her ring as a gesture of appreciation for teaching her a few words of English on their first meeting, Jim finds "something reckless and extravagant" in her wish (*Early Novels and Stories* 729). That reckless extravagance is characteristic of Ántonia

Shimerda. She is always giving something away, and what she chiefly gives is herself—to her father, to grandmother Burden, to the Harlings, to the Widow Steavens, but especially to Jim and eventually to her own family. In scene after scene in which she features, whether she is traipsing barefoot with Jim over the Nebraska prairie, popping corn in the Harling kitchen, dancing at the Vannis' tent, or sharing a midsummer picnic with Jim and the other hired girls—Ántonia is the fulcrum of the experience. Even during her bleakest days—during the first bitter winter that finds her living like an animal in a sod house, in the aftermath of her beloved father's suicide, and as she grows big with an illegitimate child while she works like a field hand for her brother—Ántonia never loses her dignity and self-respect. Despite personal loss and harsh privation, she never grows coarse like her mother, nor does she ever lose her innate understanding of and appreciation for what truly matters in life.

Cather distinguishes Ántonia from the other hired girls by contrasting her to Lena Lingard and, to a lesser extent, Tiny Soderball. Like Ántonia, Lena and Tiny have sacrificed their youths to ensuring the survival of their immigrant families. None of them has had the leisure to attend school because they have had to work in the fields or, as Lena had done, to herd cattle in the open country. When they reached their late teens, all of them are hired out to Black Hawk businesses and families, the major portion of their salaries given to their families. In Black Hawk, when they have completed their day's work, they relish their freedom to enjoy the city's amusements. Yet Ántonia remains different from Lena and Tiny, the three Bohemian Marys, and Anna Hansen, less modern and Americanized, more like the self she might have become had the hardships of life in the New World not intervened.

At Black Hawk's dances, for instance, Jim prefers to step out on the floor with Ántonia, with whom every dance is like "a new adventure" (*Early Novels and Stories* 853), rather than Lena, who "danced every dance like a waltz, and … always the same waltz—the waltz of coming home to something of inevitable, fated return" (*Early Novels and Stories* 852). Similarly, Lena's use of language amuses Jim. Although the lively young woman is "as candid as Nature," she has acquired all the platitudes and formalities, "nearly all hypocritical in their origin" (*Early Novels and Stories* 886), Jim notes, of Black Hawk's conventional citizens. Jim finds it hard not to laugh when she uses "limb" for "leg" or "home" for "house." Ántonia, in contrast, who speaks English fluently, always retains "something impulsive and foreign in her speech"

(*Early Novels and Stories* 886), something that expresses the singularity of her essential self. When, years later, Jim visits Lena and Tiny in San Francisco, the difference between their lives and Ántonia's life is not surprising. Lena, still unmarried, owns a successful dressmaking business, while Tiny, who had ventured to Alaska at the time of the Klondike gold rush, is now a wealthy woman. Neither of them has ever had the relationship to the land that Ántonia has; neither of them has ever had the capacity to nurture life that Ántonia has. Functioning essentially as foils, or contrasting characters, to Ántonia in the novel, Lena and Tiny eventually merge into the anonymous mass of modern America, losing their Old World charm and their connection to something everlasting. Ántonia, however, only ever becomes more of what she has always been, and therein lies her strength.

To the orphan Jim, Ántonia becomes and remains the most significant woman in his life, indeed, the most important person in his life. She helps him become himself, and for that, he will always have her with him. When he meets her after she gives birth to her first child, in fact, he confesses his feelings to her. "I'd have liked to have you for a sweetheart, or a wife, or my mother or my sister," he reveals, "— anything that a woman can be to a man. The idea of you is a part of my mind.... You really are a part of me" (*Early Novels and Stories* 910). Like Alexandra Bergson in *O Pioneers!*, Ántonia roots herself in the soil and thrives, and thus she becomes the embodiment of all that Jim finds of value in life.

THEMATIC ISSUES

With its retrospective first-person narrator and its elegiac tone, *My Ántonia* signals its primary theme, or central idea, memory and the memorializing of the past, and Cather develops this theme primarily as a critique of the new world order that was on the ascendancy at the beginning of the twentieth century. Like the country about which he writes, Jim Burden grows into adulthood amid change and flux, during a transitional period between the late-Victorian and the modern eras. He sees the transformation of his world from an agrarian to an industrialized economy, from a rural to an urban culture, and notes the effect of such changes on the values and ideals of its citizens. Something, Jim's sense of sadness and regret and his longing for the past conveys, something that is for him embodied in Ántonia, is missing from contemporary life, and his narrative is thus at least in part an effort to retrieve it. As the novel's epigraph from the

Latin poet Virgil, "The best days are the first to flee," suggests, the past holds much of value. In its evocation of the decline of a pioneering civilization and the intrusion of a commercial spirit, *My Ántonia* reminds readers of their loss.

Crucial to the development of this theme is Cather's depiction of prairie life in Book I. It is certainly not naive. Indeed, Cather emphasizes the extremes of temperature, the squalid living conditions, the want both physical and psychological that makes prairie life precarious, and she emphasizes this reality by positioning Mr. Shimerda's suicide as Book I's key event. Yet the overwhelming impression that Book I creates is positive. On the prairie, Jim and Ántonia have the freedom and opportunity to develop into their best selves. Attuned to the cycles of nature, they experience their connection to the primal and the universal, and their horizons stretch beyond their vision. As the tale of the Russian immigrants Peter and Pavel makes clear, even the worst that may confront them on the prairie is still preferable to the ravening realities embodied in the pack of wolves that devours a wedding party and that prompts two good and loving young men to sacrifice their friends—and their humanity—to save themselves (*Early Novels and Stories* 748–51). Prairie life demands resilience and perseverance, and it builds—and indeed requires—a sense of community that demonstrates generosity of spirit and human compassion, qualities that the Burdens and Mr. Shimerda and Ántonia possess in abundance.

From the perspective of adult wisdom, Jim, the novel's retrospective narrator, now celebrates the pioneering spirit of his youth because he recognizes its decline. Indeed, it was disappearing before his eyes even in his youth. Black Hawk's social stratification (*Early Novels and Stories* 838–41), for instance, its distinct ethnic and class prejudices, had always been a source of disdain for Jim, who even as a teen had resented the narrow-mindedness of the town's Anglicized elite but lives to take pleasure in the fact that the "best that a harassed Black Hawk merchant can hope for is to sell provisions and farm machinery and automobiles to the rich farms where that first crop of stalwart Bohemian and Scandinavian girls are now the mistresses" (*Early Novels and Stories* 840). Further evidence of decline lies in Wick Cutter, the town's unscrupulous and licentious moneylender. Although he talks much about "his pious bringing-up" (*Early Novels and Stories* 845) and contributes for sentimental reasons to Black Hawk's Protestant churches, Cutter, as his name suggests, is a destructive force within his society.

He takes advantage of the poor immigrants who borrow money from him to make possible their dreams, and he seduces the young women who, like Ántonia, seek honest employment in his household to improve their and their families' situations. So perverted are his values that he will murder his wife, with whom he has always maintained a volatile relationship, and then commit suicide to prevent her family from inheriting their property (*Early Novels and Stories* 931–32). The ambition that propels Lena Lingard and Tiny Soderball to their soft landing in San Francisco is also, as far as Jim is concerned, a dismissal of the simple life and human values that they had all once shared on the Nebraska plain. The young Jim may not have understood the implications of all that he observed, but the adult Jim clearly recognizes that the world of his youth was already in transformation, hence his effort to reclaim it.

Cather emphasizes her point about the decline of pioneering civilization in one of the novel's chief visual images—the plow silhouetted against the sun that so captures the attention of Jim and the hired girls on the day of their summer picnic. Late in the day, after Jim and Ántonia have shared confidences about Mr. Shimerda and then all the hired girls have reminisced about the old country and discussed the sacrifices they and their families have made in their new homeland, Jim, at Ántonia's request, tells them about the Spanish explorer Coronado, who had sought in vain for the Seven Golden Cities in the New World. The story prompts the girls to speculate about the motivation for such a quest and the reasons he had never returned to his homeland. Cather clearly intends the conversation and story to connect the hired girls' experiences to a long history of exploration and immigration, to a pioneering spirit that forged a destiny from a barren wilderness, and frequently at great cost. Indeed, when Jim tells the girls that history books record that Coronado "died in the wilderness, of a broken heart," Ántonia emphasizes Cather's point by responding, "More than him has done that" (*Early Novels and Stories* 865). Yet even as Cather celebrates the human capacity to dream big and the tough resilience and fierce desire necessary to achieve success, her next image, like Ántonia's remark, is an evocation of loss.

Silhouetted against the setting sun is a solitary plow, the tool with which these western pioneers have struggled to tame a resistant wilderness. Magnified by the distance, it is "heroic in size, a picture writing on the sun" that expresses Cather's awe of the pioneering spirit. Yet even as Jim and the hired girls, whose response to the image conveys Cather's point, pause to remark the truly remarkable, it is disappearing before their eyes. As the sun descends beneath the horizon and the fields grow dark around them, "that forgotten plough [sinks] back to its own littleness somewhere on the prairie" (*Early Novels and Stories* 866). Puny and insignificant against the greater forces of nature, that plow is a visible reminder that the pioneering spirit that once powered that humble machine is losing its supremacy to the new forces of mechanization and commerce that are building cities and raising factories and in the process diminishing the opportunities for heroic individual effort and achievement.

Yet as long as people like Ántonia exist, Cather ultimately concludes, that spirit will continue to animate human effort. Twenty years after Jim parts from Ántonia, 20 years during which he "parts with many illusions" (*Early Novels and Stories* 912), he returns to Black Hawk to recover the woman who symbolizes for him the "immemorial human attitudes which we recognize by instinct as universal and true." He finds her "battered" but not destroyed. Indeed, "she still had that something which fires the imagination" (*Early Novels and Stories* 926). In Ántonia's warm, generous spirit and her deep, abiding faith in possibility, Jim finds proof of the existence of such qualities. In the boundless energy and goodwill of Ántonia's happy family, Jim draws strength from the certainty that they continue to be passed down to new generations. Like the remnants of the tracks of the old road that long ago brought Jim and the Shimerdas to the Nebraska prairie and that no amount of modern construction can now obliterate from the landscape (*Early Novels and Stories* 936), Ántonia and all that she represents live still. With that knowledge, Jim anticipates a future that matters.

A MARXIST INTERPRETATION

In Book II of *My Ántonia,* titled "The Hired Girls," Willa Cather focuses on Black Hawk's "curious social situation" (*Early Novels and Stories* 838) and develops what essentially amounts to a satire, a mocking depiction of a particular human characteristic or social institution, on class and race distinctions as embodied in the traditional Anglicized elite of the United States. The hired girls, the Bohemian and Scandinavian immigrants and daughters of immigrants who are populating the prairie, may have embraced American ideals—and especially its dream of success—but Black Hawk's elite, the descendants of the original white, Anglo-Saxon Protestants who colonized and founded the nation, are reluctant to include them in their circles. Good enough to wash their clothing, clean their houses, care for their children, and serve their customers, they are, nevertheless, unsuited to marry their sons and represent a "menace to the social order" (*Early Novels and Stories* 840) that confirms and upholds the Black Hawk elite. Cather's focus in "The Hired Girls" offers the Marxist critic, who examines literature from the perspective of class consciousness and class conflict, fertile ground for exploration. Indeed, the Marxist critic who examines Black Hawk society will find in Cather's satire a challenge to tradition that is simultaneously antithetical to and affirmative of her memorializing of the past.

The Marxist critic focuses on the relation between literature and history, emphasizing particularly the social and economic factors that, according to the German philosopher Karl Marx (1818-1883), drive historical change. Like feminism, with which it shares certain basic principles, Marxism is not a single theory. In fact, several different schools of Marxist critics exist, and "all of them," according to Arthur Asa Berger, "base their criticism on varying and sometimes conflicting interpretations of Marx's theories and how they can be applied to analyzing culture in general and, more specifically, literary texts, works of elite culture, popular culture, and the mass media" (41). To understand Marxist criticism, then, we need first to explain briefly the concepts that serve as its foundation.

Marx is usually classified as a "dialectical materialist." He believed that historical transformations occur through a dialectic, or development, through the stages of thesis, antithesis, and synthesis. Each historical force, according to Marx, calls into being its Other so that the two opposing forces negate each other and eventually give rise to a third force that transcends its opposition. Unlike his great teacher Hegel, who was an idealist, Marx was a materialist who believed that social forces shape human consciousness.

For Marx, the ultimate moving force of human history is economics or, perhaps more specifically, political economy. This term encompasses political and social issues as well as economic factors. Each society, according to Marx, bases its culture on its means of production, the techniques by which it produces food, clothing, shelter, and other necessities of life, and the social relations these methods create. For example, an economy based on manufacturing demands a division of labor, cooperation among workers, and a hierarchical system of managers. These economic demands in turn shape the social relations of the people. From this basic premise, Marx argued that major historical changes occur as a result of economic contradictions, what might be termed class consciousness and class conflict. Conflict between the aristocracy and the middle classes, for example, was the source of the French Revolution of the 1790s.

In Marxist thought, the economic base gives rise to and shapes the superstructure, which finds expression in the culture's ideology, its collective consciousness of itself. This ideology comprises all the institutions of the society, such as the church, the education system, the art world, and the legal system. The ideology, which includes literature, generally conforms to and supports the culture's dominant means of production. Economic conditions alone, however, are not sufficient to explain the development and effect of its institutions. Human agency, or individual consciousness, is active in these institutions as well. Thus, Marxist criticism that focuses exclusively on economics and that celebrates the proletariat, or working class, has been termed "vulgar Marxism" for its crude tendency to oversimplify complex issues.

Marxism is primarily a political and economic philosophy, not a guide to understanding literature. As a result, Marxist criticism takes a variety of forms, depending on how the text is defined in relation to material reality or to ideology. Cather's presentation of the contrast between Black Hawk's Anglo-American elite and its disempowered underclass of ethnics, the poor, and people of color lends itself most readily to a Marxist critique based on the reflection theory. As an imitation of the culture that helped to produce it, the novel dramatizes the forces, both economic and social, that lie behind class consciousness and class conflict.

When a teenage Jim moves with his grandparents from their prairie farm to a snug, two-story house on the north end of Black Hawk, the curious young man becomes an accidental anthropologist, studying the social structures and habits of his neighbors as he reluctantly learns to accommodate to them. Black Hawk, he gradually discovers, is a conventional town with restrictive social mores and a rigid class structure. Everything about the "clean, well-planted little prairie [town's]" physical appearance, from the neat white fences that enclose the "good green yards" of the inhabitants' houses and the "shapely little trees" lining the wooden sidewalks to the "two rows" of civic and commercial buildings in the center of town, suggests order and decorum. Reinforcing that image are the town's "four white churches" (*Early Novels and Stories* 805), the source of social as well as moral life for its Baptists, such as the Burdens, Methodists, and other Christian citizens. Until the summer that the Vannis open their dancing pavilion, Jim is relatively unaware of the confining conformity that characterizes Black Hawk life. When the town's elite begins to mingle socially with its hired girls, however, Jim confronts the sterility of its values and develops contempt for them, dramatizing in his transformation Cather's awareness of and support for social change, even in the face of her traditionalism.

Cather develops her perspective by contrasting the vitality and natural intelligence of the hired girls to the complacency and insipid refinement of Black Hawk's Anglicized elite. The hired girls, Jim recalls, are "almost a race apart" (*Early Novels and Stories* 838). Hard times and physical labor in the outdoors have quickened their powers of observation, their engagement with life, and nurtured the self-confidence expressed in their "positive carriage and freedom of movement" (*Early Novels and Stories* 838). Stalwart and resolute, the hired girls willingly do what they must to assist their families to prosper, and Jim admires their generosity and goodwill almost as much as their beauty and grace. Black Hawk's daughters, in contrast, may possess all the potential of the hired girls, but their cosseted existence has made them physically inert and intellectually placid. When they danced, Jim observes, "their bodies never moved inside their clothes" (*Early Novels and Stories* 838), and they are convinced of their superiority to the hired girls simply because they are not wage earners. Indeed, many of these American girls, whose families migrated to Nebraska from Pennsylvania or Virginia, have nothing more than the hired girls, but their fathers would rather "they [sit] at home in poverty" (*Early Novels and Stories* 839) than do anything that might diminish the sense of superiority they derive from their Anglo-Saxon heritage.

Given these differences, it is not surprising that Black Hawk's sons are eager to go for a turn on the dance floor with the hired girls. They lack the "mettle" (*Early Novels and Stories* 840), however, to marry them, as the example of Sylvester Lovett indicates. Lovett, a cashier in his father's bank, pursues Lena Lingard for several months but eventually escapes into a respectable marriage with a widow six years his elder rather than risk affronting Black Hawk's conventions by following his heart. His choice, Jim observes, is typical of young men of position in the prairie town, and Jim has nothing but contempt for it, for him, and for the artificial distinctions that prevent his class from accepting the hired girls on their merit (*Early Novels and Stories* 844), especially when those girls offer the promise of reinvigorating empty and tired values and attitudes with some of the original pioneer spirit that once created a country from a wilderness.

Cather aligns her hired girls with two other examples of the dispossessed in American society, Blind d'Arnault, the mulatto pianist whose visit breaks the "dreary monotony" (*Early Novels and Stories* 828) of a Black Hawk winter, and the anonymous tramp who commits suicide, the subject of one of Ántonia's stories. Both represent persons who by virtue of race or class are unable to achieve full entry into society. Blind d'Arnault, for instance, shares with the hired girls a spontaneous appreciation of life, and he expresses it through his music. Beneath the fingers of this instinctual artist, the piano's black and white keys make sounds that are wondrously real and alive and that recall some primal force that animates all humanity. It is as an expression of his history, however, that d'Arnault's music is most significant.

Born on a southern plantation, "where the spirit if not the fact of slavery persisted" (*Early Novels and Stories* 830), (indeed, d'Arnault bears the name of the plantation's owner), he is the embodiment of racial inequality in American society. An embarrassment to his family, an affront to the plantation owner, he bears the scars of an institutionalized racism that persisted so long as to be woven into the fabric of the nation. Indeed, his music, plantation songs that evoke the romance of a bygone era and to which all the men at the Boys' Home sing along and dance tunes, the playing of which make d'Arnault look like "some glistening African god of pleasure, full of strong, savage blood" (*Early Novels and Stories* 834), is the record of that history and heritage, and it makes him an outlaw thing. The hired girls, a mulatto pianist, and the travelers who stay at Black Hawk's hotel may find common ground in d'Arnault's music, but everyone is aware that Mrs. Gardner, the hotel's manager and an arbiter of the town's morality, would not approve (*Early Novels and Stories* 833). D'Arnault is a curiosity, someone fit to entertain even a Russian nobleman (*Early Novels and Stories* 834), but he will always be marginalized in American society.

Race and ethnicity are not the only barriers to full entry into American society. Poverty, as the example of the tramp who commits suicide discloses, is another, even for those who claim an Anglo-American heritage. The tramp, who appears disheveled and distraught one summer day during thrashing season, first snidely implies that Ántonia and those with whom she is working in the fields are far more concerned about their cattle than their fellow human beings.

Then, when he learns that he has wandered into a Norwegian community, he rants, "My God! ... so it's Norwegians now, is it? I thought this was Americy" (*Early Novels and Stories* 826). Demanding work, he then climbs on the thrashing machine, cuts a few bands of wheat, and throws himself into the blades. Although Ántonia cannot understand why anyone would commit suicide during thrashing season, when the warm summer days and the bountiful harvest erase all reminders of want and hardship from memory, her failure to understand makes Cather's point. She and the tramp are united in their poverty, and yet neither feels solidarity with the other. In fact, Ántonia finds hope in her situation. The tramp, in contrast, finds himself displaced once again, his words imply, by the encroachment of foreigners whose presence is ruining the country. Like the American farmers who would rather suffer than permit their daughters to work for wages, the tramp cannot see that his enemy is a class system that discards the poor of any race or nationality as easily as it marginalizes ethnics and persons of color, so he chooses death over solidarity with people like him in every other way but national origin. Indeed, his method of suicide is a blow to the very lifeblood of the immigrants.

Cather intensifies the irony in the tramp's failure to identify his own self-interest through her depiction of Wick Cutter, Black Hawk's moneylender and the person who exemplifies, to use Hermione Lee's terms, "the debased American currency which Cather saw buying out the pioneers' values" (152). Fond of quoting "Poor Richard's Almanack" and of talking much about his "pious bringing-up" (*Early Novels and Stories* 845), Cutter is, nevertheless, far removed from Benjamin Franklin's ideal of the self-made man. Not only is he an unscrupulous businessman and a monstrous husband who hoards his wealth against the fear that his wife's family will some day inherit it, but he is also an example of licentious masculinity, preying on the hired girls and attempting to rape Ántonia. Like his childless marriage, Cutter's life is barren of any human emotion and produces nothing but anger and hurt. When Cutter murders his wife and then commits suicide, orchestrating his actions to ensure that Mrs. Cutter's family is denied his fortune, he reveals his monstrous depravity to the world. Yet this is the man who determines the fate of many of Black Hawk's citizens, regardless of their nationality. He lives smugly in a big, fine house, having prospered on both their labor and their misfortune, his money protection against the townspeople's disapproval and distress. In America, his example implies, where success is now measured by material possessions and money now constitutes power, Wick Cutters are everywhere despoiling with impunity the values and ideals that shaped the nation and attacking the people who are building it.

Cather's depiction of class consciousness and class conflict in *My Ántonia* underscores the changes in American culture at the turn of the twentieth century to which she responds in all her fiction with a profound sense of regret. The prairie world in which Jim and Ántonia formed their essential selves certainly could be harsh and trying, but it also provided individuals with the freedom and scope to reach for something beyond dull realities and crass materialism. It also tended to unify disparate peoples in the common struggle to survive, for the will to prevail, not race and ethnicity, was the only distinction that mattered between such people. Cather mourns the loss of that world and celebrates its values, especially as they are embodied in Ántonia.

Yet even as she memorializes that past, Cather is mindful that change may be necessary to keep alive what is most valuable about it. America's original English settlers had never had exclusive ownership of the pioneer spirit, yet in the course of the nation's history, their descendants had become the country's elite. Their rise to power gradually mandated that full entrance to American society depended on achieving an Anglo-American ethnicity, thereby creating and reinforcing class distinctions in a nation that took pride in the democratic principle of equality. In confronting those class distinctions, however, Cather suggests the need to dismantle them. The sterility of Wick Cutter's values and the superficial basis for the sense of superiority among Black Hawk's American farmers present a sharp contrast to the bold spirit of life that animates the hired girls and that Blind d'Arnault releases in his music. That contrast makes clear the need for change, or at least for a redefinition of America's elite, and that redefinition would be inclusive rather than exclusive, based on shared traits of mind and being rather than meaningless distinctions of race, economic status, and ethnicity. In celebrating the pioneer spirit, Cather thus puts her traditionalism to use in the service of social change.

My Ántonia is clearly a novel with many angles. As a *bildungsroman,* or novel of maturation, it charts the development of Jim Burden's spiritual and intellectual growth and his discovery, indeed, his recovery, of what matters most in life. As a novel of the soil, it extends and essentially concludes her exploration of the immigrant experience that Cather had begun in *O Pioneers!*. As a critique of early twentieth-century American society, it charts a world in flux. At the center of all these stories, however, is Ántonia, the Bohemian immigrant who embodies Cather's conviction that primary human values will persist and indeed prevail. *My Ántonia* is thus Cather's testament of faith.

7

After "the World Broke in Two": *The Professor's House* (1925)

The best of Willa Cather's midcareer novels, *The Professor's House* (1925) is, appropriately, a transitional work, bridging the gap between the novels of the soil on which her reputation flourished and the historical novels on which her late career rests. It is also one of her best. The story of Professor Godfrey St. Peter, a sensitive and an intelligent man in the midst of a midlife crisis, *The Professor's House* explores the conflict between individual sensibility and the demands of the conventional world. The theme, of course, was not new to Cather, who had developed it to some extent in both her first novel, *Alexander's Bridge* (1912), and her third, *The Song of the Lark* (1915). In *The Professor's House,* however, Cather gives it full treatment, exposing the inevitable disappointments and disillusionment that result from compromised ideals.

The Professor's House opens in the midst of quiet crisis. Professor Godfrey St. Peter, the recent recipient of an Oxford prize in history for his study of *Spanish Adventurers in North America,* should be preparing to move into the new house that the prize has enabled him, at his wife's suggestion, to build. Instead, he sits contemplatively in his old attic study, reviewing his life and relationships, having determined to retain his habitual retreat and continue his research amid the dress forms and patterns that had long shared the space and that connect him to his life outside its door. That life involves a daily routine of university lectures, the too-frequent intrusion of university politics into his scholarly pursuits, and, increasingly, the petty irritations between his two adult daughters, Rosamond and Kathleen, and an indefinable rift between the Professor and his wife, Lillian. In his attic retreat, however, the Professor escapes these conventional demands in memories of and research into the preferable past.

The past to which St. Peter chiefly retreats during the summer term in which the novel's key event is set recalls his deep and fervent friendship with Tom Outland, a brilliant former student who had been killed in Flanders fighting with the French Foreign Legion in World War I. As he prepares for publication Outland's life story, which includes the discovery of an ancient cliff-dwelling civilization in New Mexico and the invention of a vacuum with the potential to revolutionize aviation (*Later Novels* 121), St. Peter measures his pupil's remarkable achievements against his own youthful dreams and meager accomplishments to confront his nagging sense of failure, the result of the compromises life forced him to make between competing needs and desires and obligations. Enervated by his state of mind and being, St. Peter thus fails to rouse himself from dreamy reverie on the sofa on the day that the wind blows closed the attic window, trapping the gas from a tiny heater that only the fortuitous arrival of the family's German seamstress, Augusta, will prevent killing him. While *The Professor's House* is not without scenes of action and adventure, it is primarily a novel that explores an individual sensibility. It is Cather's artistic genius that makes this exploration as moving and significant as Outland's New Mexico discoveries.

GENESIS AND CRITICAL RECEPTION

The genesis of *The Professor's House,* Cather's seventh novel, lies, somewhat surprisingly, given the novel's title, not in Professor St. Peter's story but in Tom Outland's. In 1912, Cather had made what a biographer, Hermione Lee, characterizes as a "crucial, transforming journey to the Southwest" (23). The significance of this experience she captured in Thea Kronborg's artistic development in *The Song of the Lark.* In 1914, Cather, accompanied by her friend, the magazine editor Edith Lewis, made a second trek into the Southwest's high mesas, a landscape that clearly touched a chord in her.

Their week's exploration of ancient cliff dwellings, including an unexcavated cliff village, climaxed with a harrowing 24 hours during which the friends, lost in uncharted territory, were left to fend for themselves while their guide went in search of help. Rescued by men from an archaeological dig, Cather and Lewis made a rough and difficult climb to safety and returned to civilization as local sensations (Lee 230–32). Cather would later play down the adventure, but the experience was in fact significant, prompting her to write an essay in which, according to Lee, she "grafted her own responses [to the mesa's profound beauty and significance] onto the witness of" other explorers and historians of the region (232). She began almost immediately to think as well of transforming her experience into story, but she never completed the tale that she intended to title "The Blue Mesa." Seven years later, however, when she began work on *The Professor's House*, it was "Tom Outland's Story," the novel's self-contained second section, that Cather first composed (Lee 232). The resonance of her intellectual, aesthetic, and emotional experience of the Southwest thus lies at the novel's heart.

Onc of Cather's early stories, "The Enchanted Bluff," written in 1909, also anticipates in setting and theme the achievement of *The Professor's House.* In the story, six boys set up camp, as they have habitually done for years, on one of the sandbar islands created by the changing course of the Nebraska River. The narrator, who is preparing to leave behind his mates to teach school on the Divide, is already suffering homesickness. The story's plot, such as it is, seems relatively inconsequential. The boys swim, eat, and build a fire around which to talk about the stars as they appear in the night sky and to watch the moon rise over the bluffs. Their conversation eventually centers on heroes and legends of conquest and exploration, on Columbus and Napoleon, on Aztec sacrifices and Mound Builders, and on Coronado's quest for gold along their river and finally shifts to the places they dream one day of going. Tip Smith, the grocer's son, then shares the "dolorous legend" (*Collected Stories* 417) that his Uncle Bill had told him of a vanished cliff-dwelling civilization in New Mexico and his own intention to find and climb the bluff on which it once stood, inspiring his companions to commit to his resolution. In the night, the narrator dreams that he is racing the others to the bluff and wakes in a "kind of fear" (*Collected Stories* 419) that he has missed his chance. At dawn, the boys swim again before returning to their separate lives. They next meet at Christmas, when they skate to their island and "[renew] their resolution" (*Collected Stories* 419) to find the bluff. Cather concludes her tale with a coda that describes their destinies 20 years later. None of them, sadly, has achieved his dream. Percy Pound, for instance, is a Kansas City stockbroker, the German tailor's sons have inherited their father's business, and the charming and clever Arthur has drunk himself to an early death. Tip Smith, whose tale had so inspired his friends, is now a shopkeeper married to a "slatternly" (*Collected Stories* 420) wife. His son Bert, however, with whom Tip has shared the wondrous legend, is now in its thrall and "thinks of nothing but the Enchanted Bluff" (*Collected Stories* 420).

Although "The Enchanted Bluff" pre-dates the publication of *The Professor's House* by 14 years, the story certainly gives evidence of the landscapes and subjects that inspired Cather's imagination. Adventurers and pioneers, conquerors and explorers, and always the presence of the past, the heroic past that even included anonymous and long-vanished civilizations, presented Cather with proof of the achievements of which humans were capable. Yet as the story's theme also makes clear, far too often and despite their best intentions, humans fail to realize their dreams and settle instead for ordinary existence. Such compromise betrays the best of their humanity and accounts, perhaps, for life's ineffable sadness. Fourteen years after her initial exploration of these landscapes, subjects, and themes, Cather would still be probing them in *The Professor's House.*

Critical reception of *The Professor's House* on its publication in 1925 was generally unfavorable. While virtually all the reviewers praised Cather's characterization of Godfrey St. Peter, they were uniformly confused by and critical of the novel's structure. The critic for the *New York Evening Post's Literary Review,* for example, could think of no reason to include Tom Outland's story unless, in an allusion to the novel's epigraph, it were "the 'turquoise' set in the 'dull silver' of the other lives." Interrupting the Professor's story with Outland's, he went on to assert, "is an extraordinary thing to do in point of technique, because to all intents and purposes, it has nothing to do with the story" (O'Connor 234). That opinion was shared even more vehemently by the critic for the *New York Times Book Review,* who claimed that the novel's first book was "ingeniously invented and admirably carried along as far as it goes," its second book was "an amateurish essay in archeological adventure," and its third was "far beyond [Cather's] philosophic depth without adequate equipment of water-wings for keeping afloat what is left of the story so inconsiderately abandoned at the end of book one" (O'Connor 235). Even those few critics who praised *The Professor's House* found themselves apologizing for Cather's narrative form. Henry Seidel Canby, for instance, writing in the *Saturday Review of Literature,* began his review with an implied justification of the novel's structure: "This is the age of experiment in the American novel." Cather, in other words, was merely attempting what others of her generation of writers were doing, searching for "new methods of story telling, new angles of approach." Thus, he dismissed any technical flaws by asserting "if the new technique of *The Professor's House* creaks a little, a method is only machinery after all" (O'Connor 252). He then offered a thoughtful assessment of the novel's strengths, particularly its study of an "old soul" (O'Connor 253), that ended by claiming that *The Professor's House,* "more than *O Pioneers!,* is a pioneering book" (O'Connor 254).

PLOT DEVELOPMENT

Perhaps Cather's first critics were unprepared for the new direction of *The Professor's House,* expecting another novel of the soil and thus disappointed that she did not deliver on form, but contemporary critics would generally concur with Canby's assessment. Indeed, most now consider *The Professor's House* one of Cather's most important works. But at the time of its publication and even years afterward, Cather found herself explaining her novel's structure. Eventually, she offered two reasons for it. The first, she explained to Fanny Butcher of the *Chicago Tribune* and reiterated 15 years later in *The News Letter of the College English Association,* was an effort to bring musical form, specifically, the sonata, to the novel ("On *The Professor's House,*" *Stories, Poems, and Other Writings* 974). "This story," she explained to Butcher, "is built like a piece of music, the theme of St. Peter, then the theme of Tom Outland, and the last part of the book the mingling of the two themes" (O'Connor 237). The second, she revealed to the academics, was an attempt to use a literary "device" characteristic of the "early French and Spanish novelists; that of inserting the *Nouvelle* into the *Roman*" ("On *The Professor's House,*" *Stories, Poems, and Other Writings* 974), in other words, of embedding a short story into a novel. "Tom Outland's Story," she went on to note, had an independent life, having been published in French, Polish, and Dutch for "school children studying English" ("On *The Professor's House,*" *Stories, Poems, and Other Writings* 974).

Cather's comments confirm the novel's deliberate if somewhat unconventional plot structure. Writing *The Professor's House* during the heyday of the period of American literary history known as modernism, when, as Canby noted, experimentation was an expectation of literature, Cather may indeed have been influenced by the spirit of the age. Not only does she attempt to inject musical form into the novel's structure and to adapt European forms to her American subject, but she also experiments with the linear structure of the two books devoted to the Professor's story. While she does not use the technique known as stream of consciousness, which transforms the flow of human thought into narrative form, she comes close to it by limiting point of view, or the perspective from which events are related, to the Professor's. The effect is to place readers within his consciousness, where the ebb and flow of memory is as real and compelling to him as the events of daily life. Indeed, they may be more so. Cather's narrative captures this ebb and flow of human thought in all its depth and variety, producing the nonlinear structure of Books One and Three. The strategy also connects Tom Outland's story to the Professor's, for its prominent position in the novel indicates that it is his key memory. As the novelist who uses the stream-of-consciousness technique does, Cather asks readers to close the gap between what seem to be disconnected experiences to discover their meaning. Thus, the plot of *The Professor's House* is a deliberate and even modern design, as complex as its subject, and its three-part structure gradually unfolds its source and its resolution.

Book One, titled "The Family," introduces the novel's protagonist, or central character, Professor Napoleon Godfrey St. Peter, and places him in relation to the members of his household, his profession, and his own bittersweet memories of his past. Cather establishes a sense of dislocation and disillusionment in the novel's opening chapter, which she sets on the September day on which the St. Peter family completes its move into a comfortable new house, built with the proceeds of a £5,000 Oxford prize in history awarded for Professor St. Peter's eight-volume work *Spanish Adventurers in North America*. Surveying the dismantled rooms of the shabby old house where he had lived since his marriage, raising his two daughters and building his career, the Professor then mounts the wobbly stairs to an attic workplace that he has shared for years with the dress forms, paper patterns, and sewing machine of the German seamstress the family employs. This attic study, not the "sham" (*Later Novels* 106) one below, has always been the Professor's true retreat. Now he refuses to be dislodged from it, brooking his wife's disapproval of what she considers his intolerance (*Later Novels* 117) and the community's disbelief of what they perceive as his eccentricity to remain in the place he associates with all that matters most in his life. St. Peter's breach of familial and social customs clearly signals both the internal and the external distress that threatens the integrity of the Professor's house.

The remainder of Book One details the significant events of the next eight months of the Professor's life, placing them within the context of his remembered past. Cather introduces Lillian St. Peter, the Professor's wife, and reveals the history of their courtship, their current estrangement, and, in an emotionally complex scene during which the long-married couple attends a performance of the opera *Mignon,* the mutual sadness it gives them both (*Later Novels* 153). She also exposes the prickly relationship between the St. Peters' two daughters, Rosamond and Kathleen. Rosamond, the eldest, is happily married to Louis Marcellus, a charming and generous electrical engineer by profession who discovered a way to exploit commercially a patent that his wife inherited and thereby created for them a life of material ease and comfort of which Kathleen is rather envious. Happily married to a young journalist, Scott McGregor, Kathleen also disapproves of the changes she notes in her elder sister's attitudes and behavior, and Rosamond feels the silent sting of the McGregors' judgments. It is the absent presence of a mysterious young man who had one day, more than a decade before, appeared at the Professor's house, eager for an education, that lies at the center of all their lives. Cather, however, unfolds his story elliptically in Book One, presenting him only in relation to others and thereby creating of him a bit of an enigma. In Book Two, "Tom Outland's Story," she provides the background that explains the reason he remains "a glittering idea" (*Later Novels* 164), as Scott McGregor remarks, in all their lives.

"Tom Outland's Story" is a narrative complete in itself, yet its placement within the novel and the manner of its telling make clear its importance to the entire work. At the center of the novel's three-book structure, "Tom Outland's Story" solves, of course, the riddle of the mysterious young man's history and character. A railroad call boy in Pardee, New Mexico, Tom, who had been orphaned as a baby, one day befriends Rodney "Roddy" Blake, a rough-and-ready railroad fireman who becomes Tom's surrogate father as he nurses him through a bout of pneumonia. When Tom recovers, the two men abandon the railroad to herd cattle near the Blue Mesa, a geographical maze of seemingly impenetrable canyons and impregnable cliffs whose mystery and beauty gradually seduce them. After Tom unearths some pottery shards, arrowheads, and a perfectly preserved stone pick ax (*Later Novels* 216), they determine to scale the cliffs and explore the mesa. What follows is a thrilling but sad tale of discovery, disappointment, and betrayal.

Roddy, Tom, and Henry Atkins, a "castaway Englishman" (*Later Novels* 218) who accepts their offer to join them as cook and dies of snakebite during their adventure, spend a summer excavating the remnants of an extinct civilization that they christen Cliff City. Eager to share their discovery of what their friend Father Duchene calls "a sacred spot" (*Later Novels* 234), Tom travels to Washington, D.C., to enlist the aid of archaeologists at the Smithsonian Institution. Six months later, destitute and disillusioned by official bureaucracy, Tom returns to New Mexico and a more profound betrayal. In his absence, Roddy had misunderstood his motives and sold their collection of artifacts to a German. The two friends quarrel and then separate forever, the legacy of their adventure a bank account into which Roddy had deposited the proceeds of the sale in Tom's name and which the disillusioned young man refuses ever to tap.

Cather makes Tom's tale of youthful idealism all the more compelling and significant in the manner of its telling. It may be a self-contained narrative, but it exists as the Professor's memory. During the summer hiatus from lecturing, St. Peter has declined an invitation to accompany the Marcelluses and Lillian on a holiday to France in favor of editing for publication Tom Outland's journal, the tale that ostensibly constitutes Book Two of Cather's novel. Yet Book Two takes the form not of a written work but rather of an oral recitation. It re-creates Tom's turns of phrase and rhythmic patterns and thereby re-creates the man. For St. Peter, Cather's narrative strategy makes clear, Tom Outland lives still. This man and his adventure are the embodiment of the Professor's own idealistic youth, his own mature disappointments.

Book Three of *The Professor's House,* titled "The Professor," now brings to conclusion the meaning and consequence of St. Peter's heroic but failed dreams. In five brief chapters, one no more than two pages, St. Peter surveys the meaning of his life and finds again his essential self. So when a summer storm blows shut the tiny attic window and extinguishes the gas stove, he briefly considers his responsibility to family and society to rouse himself from the sofa bed on which he is comfortably drowsing (*Later Novels* 267). Chance, however, as it has so often in the Professor's life (255), intervenes when Augusta, come to retrieve the keys to the new house, discovers St. Peter lying unconscious on the attic floor and saves him, not without some gratefulness, for his compromised life.

As its plot makes clear, *The Professor's House* is a novel of sensibility rather than event. In it, Cather seems to abandon the land beneath her feet, the tales of midwestern pioneers in which she had discovered her unique voice and subject, to return to the Jamesian roots of her first novel, *Alexander's Bridge* (see Chapter 3). By grafting Tom Outland's adventure onto the Professor's life, however, she manages to retain the strengths of her characteristic work—her wonder and respect, for instance, for human striving and achievement of which the past gives evidence—while achieving a sensitive and complex portrayal of the inner workings of one man's heart and mind. Character is event in *The Professor's House*.

CHARACTER DEVELOPMENT

Cather assembles her cast of characters as individuals and in ever-shifting pairs to reveal their complex personalities and relationships. As the novel's protagonist, Professor Godfrey St. Peter factors in the most significant pairings, each representing one of the "two romances" in his life: "one of the heart . . . and a second of the mind—of the imagination." The first, with his wife Lillian, "had filled his life for many years." The second, with Tom Outland, came "just when the morning brightness of the world was wearing off for him, . . . and brought him a kind of second youth" (*Later Novels* 255). These "romances" signify the Professor's competing needs and desires, the reasons for life's compromises.

When St. Peter accepts one of the first university positions offered to him, his purpose is clear: the new scholar, in his mid-twenties and fresh from his doctoral studies, wants nothing more than to marry the beautiful American he had met while earning his degree in Paris. The position also returns him to the shores of Lake Michigan, the "inland sea" (*Later Novels* 114) from which he had been wrenched as a boy when his parents moved their family to Kansas and a geographical feature that is essential to his emotional well-being (*Later Novels* 115). A deeply introspective man, St. Peter has always responded to its "innocent blue" (*Later Novels* 115), the color of youth, which "kindled him" to life (*Later Novels* 113). Matched now, he believes, with a wife in possession of an "interesting mind" (*Later Novels* 126), the Professor settles into professional and domestic routines, but neither is entirely fulfilling. In fact, he lives his real life in his attic study, where his mind has free rein to pursue his research into the historical past. Indeed, he prefers his singularity. Like those Spanish adventurers and his namesake emperor and general, he cares only to conquer new territory, intellectual perhaps, but his own nonetheless, territory from which he can know the thrill of discovery and on which he can leave his mark. This aspect of the Professor's essential self, which provides a second connection to youth, helps to explain the restlessness and vague dissatisfaction that have entered his middle age. Indeed, the narrowness of his conventional life, the creeping commercialism undermining his profession (*Later Novels* 182), and the nagging sense that his best years are behind him combine to make him feel like his namesake, who, he reminds his wife, also fell into a slump after spending his energy in conquest (*Later Novels* 197).

During their early married life, Lillian had been the Professor's primary source of intellectual companionship. Yet it was not so much her mind as her "richly endowed nature that responded strongly to life and art," giving her "vehement likes and dislikes" (*Later Novels* 126), that St. Peter had found interesting. In the intervening years, however, her "prejudices" and "divinations about people and art" (*Later Novels* 126), however correct they proved to be, have grown less and less charming to him. Certainly, the Professor appreciates his wife's "fastidiousness," her instinctual understanding of the right and proper that has kept her family from being "drab" and "absurd": "If they couldn't get the right thing, they went without" (*Later Novels* 196). But Lillian's fastidiousness has begun to harden into an attitude that St. Peter finds distasteful. Regretfully aware that a rift has developed between them, Lillian now transfers her attention to and seeks the approval of her sons-in-law. With them, the Professor bemusedly reflects, "She had begun the game of being a woman all over again" (*Later Novels* 144). He dates the beginning of the change in their relationship to the morning Tom Outland walked into their lives. Nothing has been the same since.

Despite his early death on Flanders fields during World War I, the aptly named Outland had led a remarkable life, including the daring but disheartening adventure that constitutes Book Two of the novel. But everything about Tom's life beyond that adventure is equally remarkable. With little more than a sporadic education in Latin acquired from Father Duchene in New Mexico (*Later Novels* 165) and knowledge of two classic adventure tales, *Robinson Crusoe* and *Gulliver's Travels* (*Later Novels* 212), the brilliant young man who appears at the

Professor's door eager for an education manages in a summer to learn enough mathematics to qualify for admission to university in the fall. There, he distinguishes himself in his studies to become a brilliant physicist and inventor of the Outland vacuum.

Yet it is not Outland's accomplishments but his spirit that resonates for St. Peter. With his "sumptuous generosity" (*Later Novels* 178), his deep and instinctive appreciation for the human history in the Cliff City artifacts, his "quixotic" (*Later Novels* 203) personality, and his innate moral sense, Outland was a romantic idealist. He wanted, for instance, not to make money (or at least not a fortune) from his New Mexican discoveries (*Later Novels* 247) but to share them with his country, to which he believed they belonged. He was also determined never to profit materially from personal friendships (*Later Novels* 203). The Professor had found his attraction irresistible. Such a companion returned him to his essential self, the person he was and intended to be before social responsibilities impinged on his life and molded him into husband, father, professor and scholar. He and Outland had explored the Blue Mesa and climbed to Cliff City; they had traveled through Old Mexico and planned, before war intervened, to visit Paris together. Through Outland, St. Peter "[experienced] afresh things that had grown dull with use" (*Later Novels* 256), and the later volumes of his life work were steeped in authenticity both physical and spiritual because they had traced the journey of his Spanish adventurers. Lillian St. Peter thus had reason to be "jealous" of Tom Outland (*Later Novels* 126), for she could never compete with her husband's attraction to his ideal self-image.

In his own way, Tom Outland also factors in the lives of the St. Peters' daughters. Rosamond, the elder, beautiful and worldly and so like her mother, had been engaged to marry him and had inherited on his death the patent to the invention that would make her a wealthy woman. Kathleen, however, the younger, less certain of her worth (*Later Novels* 135), more sensitive than her sister, for whom her father has "a special kind of affection" (*Later Novels* 149) and with whom she shares fond memories of "our Tom" (*Later Novels* 17), had secretly loved him, too (*Later Novels* 150, 163). Inseparable as girls, Rosamond and Kathleen had adored Outland and lived in his stories (*Later Novels* 171). But now, as adults, his memory is the source of friction between them. Kathleen resents her sister's wealth, not so much because she envies Rosamond's possessions but because she believes the use to which she puts Outland's legacy betrays his spirit and is twisting her priorities (*Later Novels* 146–50). When their seamstress Augusta, for example, loses much of her savings in a bad investment, Rosamond meanly declines to assist her until she "[admits] her folly" in not following Louie's warning against her action (*Later Novels* 175), whereas Kathleen immediately appeals to her father to add to her own contribution to the hardworking woman's security. Rosamond, for her part, is sensitive to her sister's disapproval but too proud and self-satisfied to admit any fault, and with her expensive furs and designer frocks as armor, she effectively blunts any criticism.

The sisters' husbands' conflicting values and attitudes reflect and extend their wives', and once again, Tom Outland is the unspoken focus of the couples' differences. Kathleen has married Outland's best friend, Scott McGregor, a young journalist who, among other things, contributes a daily "prose poem" (*Later Novels* 135) to a newspaper syndicate but now that the thrill of first success has passed deeply loathes his profession, which he feels is beneath his talents. McGregor longs to do something meaningful, something, perhaps, commensurate to his friend's achievements. Indeed, Outland represents a "glittering idea" (*Later Novels* 164) to him, something untranslatable into crass materialism. Like Kathleen, therefore, he disapproves of the use to which his sister- and brother-in-law put Outland's memory and shares with the Professor the view that the Marselluses' intent to call their new country house "Outland" is pretentious and presumptuous (*Later Novels* 139–40).

Louis Marsellus, in contrast, Rosamond's gregarious and generous husband, believes that he is merely completing Outland's work. His foresight and initiative had been responsible for the development of the potential in the Outland vacuum. Now he feels an obligation to preserve the memory of the man who had been the source of his and his wife's material bounty. Louie's purpose in building "Outland" and endowing scholarships in the inventor's name is certainly well intentioned (*Later Novels* 121–22), but it still smacks to the McGregors of self-aggrandizement. Moreover, from their (and even the Professor's) perspective, his efforts have transformed Outland into "chemicals and dollars and cents" (*Later Novels* 177). Marsellus, however, is too good-natured to take such a view. Capable, certainly, of feeling the McGregors' slights, as when he learns that Scott had prevented his membership in the exclusive Arts and Letters society, but gracious enough not to bear them ill will, Louis genuinely believes that he can win Scott's friendship simply by treating him well (*Later Novels* 200–202).

Cather aptly conveys the differences between the Professor's sons-in-law when St. Peter recalls a picture he had painted of them for a college function: Louis he imagined as the Saladin, patiently and reasonably arguing with an arrogant and "unthoughtful" (*Later Novels* 141) Scott, as Richard Plantagenet, before the walls of Jerusalem during the Crusades. Like their historical counterparts, each of them represents opposing worldviews that are exactly right for themselves but exactly wrong for the other. In this way, the tableau represents as well St. Peter's own situation: to please himself is to neglect and disappoint others. The resolution of this conflict, like the historical one, promises to satisfy nobody.

The resolution of this conflict, however, is the direction toward which the novel's plot has been moving, and at its end and therefore integral to the development of its major thematic subject is one other character, Agatha, the St. Peters' dour and dependable German seamstress. A devout Roman Catholic, Agatha embodies as no other character fully does the conventional world. She has little patience with the pretentious, with women, for instance, who conceal the signs of age in graying hair beneath "switches and rats" and other sorts of hair pieces (*Later Novels* 110–11). Nor is she afraid to discuss life's unpleasant facts, including death (*Later Novels* 269–70). For all the years that they have shared the attic workplace, she has worried about the state of the Professor's soul (*Later Novels* 111), and he has humored her piety and solid respectability. Yet she has been a necessary tonic throughout those years, "like the taste of bitter herbs," St. Peter reflects on the day she inadvertently saves his life, a reminder of the "bloomless side of life" (*Later Novels* 270) that he had always attempted to avoid. Augusta, in other words, like Tom Outland, is a symbolic character in *The Professor's House*. In fact, she signifies Outland's opposite.

THEMATIC ISSUES

The oppositions embodied in Augusta and Tom Outland and the Professor's struggle between them reveal Cather's primary thematic preoccupation, or main point, in *The Professor's House*. Throughout his life, St. Peter has yearned for the ideal. He has valued above all else the heroic aspirations that he associates with youth. It is not by accident that St. Peter has become an historian and especially the chronicler of bold adventurers. If he cannot duplicate their achievements, he can at least vicariously experience them through his research. But now, in middle age, no matter how he tries to work off in his garden his vague "discontent," his "home-sickness for other lands and the fret of things unaccomplished" (*Later Novels* 105), St. Peter finds unsatisfactory the compromises he has made in life. In the year during which the novel is set, he wrestles with those compromises and, in the aftermath of crisis, accepts them. In her study of Professor Godfrey St. Peter, Cather thus explores the pathos of all human endeavors, the gap between desire and achievement that constitutes human existence.

The inspiration for St. Peter's life's work reveals the romantic idealism that has fueled the imagination of the scholar. He can still recall the summer in France during which he had conceived the idea of his study and determined to pursue it. The married father of two little girls was so taken by his idea that he left his family with enough money to finish the summer and make their way home without him while he traveled to Marseilles to seek the advice and assistance of Charles Thierault, a French friend. For the next three weeks he lived in Thierault's house in the Prado, preparing the ground for his work, but it was a journey by sea to Algeciras that crystallized his vision. Everything, St. Peter recalls, "seemed to feed the plan of the work that was forming in [his] mind" (*Later Novels* 160): the captain and his crew of Provençal seamen, the Catalan second mate, the sea itself, but chiefly the snow-covered peaks of the Sierra Nevadas, "high beyond the flight of fancy" (*Later Novels* 161). The very image of aspiration, they led St. Peter to an understanding of his Spanish adventurers, whose yearning, like his own, for that beyond was the source of their achievements.

What is remarkable about this incident in the Professor's life is not just the insight it gives into his imagination but also the evidence it provides of his dedication. In pursuit of his idea, he virtually abandons his family on their summer holiday, and he will spend many subsequent summers conducting his research, including those journeys to Mexico and the Southwest with Tom Outland. During the 15 years that he is writing his study, St. Peter will meet his professional obligations and his social responsibilities, but his real life he lives in his attic study. In other words, St. Peter is almost single-minded in pursuit of his idea, and nothing but his idea motivates his scholarship. His subject, for instance, lacks commercial value (*Later Novels* 182–83). Although the scholarly community, moreover, initially underestimates his achievement, St. Peter cares not "a whoop" (*Later Novels* 116) what others think of his approach. His conception drives him to the end, and thus the "house" that the Professor truly inhabits is his mind.

Yet despite his success, St. Peter feels a failure and believes that "life," as he tells Augusta, "doesn't turn out for any of us as we plan" (*Later Novels* 110). He had never been an "ascetic" (*Later Novels* 112). Indeed, he "was terribly selfish about personal pleasures" and would sacrifice "so-called necessities" (*Later Novels* 112) for them. He had also wanted to be loved, and that desire had transformed him into his "secondary social" (*Later Novels* 259) self and circumscribed his life. The dress forms with which he has shared his attic workplace all these years have been constant reminders of the social self's "cruel biological necessities" (*Later Novels* 109), the sexual desire that compelled him into marriage and a professional position at a pedestrian institution incommensurate with his intellectual self (*Later Novels* 115). They have also connected him to the "engaging drama of domestic life" (*Later Novels* 112) unfolding beneath his attic retreat. Now St. Peter must confront and accept their implications. He must not only acknowledge "the bloomless side of life" (*Later Novels* 270) that Augusta embodies but also embrace an image of self that is so much less than he had conceived it to be, for such is the nature of his common humanity.

When St. Peter awakens from his near-death experience, he is a changed man. No longer does he cling to the romanticized and unrealistic ideal of self embodied in Tom Outland. Indeed, his change is a reminder that Outland died before he had faced and perhaps surrendered to his own social self. After all, he was engaged to marry Rosamond St. Peter at the time of his death and would inevitably have faced the same compromises that had undermined the Professor's resolve. Only his premature death on Flanders fields had perhaps made possible his heroic image. Now St. Peter finds in Augusta's solid reality and uncompromising practicality proof that life "without delight" is possible (*Later Novels* 271) and accepts that sort of life as his own. During his lapse into unconsciousness, he has let go "something very precious, that he could not consciously have relinquished, probably" (*Later Novels* 271). All passion spent, he is no longer a man divided against himself but simply a man who feels "the ground under his feet" (*Later Novels* 271). If he no longer possesses desire, the quality, he had been convinced, from which all great human endeavor springs (*Later Novels* 104), neither does he risk more disappointment and pain. What he possesses instead is the "fortitude" (*Later Novels* 271) necessary to face his future, and while fortitude may seem too little compensation for St. Peter's diminished sense of self, it is the quality, Cather implies, essential to living the life he has made.

The Professor's House ends on a somber note that underscores Cather's central theme. St. Peter does not triumph over his predicament any more than Tom Outland conquered his. Indeed, that is the meaning of Tom Outland's story, which parallels the Professor's in its downward arc: Bouyed by the thrill of a discovery that connects him to great human endeavor, Outland lives his own heroic adventure and wants only to share it with others, but official bureaucracy, petty greed, and human misunderstanding stymie his efforts and diminish his achievement, leaving him sad and disillusioned to forge ahead into his future. His heroic failure was the Professor's, struggling to give life to an idea amid the trivialities of daily existence, and even the ancient cliff dwellers', whose efforts to prevail over nature and man left only magnificent ruins. But that seems to be the point of Cather's intertwined stories. Seldom, if ever, does human endeavor achieve its object, and yet we press on. It is what we must do.

A FEMINIST INTERPRETATION

A novel that locates its male protagonist's failures within the sphere of domesticity, *The Professor's House* certainly lends itself to a feminist interpretation. Such an interpretation, based on precepts outlined in Chapter 5, confirms traditional gender stereotypes. What it does not do, however, at least intentionally, is critique those stereotypes. Indeed, what is surprising for a woman writer is Cather's masculine-identified stance, her clear privileging of heroic endeavor and moral struggle of the sort experienced by Tom Outland and Godfrey St. Peter. Measured against the lives of her male characters, those of her female characters are shallow and conventional, and because Cather never truly explores them, the novel's women are interesting only as they affect the destinies of its men. Thus, from a feminist perspective, *The Professor's House* is a misogynistic novel. In fact, one of the novel's first reviewers, Schuyler Ashley of the *Kansas City Star,* noted at its publication that "in this book Miss Cather is very hard on her own sex" (O'Connor 254). So hard is she, feminist critics would argue, that she reinforces deeply entrenched cultural stereotypes about gender roles and expectations rather than challenges their validity.

Cather's choice of point of view, or the perspective from which the narrator tells the story, gives her novel a masculine-identified stance. In narrating her story from the Professor's and Tom Outland's points of view, Cather lends these men her sympathies. Through their eyes, readers understand their motivation, experience their exhilaration and defeats, and gradually, like their creator, come to identify and empathize with them. For Lillian St. Peter as well as her daughters, however, readers develop no such understanding and reactions, for Cather never deeply probes their psyches. Their disappointments and dismay all too often seem merely pettiness or querulousness rather than appropriate responses to events in their lives because Cather makes it difficult, for instance, to empathize with sibling rivalry when the source of jealousy between Rosamond and Kathleen is a fur coat. So much more, she makes readers understand, is at stake in St. Peter's and Outland's lives, and it is that understanding that confirms Cather's masculine-identified stance and prepares readers to accept without question a masculine perspective on the female world of domesticity.

Almost uniformly, the women in *The Professor's House* are defined and effectively confined by their domestic world. Daughters who claim adulthood by marriage and the establishment of their own homes, they devote virtually all their effort and energy to homemaking and to facilitating their husbands' careers. They may be intelligent and well educated. They may even possess, as Lillian St. Peter does, an intuitive understanding of life and art that gives them charm, wit, and taste and an unerring ability to evaluate others (*Later Novels* 126). But they subsume these qualities into their domestic roles. Any personal ambition they may have they realize through their husbands' successes.

These attributes and actions are not necessarily deficient in quality or morality. Indeed, they were characteristic of women during Cather's time, whose understanding of their roles had been shaped by patriarchy, or male domination. The St. Peter women, in other words, become exactly what their society would expect of them—good wives, daughters, and mothers within their households. Yet from the Professor's perspective, they seem self-absorbed women who lead trivial lives in which men become ensnared. Thus, the domestic world that they create is an insidious trap that prevents men from fulfilling their different and, by implication, more worthy destinies.

Cather's characterization of Lillian St. Peter carries the weight of these ideas. When the Professor had rushed into marriage nearly 30 years before the novel's contemporary events, he had been captivated by Lillian's "interesting mind," or, more accurately, her "prejudices" and "divinations" (*Later Novels* 126), indeed, her idiosyncratic view of the world. In the intervening years, however, an indefinable but unmistakable chasm has developed between the St. Peters, and those idiosyncrasies seem to the Professor to be no longer "mere fastidiousness" but to have hardened into an unbecoming "worldliness" (*Later Novels* 196). In response, the Professor increasingly retreats to his study, assuming, in his mind, the moral high ground, while Lillian compensates for loneliness and for "something that spoke of an old wound, healed and hardened and hopeless" (*Later Novels* 153), by a "willingness to [profit from] occasions and people" (*Later Novels* 196) that her husband finds unseemly. She also begins to play "the game of being a woman all over again" (*Later Novels* 144) by seeking the attention of her sons-in-law as a substitute for her husband's. For them, she now fusses with her appearance, entertains, and plans for their futures, "[living] in their careers as she had once done" for her husband's, a "splendid" course of action, the Professor reflects, that will, now that her children are married, give purpose to the blank space in her life between motherhood and grandmotherhood (*Later Novels* 144).

To be fair, the Professor feels uncomfortable about his judgment of his wife. After all, to her sophistication, he acknowledges, he owes the comforts that have kept his life from being a "drab" and "shabby" thing (*Later Novels* 196). On another occasion, when the St. Peters attend the opera, Lillian's confession that she, too, has wished for a different sort of life, a different sort of marriage, astonishes him into the poignant reflection: "The heart of another is a dark forest, always, no matter how close it has been to one's own" (*Later Novels* 153). This partial acknowledgment of his own failures in their marriage (partial because it also offers an excuse for them) does not, however, reverse the impression of Lillian St. Peter and the domestic world that she represents. Throughout the novel, she is the voice of the mundane. A grasping and demanding woman, encased in a patina of sophistication, she orchestrates others' lives to suit her narrow vision of the social world and is thus a perpetual reminder of commonplace realities and responsibilities from which St. Peter cannot escape. Indeed, Lillian so embodies the enervating demands of domesticity that it is hard not to sympathize when the Professor reveals that on the night of the opera performance, even after their moment of mutual understanding, his ideal of the perfect ending to his life does not include her (*Later Novels* 153).

To reinforce her impression of domesticity, Cather depicts the whole of the Professor's family life, including his relations with his daughters and sons-in-law, through what Hermione Lee calls "little dramas of greed and malice" (227). Rosamond and Kathleen and their respective husbands, Louis Marsellus and Scott McGregor, live amid a minefield of unexpressed hurt and resentment. Rosamond, for example, who has profited immensely from Marsellus's exploitation of Tom Outland's invention, engages in conspicuous display of their wealth, especially in the construction of their country house, "Outland," and orgies of consumption that disgust Kathleen, not least because they make her purchase of a new fur coat shabby in comparison to her sister's (*Later Novels* 146–49). And while Kathleen may seem to take the high moral ground when she champions Augusta's fortunes following the seamstress's disastrous financial investments, she and Scott are jealous enough of the Marselluses to wound both by preventing Louie's admission to a prestigious private club with Scott's blackball of his nomination (*Later Novels* 201). With nothing but domesticity to fill their lives, Rosamond and Kathleen, in their own ways, have become versions of their mother, and Scott and, to a lesser extent, Louis, whose inherent magnanimity saves him from meanness, have been drawn inevitably into the sisters' complex relationship. Thus, St. Peter, who increasingly finds himself soothing hurt feelings and mediating between competing factions, again falls prey to his domestic life.

While feminist critics would argue that patriarchy, which imposes this domestic role on women, must bear primary responsibility for its shape and effects, Cather, who has supplied the evidence from which to develop such an interpretation, never explores it. Indeed, as her masculine-identified perspective makes clear, patriarchy had never been her subject. What interests Cather in *The Professor's House*, as it has always interested her, is individual—and even heroic— achievement, and as her great heroines—Alexandra Bergson, Thea Kronborg, and Ántonia Shimerda—testify, such achievement is not a matter of gender. Yet the novel's subdued tone and qualified resolution, both of which arise from the Professor's reluctant acceptance of the inevitable compromises that hinder such achievement, certainly arise from gendered conditions. If St. Peter had been shipwrecked alone on his island, as he imagines himself in his ideal scenario (*Later Novels* 153), he might have achieved all he intended from life, but he was not. He desired as well a companion, a wife, and was soon entangled in domestic life, and that entanglement impinged on St. Peter's ideal of self. In *The Professor's House*, domesticity is thus the ultimate trap for men. That women are ensnared in it as well seems of little concern to Willa Cather.

Indeed, in the end, what moves readers of *The Professor's House* is Cather's poignant dramatization of human limitation. Godfrey

St. Peter and Tom Outland—even those ancient cliff dwellers—had such dreams, and they came so close to realizing them. But they did not. Nature, circumstance, and even conflicting human desires impinged on them, leading inevitably to disappointing compromises and tragic losses. By the end of *The Professor's House,* Tom Outland has died on Flanders fields, and Napoleon Godfrey St. Peter seems as defeated as his namesake gone into exile on Elba. That his defeat comes as a consequence of the demands of the conventional world makes it all the more disheartening, for that is the world in which we all must struggle.

8

Death Comes for the Archbishop (1927)

In *Death Comes for the Archbishop* (1927), Willa Cather abandoned the midwestern prairies of her youth for the southwestern desert of the historical past. She did not, however, forsake the ideals that her midwestern novels had previously affirmed. She merely relocated them. If the qualities that she so admired in Alexandra Bergson and Thea Kronborg, Ántonia Shimerda and Godfrey St. Peter seemed to have vanished from postwar America, then she could assert their value and meaning, indeed their very existence, by retreating to history and to a place that offered a vision of the continuous past, and that is what she did. In the lives of Father Jean Marie Latour, the vicar apostolic of the newly annexed New Mexico territory, and his faithful companion Father Joseph Vaillant, Cather drew on the historical record to find evidence of the beauty, order, and heroic action that she had celebrated in her novels of the soil—*O Pioneers!* (1913), *The Song of the Lark* (1915), and *My Ántonia* (1918)—and of which she had lamented the disappearance in *The Professor's House* (1925). Indeed, in *Death Comes for the Archbishop*, Willa Cather re-created a world in which her ideals could be realized.

On its surface, *Death Comes for the Archbishop* is the fictional biography of two pioneer priests. Sent by the Roman Catholic hierarchy into New Mexico, a territory "larger than Central and Western Europe, barring Russia" (*Later Novels* 279) that had been annexed by the United States in 1848, Father Jean Marie Latour and Father Joseph Vaillant, friends since their seminary days in their native France, make their long and arduous journey into a land that had defeated others before them. Their mission is to complete the task begun by Spanish priests at the time of the conquistadores, to minister to a native population of Indians and Mexicans and now the encroaching Americans, to bring spiritual order to a recalcitrant land and peoples. In a series of self-contained episodes that spans nearly 40 years of dedicated effort, Cather charts their success. By the time Father Vaillant dies in Colorado, where his ministry had taken him during the lawless days of the gold rush, and Father Latour dies in Santa Fe, the golden stones of the Romanesque cathedral that he had built to the glory of God towering above the city, their lives, especially Latour's, bear witness to the greatness that exists in humanity. It is that truth that lies beneath the surface of one of Cather's most enduring classics.

GENESIS AND CRITICAL RECEPTION

The Southwest, of course, had long held a special place in Cather's imagination. Indeed, it was almost as important to her as the Midwest. In 1912, the novelist had made the first of many extended visits to the region, and she had already exploited its significance by setting sections of *The Song of the Lark* and *The Professor's House* there. Cather, as she had admitted in an essay published in *The Commonweal* in 1927, had been intrigued by the tales of the Spanish missionaries, but she "hadn't the most remote idea" of writing about them, at least in part because the author, who had been confirmed in the Episcopal church in 1922, was convinced that "any story of the Church in the Southwest was certainly the business of some Catholic writer." She was also inspired by the bronze memorial to New Mexico's first Archbishop, Jean Baptiste Lamy, "who looked so well-bred and distinguished," and the "interesting stories" that "old Mexicans and traders" told of him. "What I felt curious about," she revealed, "was the daily life of such a man in a crude frontier society." And then, a fortuitous discovery—a biography of Father Joseph P. Machebeuf, the first archbishop of Colorado, written by William Joseph Howlett, a priest who had assisted him in his mission—provided Cather with the information she needed to tell the story of this "pioneer churchman" ("On *Death Comes*," *Stories, Poems, and Other Writings* 959).

Howlett's biography was, according to Cather, "almost as revelatory about Father Lamy as about Father Machebeuf," for the two priests had been associates from early youth and had gone together first to Ohio and then to New Mexico to fulfill their mission in America. In writing Father Machebeuf's life story, Father Howlett had traveled to the priest's native France to acquire knowledge of his subject's background and to interview his sister, Philomèna, who gave him her collection of her brother's letters to her, letters detailing his experiences as well as his thoughts and feelings about them. Many of these letters, "splendidly translated," Father Howlett inserted into the biography, and Cather later acknowledged that without them, "I would certainly never have dared to write my book." She may have included many of her own experiences in re-creating her subjects', but from the letters, she was able to understand how similar experiences affected these men with a mission (*Stories, Poems, and Other Writings* 960). "What I got from Father Machebeuf's letters was the mood," she asserted, "the spirit in which they accepted the accidents and hardships of a desert country, the joyful energy that kept them going" (*Stories, Poems, and Other Writings* 960–61). Within two years of finding this inspirational work, Cather had reimagined their experiences, created their fictional counterparts, Father Jean Marie Latour and Father Joseph Vaillant, and published their fictional biography as *Death Comes for the Archbishop*.

At its publication, in September 1927, following serialization in *The Forum* earlier that year, critical consensus about *Death Comes for the Archbishop* was favorable and even enthusiastic. The critic for the *New Republic,* for instance, Robert Morss Lovett, proclaimed that Cather had "produced a book which will remain an American classic" (O'Connor 338), while Joseph Wood Krutch, writing in *The Nation,* observed that Cather had transformed material that in the hands of another writer might have become "some exciting and dramatic narrative" into something wholly original. She "softens the epic," he observed, "until it becomes an elegy," and thus, it is a "book to be read slowly, to be savored from paragraph to paragraph" (O'Connor 337). Henry Longan Stuart, writing in the *New York Times Book Review,* expressed some minor reservations about the novel's departure from the traditional form of the historical novel and further misgivings about the tendency among contemporary writers of the genre to dispense with the "tyranny of fact" long considered one of its conventions. But even his criticisms were backhanded compliments of Cather's achievement: "May not the new fashion [of the historical novel] quite possibly be laying down snares for the feet of generations to come, little versed in documentation and quite ready to take the word of so fascinating a writer in matters of fact as well as of fancy?" (O'Connor 312). In the *Saturday Review of Literature,* Lee Wilson Dodd shared some of Stuart's confusion about the novel's form, but then, making an important distinction between fact and truth, he asserted, "By putting unforgettably before us the life (actual, wholly imagined, or partly imagined) of Father Latour, Miss Cather has also given us *truth*," an "artistic purpose ... difficult of fulfillment," but one that *Death Comes for the Archbishop* "serenely and triumphantly carried through" (O'Connor 316–17). Only a fellow novelist could, perhaps, offer higher praise, and Cather had that from the British writer Rebecca West in a long, thoughtful appreciation published in the *New York Herald Tribune Books* in which she asserted about *Death Comes for the Archbishop* "great is her accomplishment" (O'Connor 318).

PLOT DEVELOPMENT

Critical comment about its form gives some indication of the difficulty of defining the genre, or literary type, and describing the plot of *Death Comes for the Archbishop.* Because it is based on historical record and features historical persons, however fictionalized, *Death Comes for the Archbishop* is properly an historical novel. Yet Henry Longan Stuart, in his review of the novel, was correct in asserting that while Cather may have followed, "chronologically at least," the events of Father Lamy's life and may also have "enshrined" a great many traditions in her novel, she was not particularly interested in fact. Among her cast of characters, for instance, she includes the frontier scout Kit Carson, whose exploits could have filled pages of her novel, but keeps him on the periphery of her narrative until she needs his presence to achieve her ends. In his brief appearances, he is a devoted friend to Latour (as he was to Lamy) and respects the native cultures. In fact, he is married to a "native woman" (*Later Novels* 322). His most sustained appearance, however, as the "misguided" (*Later Novels* 455) legend who eventually betrayed the Navajos, allows Cather chiefly to expose the cruelty and injustice of government policy in the region. This example validates Stuart's contention that Cather, like other contemporary practitioners of the genre, had created "not so much an historical novel, as a superimposition of the novel upon history" (O'Connor 311), and Cather admitted as much. Indeed, by her own account in *The Commonweal* essay, she acknowledged her interest in the *affect* of historical event on character (*Stories, Poems, and Other Writings* 960–61), and such an interest requires the imaginative leap into consciousness and the selective inclusion of event that reveal such information and that are characteristic of the novel.

Yet as Cather's title suggests, *Death Comes for the Archbishop* is so narrowly focused on one man, Father Jean Marie Latour, the historical Archbishop Lamy (who was not, rather surprisingly, the subject of her historical source), that it is not, according to another contemporary reviewer, a novel at all. Rather, it is an "imaginative biography" in which Cather "corroborates with a wealth of imaginary detail the historical data concerning the Archbishop and his diocese" (O'Connor 340). The reviewer, Frances Lamont Robbins, goes so far as to classify the work as hagiography, a saint's biography. Once again, Cather's own observations about her novel, which clearly resists easy classification, affirms the comparison. They also provide a metaphor for the novel's plot structure.

In *The Commonweal* essay, Cather revealed a desire to write "something in the style of legend" ("On *Death Comes*," *Stories, Poems, and Other Writings* 960) and mentioned specifically the "Golden Legend," the collected lives of the saints. What struck Cather about the legends was the fact that "the martyrdoms of the saints are no more dwelt upon than are the trivial incidents of their lives; it is as though all human experiences, measured against one supreme spiritual experience, were of about the same importance." Such a quality seems also to have characterized Puvis de Chavannes's frescoes of the life of Saint Geneviève, and Cather confessed that since her student days she had wanted to "try something a little like that in prose; something without accent, with none of the artificial elements of composition."

With the frescoes and the legends as her models, Cather structured her novel as a series of episodes or, perhaps more accurately, as an episodic collection of stories about Father Latour. It is a stylized narrative, dependent, in other words, on "the artificial elements of composition," despite Cather's protestations to the contrary, in which she subverts chronology, sometimes withholding dates, sometimes working backward in time, and frequently includes a number of seemingly unrelated stories, such as the incident about Doña Isabella or the legend of Fray Baltazar, that function as parables about human behavior. This juxtaposition of episodes makes all of them equally important to her central character and to her themes and creates a series of timeless moments that effectively substitutes for a chronological plot.

The accretion of incidents that functions as plot in *Death Comes for the Archbishop* begins with a prologue set in Rome in 1848 that establishes a sharp contrast between the Church as a political and social institution and the mission of the Church in the wilderness. At issue in this prologue is the founding of an apostolic vicarate in the newly annexed territory of New Mexico and chiefly the selection of a priest to conduct the "Augean" (*Later Novels* 279) task of reestablishing proper religious discipline in a land where Catholicism has been "allowed to drift for nearly three hundred years" (*Later Novels* 279). There, from his mission on the Great Lakes, is Bishop Ferrand, come to champion the appointment of Father Jean Marie Latour before three cardinals at the Vatican. Connoisseurs of art and wine and clever conversationalists, the sophisticated cardinals make Bishop Ferrand, who would have been their equal prior to his missionary work, seem a rather crude and uncivilized specimen of humanity, and indeed, he courts defeat by his insistence on discussing business with men who would prefer to concentrate on a good meal. Yet Bishop Ferrand's sincerity and his dedication to the arduous task that he describes to his colleagues make their religious feeling seem tepid and their views uninformed. After all, men whose knowledge of the New World has been acquired from the romantic adventures of the American novelist James Fenimore Cooper's Leatherstocking tales (*Later Novels* 282) can hardly be expected to understand the risks that the new bishop will face from not only the savage environment but also its hostile inhabitants, including the native priests. By the end of the prologue, Father Latour's appointment is assured, but given the contrast between the life of ease in Rome and the perils of the missionary existence, readers must wonder at the man who would choose such a difficult task.

Such wonder is the purpose of Cather's prologue. It provides readers with the backstory to Father Latour's circumstances and foreshadows the difficulties he will face at his new post. It also offers insight to the personal qualities—the fortitude and determination, the zeal and commitment, and, above all, the rage for order (*Later Novels* 28)—necessary to success. In consequence, when readers meet Father Latour three years later in the novel's first book, "a solitary horseman" (*Later Novels* 285) lost in the New Mexican desert, they possess an image of the man that subsequent events simply corroborate and even enhance.

While the remainder of the novel may seem a series of haphazardly organized events, given their lack of strict linear chronology, the eight books actually form four units of two related books and thus give shape to Father Latour's life and works. Books One and Two chronicle Father Latour's experiences among the Mexicans and his initial efforts to assert his authority in a land where Church authorities would no longer recognize Catholicism as practiced there. Indeed, one of Latour's first duties following his arrival in Santa Fe is an arduous 3,000-mile trek into Old Mexico and back to collect the letters authorizing his jurisdiction over the recalcitrant native priests with which Book One begins. The books' events include moments of quiet domestic harmony such as Father Latour's first Christmas celebration with his faithful friend and assistant Father Vaillant, who had cooked a meal worthy of any French table, as well as harrowing tales of danger and escape such as the priests' encounter with a murderous American in "The Lonely Road to Mora." During this incident, the priests also save Magdalena from her vicious husband and earn her devoted service, just as her biblical counterpart, Mary Magdalene, devoted herself to Christ following her salvation. They also dramatize the priests' missionary work, such as the marriages and baptisms on Manuel Lujon's ranch (that culminates in the acquisition of their two white mules, Contento and Angelica). Both books, however, emphasize chiefly the miraculous nature of human existence. Father Latour, for instance, survives his perilous trek to Old Mexico (after having previously survived shipwreck in Galveston Bay and recovered from a leg injury that resulted when he jumped from an overturning wagon near San Antonio) because a cruciform tree, the sign of the Cross, points him to safety. Cather also inserts the miracle of Guadaloupe, the patron saint of Mexico, into the narrative, providing Latour the opportunity to advise Vaillant, "Where there is great love there are always miracles" (*Later Novels* 30). Latour's life will gradually become proof of this truth.

Books Three and Four find Father Latour and Father Vaillant extending their mission into the tribal communities. Latour acquires Jacinto, a tribal guide, who accompanies him to Ácoma. There, he conducts Mass for native peoples who juggle their Christian beliefs with their traditional myths and actually experiences the vitality of those myths when he and Jacinto must shelter from a storm in a cave that serves as a Pecos place of worship. He also hears the legend of Fray Baltazar, another of the inset stories that function as parables, in this case, cautioning against greed, pride, and anger.

Cather uses Books Five and Six to explore the passing of the old order for the new through the tales of two contrasting personalities.

Book Five focuses on Padre Martinez, a priest who has forgotten his true mission, rules by the assertion of his "imperious will" (*Later Novels* 362), and uses his position for self-gratification. His contest of wills with Father Latour, however, never really materializes because his adversary understands that "the day of lawless personal power was almost over, even on the frontier" (*Later Novels* 362). Father Latour, in other words, uses his wits to effect inevitable change. Book Six focuses on another anachronistic character, Doña Isabella, whose vanity nearly proves her undoing. Father Latour, however, who admires her graciousness and sensibility, reverts to an ancient code of chivalry to preserve her peace and dignity.

Books Seven and Eight return the focus of *Death Comes for the Archbishop* to Father Latour. His mission well established, he now has time to face the doubt that has often shadowed his efforts, but an encounter with Sada, a Mexican woman enslaved to an American family hostile to Catholicism who briefly escapes to the church one cold December evening, restores his faith and purpose. Yet he struggles with his need of Father Vaillant's presence as friend and confidant in his life, and even a retreat to the Navajo territory, where he finds comfort in the counsel of the Navajo priest Eusabio, cannot help to reconcile him to his friend's need to minister in the field. In Book Eight, however, Latour must bid farewell to his fellow priest when the discovery of gold at Pike's Peak, Colorado, demands Father Vaillant's special skills. Both men will now be free to fulfill their destinies: Father Vaillant to establish a mission in a place of cruel materiality, Father Latour to build a Romanesque cathedral in the desert.

When death comes for the archbishop in Book Nine, it seems right and proper. Father Latour has completed his mission, bringing the beauty and order in religion to a hostile landscape and fallible humans. Now he needs only to leave his past behind him (*Later Novels* 453), and following a series of personal reminiscences of his life in France, his friendship with Father Vaillant, and his decision to become a missionary, he passes quietly to death. These reminiscences provide the missing elements of Father Latour's backstory, and with that information, his life is indeed complete. *Death Comes for the Archbishop,* despite its episodic plot and lack of linear chronology, thus concludes on a more hopeful note than many of Cather's other novels. It lacks, for instance, the melancholy of Jim Burden in the face of Ántonia's happiness in *My Ántonia* and the sense of heroic failure in Godfrey St. Peter's acceptance of conventional life in *The Professor's House.* Meaning and purpose unify the discrete incidents of a life, Cather's novel suggests, providing order and creating a sense of completeness, and Father Latour's life has both.

CHARACTER DEVELOPMENT

Indeed, the beauty and perfection of Father Latour's life create some of the difficulties Cather faced in developing his character. So, too, does the novel's form. In the first instance, Father Latour's vocation threatens to make him a one-dimensional figure, all goodness and dedication, all idealistic believer, especially since he has already joined the priesthood and even committed his life to missionary work prior to the novel's beginning. Cather, in other words, has no opportunity to explore the psychological drama of those decisions. She is equally frustrated in her efforts to probe his psyche because the dedicated priest follows directives from Rome that resolve for him other personal issues, perhaps most crucially his dependence on Father Vaillant. In the second instance, Cather, like other writers of biography and history, even fictionalized forms of the genres, faced the problem of remaining true to the historical record and simultaneously ascribing motivation and giving psychological depth to real persons she had never known. To resolve these difficulties, Cather relies primarily on incident to reveal character, and in this case, the novel's episodic structure works to her advantage. She also relies on contrast, chiefly between the renegade priests and Father Latour and Father Vaillant, to reveal habits of mind and being that constitute character. Nevertheless, Father Latour and Father Vaillant, the principal characters in *Death Comes for the Archbishop,* lack depth and complexity. They are heroic figures, brave, utterly committed to their faith, and willing to sacrifice all to its demands.

Father Jean Marie Latour, "a priest in a thousand" (*Later Novels* 286), is everything he was purported to be by his champion, Bishop Ferrand, in the novel's prologue. In fact, as his name suggests, he is a towering figure in the wilderness, someone up to whom others can genuinely look. A native of France, he shares his countrymen's passion for order (*Later Novels* 280–81) and brings his fine intellect to the logical solution of any problem. Appointed vicar apostolic of the New Mexico Territory, he systematically surveys the whole of his diocese to determine its needs and to understand its perspectives, and he is sensitive to and appreciative of the native peoples. Thus, he does not rush to displace the corrupt Padre Martinez and risk alienating his congregation. Nor does he deny the tribal people their traditional beliefs. Instead, he asserts his authority by earning the respect and trust of the people by extending the same qualities to them. When death comes for the archbishop, Mexicans, Americans, and Native Americans genuinely feel his loss (*Later Novels* 459).

For all his heroic qualities, however, Father Latour is not without weaknesses. He is a quiet, dignified man, for instance, and relatively reserved, not the sort of person who exudes warmth and enthusiasm, especially in comparison to his great good friend Father Vaillant. In consequence, he relies on his friend to sound his thoughts and ease his loneliness. Father Vaillant is, after all, a connection to France. They share a personal past, social customs, and national traditions that transcend time and distance, a point that Cather poignantly illustrates with the Christmas dinner, complete with onion soup, lovingly prepared by Father Vaillant, that the priests share shortly after their arrival at Santa Fe. Despite his commitment to his faith and his mission, Father Latour is emotionally vulnerable: at one point, he selfishly recalls Father Vaillant to Santa Fe from missionary work in the desert because he has need of his companionship (*Later Novels* 430), and he struggles uncharacteristically for a man whose vocation has trained him to "[blot] himself out of his own consciousness" (*Later Novels* 287) with his duty to appoint his friend to the Colorado mission (*Later Novels* 430). He also struggles occasionally with doubt, as the encounter with Sada, the Mexican woman who seeks temporary refuge from persecution and servitude, reveals, and suffers at times from homesickness. These weaknesses, however, are the sign of his common humanity, and his ability to overcome them contributes to his heroic stature. Indeed, by the end of his life, when he returns to France intending to retire, he finds himself nostalgic for his desert home and returns to New Mexico, having reconciled the Old and New Worlds in his soul.

In marked contrast to Father Latour, Father Joseph Vaillant is an ebullient, generous-spirited man with a genuine love of people. Where Father Latour is elegant in bearing (*Later Novels* 286), Father Vaillant is homely, his body aged beyond his years (*Later Novels* 298), his nearsighted eyes focused always on the distance (*Later Novels* 299). Indeed, there is "nothing in his outer case to suggest the fierceness and fortitude and fire of the man" (*Later Novels* 298), yet the Mexicans and Native Americans respond instinctively to his personality, believing in him, eager to assist his efforts. Thus, his finely honed talent of begging for the Church (a quality that causes Father Latour great embarrassment) makes it difficult for people to deny him any request, even a hint. The nuns in the French convent where his sister serves the Church, for instance, supply him with fine linen vestments, and when he builds his church in Denver, the poor Mexicans not only donate sufficient funds to pay for windows but also provide him with feather beds, linens, and even a roll of the finest blankets (*Later Novels* 434–35). In one of the novel's comic scenes, Father Vaillant's rather dubious talent even helps him acquire the prized white mules of the wealthy rancher Manuel Lujon following two days of performing marriages and baptisms for his Mexican workers. The mules, named Contento and Angelica, transport Father Latour and Father Vaillant through all the days of their southwestern mission, a touching symbol of the priests' enduring friendship and a testament to Father Vaillant's devotion not only to his friend but also to his vocation. Father Latour may have had to stand firm behind Father Vaillant, who on the day of their departure from family and home for the vast unknown of the Great Lakes region, where they began their missionary work, nearly lost his resolve, but he proves, as his name suggests, a most valiant servant to the Church. Indeed, for sheer enthusiasm for missionary work, Father Vaillant far exceeds Father Latour.

Cather's characterization of Father Latour and Father Vaillant is undeniably positive, and she emphasizes her point by offering portraits of renegade priests who have forgotten their vows and abandoned their mission primarily because they lack the self-discipline and generosity of their French counterparts. The genial Padre Gallegos, for instance, Albuquerque's popular priest, plays poker, enjoys hunting, and, though 10 years older than Father Latour, "would still dance the fandango five nights running, as if he could never have enough of it" (*Later Novels* 324). Father Latour quickly moves him from his position as a lesson to others (*Later Novels* 327). A more formidable adversary is the powerful Padre Martinez, who, it was popularly believed, had instigated a revolt among the Taos tribes against the Americans in the region. The richest man in the parish, Padre Martinez is greedy, insolent, and contemptuous of Church doctrine (*Later Novels* 365–67) and brazenly claims "a gawky lad of ten or twelve" as his son (*Later Novels* 363). During his day and a half visit to Albuquerque, Father Latour is physically and morally repulsed by Padre Martinez, who is anathema to all that the Frenchman embodies.

Father Vaillant, too, has his negative counterpart in Father Lucero, Padre Martinez's associate (to call him friend and confidant of the renegade priest would be too kind). A miser by nature, Father Lucero lives in abject poverty, relying on the generosity of his parishioners for even minor extravangances, such as meat instead of beans, although everyone believes that he is a wealthy man (*Later Novels* 375). On his deathbed, he is less concerned for his soul than he is for the $20,000 hidden beneath the floorboards of his house, and he exacts promises from all who attend him for the disposal of his hoard (although he had failed to honor his own promise to Padre Martinez to offer masses for his soul and pocketed the money he had entrusted to him for that purpose [*Later Novels* 380]). So different is he from Father Vaillant, who, ironically, administers the last rites to him, that it seems wrong to link them together, but that is exactly Cather's point.

Indeed, the Padre Martinez–Father Lucero relationship is itself a travesty of the Father Latour–Father Vaillant relationship. Where the Mexican priests are united only by their "love of authority" (*Later Novels* 375) and eventually mutiny against Rome's control, establishing a "schismatic church" (*Later Novels* 376) rather than reform their behavior, the French priests support each other in their mutual work for the Church from their first meeting. Where the Mexican priests "[talk] shamelessly about each other" (*Later Novels* 375), the French priests hold each other in high esteem, each measuring himself against the other. Father Latour, for instance, easily concedes that Father Vaillant "excelled him in the fervour of his faith" (*Later Novels* 414), while Father Vaillant has always wondered that "a priest with Father Latour's exceptional qualities" should have been consigned to such an uncivilized place, "where scholarship, a handsome person, and delicate perceptions" could have so little effect (*Later Novels* 430). Finally, where Father Lucero betrays Padre Martinez in death, Father Latour honors the spirit of Father Vaillant until he, too, dies. Measured against the Mexican priests, Cather's French priests are clearly worthy of remembrance.

Cather relies on one other narrative strategy—using physical appearance as symbol—to reveal character in *Death Comes for the Archbishop*. One need only glance at Father Latour's head, for example, which was "built for the seat of a fine intelligence," his "open, generous, reflective" brow, and the "singular elegance about the hands" to recognize his exceptionality (*Later Novels* 286). Similarly, Father Lucero's wasting disease is an ironic punishment for someone whose "lust for money" (*Later Novels* 375) had perverted his being. Cather uses her strategy most effectively, however, in her scathing description of Padre Martinez, whose "broad high shoulders were like a bull buffalo's." With "his big head set defiantly on a thick neck" and his "brilliant yellow eyes set deep in smooth arches, and full, florid cheeks," Padre Martinez is clearly a force with which to be reckoned. It is his final physical feature, however, that defines the nature of that force: "His mouth was the very assertion of violent, uncurbed passions and tyrannical self-will; the full lips thrust out and taut, like the flesh of animals distended by fear or desire" (362). Padre Martinez, as his physical appearance symbolizes, may have the features of a man, but he is little more than a beast. In a realistic novel such as *Death Comes for the Archbishop,* Cather's use of unobtrusive physical detail as symbol is the perfect strategy by which to achieve her effect and to make her point.

THEMATIC ISSUES

Willa Cather's noble archbishop and his faithful assistant embody her novel's highest ideals and thus point the way toward its thematic issues, or main points. For most of her career, Cather had been celebrating heroic achievement in her fiction. Her novels were filled with pioneers and idealists determined to achieve their ambitions and to realize their dreams and generally succeeding. Yet the tone, the author's attitude toward her subject, of those works had been nostalgic, tinged with a sense of sadness that reflected Cather's clear-sighted recognition that her world had changed so much that the values she championed, the world she envisioned, were irrecoverable. *Death Comes for the Archbishop,* however, lacks that tone. In turning to the historical past and indeed to historical record, Cather found evidence to support her beliefs. Into a harsh but beautiful environment where civilizations had thrived and died and now uneasily coexisted came two priests with a belief in a vision of the eternal and a plan to order this world to its specifications. Their success, Cather's novel suggests, should inspire generations to come.

Crucial to the development of theme in *Death Comes for the Archbishop* is form. Conceived as a series of incidents, like Puvis de Chavannes's frescoes of the life of Saint Geneviève, and written "in the style of legend" ("On *Death Comes,*" *Stories, Poems, and Other Writings* 960), Cather's novel has a timeless quality that makes everything immediately present and significant. The landscape, the incidents, and the people in each chapter form a series of pictures, providing signs by which to read their meaning or meanings, for Cather is ever aware of the role of the individual consciousness in interpreting its world. Father Latour and Father Vaillant, for instance, differently interpret the meaning of the tamarisk tree (*Later Novels* 399), and on the crucial subject of miracles, Father Latour understands that Father Vaillant "must always have the miracle very direct and spectacular, not with Nature, but against it" (*Later Novels* 293) while he finds the miraculous wherever "there is great love" (*Later Novels* 306). Like Father Latour, Cather takes her miracles where she finds them—in a bowl of onion soup that is "not the work of one man" but rather "the result of a constantly refined tradition" and thus contains "nearly a thousand years of history" (*Later Novels* 299); in the "comely figure and deep claret colour" of Magdalena, transformed by love, her arms and shoulders lined with doves that eat from her hands (*Later Novels* 404); in the rock of Ácoma, the "utmost expression of human need" (*Later Novels* 335) for something "permanent, enduring, without shadow of change" (*Later Novels* 336). She fills her novel with such signs, such images, that are themselves timeless and that contain tradition, creating a sense of stasis that is part of her larger design. From this series of images, she constructs her novel's theme.

Landscape is a key element of these images. New Mexico is a land of stark contrasts, of "monotonous red sand-hills" (*Later Novels* 285), with thin ribbons of verdure "greener than anything Latour had ever seen, even in his own greenest corner of the Old World" (*Later Novels* 289), of trees "so large that they seemed to belong to a bygone age" and twisted into strange shapes by "the ceaseless winds that beat them to the east and scoured them with sand" (*Later Novels* 412), and always the sky, that "brilliant blue world of stinging air and moving cloud" creating ever-changing contrasts of light and shadow (*Later Novels* 419). "Elsewhere," Cather writes, "the sky is the roof of the world; but here the earth was the floor of the sky" (*Later Novels* 419). Descriptions of landscape fill *Death Comes for the Archbishop,* and in each, Cather emphasizes its elemental quality. Everything about this landscape contrasts with the natural features of the civilized Old World. Indeed, at its most elemental, on the Ácoma plain, the mesa has "the appearance of great antiquity, and of incompleteness; as if, with all the materials for world-making assembled, the Creator had desisted, gone away and left everything on the point of being brought together, on the eve of being arranged into mountain, plain, plateau. The country was still waiting to be made into a landscape" (*Later Novels* 334). This world is on the verge of something that is already there, something that needs only the vision and dedication of persons such as Father Latour to achieve.

Cather sounds this point, her primary theme, most clearly in Book One, where Father Latour makes his first appearance in the novel. Lost amidst the "interminable desert of ovens" (*Later Novels* 287) in New Mexico, a "geometrical nightmare" (*Later Novels* 285) that threatens to overwhelm the solitary traveler, he suddenly sees the cruciform tree that points him to salvation. In the days that follow, as he regains his physical health and performs the sacraments that restore spiritual health to a people "trying to remember their catechism" (*Later Novels* 294), Father Latour will reflect on his experiences, finding the meaning of this foreign land in the remembered past of his original French birthplace. The arrowheads and the Spanish sword hilt that an old Mexican grandfather show him one day remind him of the land's long history, indeed, of a past that stretches beyond history, enfolding countless civilizations into the present one: this place, he thinks, is "like those well-heads in his own country where the Roman settlers had set up the image of a river goddess, and later the Christian priests had planted a cross" (*Later Novels* 294). At several other points in the book—when, for instance, the priests discuss the significance of the onion soup and Father Latour reflects on the history of bells (*Later Novels* 302-3)—Cather reinforces her point, and the repetition effectively supports the conclusion that Father Latour reaches at the beginning of the book: that "faith," and the beauty and order that come of it, "awaited only the toil of the husbandman" (*Later Novels* 295). In *Death Comes for the Archbishop,* Father Latour is that husbandman.

Indeed, just before he departs for Colorado, Father Vaillant reflects on God's choice of missionary to build a diocese in a wilderness. The intelligent and cultured Father Latour seems to him to have been misplaced in New Mexico, but then he concludes that something of his "fine personality" (*Later Novels* 430) may persist into the future, "some ideal, or memory, or legend" (*Later Novels* 431). And it does. It remains in Father Latour's garden, for instance, a well-ordered image of life giving life recalling Eden, so different in purpose from the tyrant Fray Baltazar's cultivated kingdom. Its fullest expression, however, Father Latour's Midi Romanesque cathedral, towers triumphantly over the city of Santa Fe. Designed by a French architect in the style of the cathedral of Father Latour's native Auvergne and constructed of New Mexican stone just the color of those Old World expressions of religious faith (*Later Novels* 423), the cathedral at Santa Fe is part of the fabric of the landscape. It rises from the "rose-coloured hills" to lie against the "pine-slashed slopes" and "with a purpose so strong that it was like action" (*Later Novels* 441). Long after his death, the cathedral in which Father Latour lies buried stands testament to and inspiration for the human endeavor that transforms faith into being. Cather's persistent theme is here given its most positive expression, and that, too, is tribute to the example of Father Latour.

A POSTCOLONIAL INTERPRETATION

Father Latour's Romanesque cathedral may be the triumphant symbol of beauty, order, and heroic endeavor that Cather had consistently celebrated in her fiction. For postcolonial critics, however, who examine literature through the lens of power relationships between indigenous, or native, peoples subdued and transformed by foreign invaders, it is instead disturbing evidence of political and cultural subjugation. Father Latour may have come to New Mexico with what seems a noble mission. He may even have respected the native peoples and cultures that he finds there. Yet for postcolonial critics, he is merely another in a long line of European and Europeanized colonizers that stretches back to the Spanish conquistadores and their missionary priests and forward to the American pioneers in process of claiming a continent. His success, signified in his Romanesque cathedral, effectively legitimizes the colonizer's superiority over the inferior colonized, and thus, from this perspective, *Death Comes for the Archbishop* is a profound expression of the American belief in manifest destiny and a melting-pot ideology.

Such an interpretation depends, of course, on an understanding of postcolonial literary theory, a critical approach that developed primarily in the aftermath of World War II, when writers in former European colonies began a project of cultural self-definition that, in conjunction with a project of political self-determination, challenged Eurocentric views of the colonial experience that had effectively legitimized it. Just as politicians in the former European colonies began the process of nation building, writers in these countries began to create—and in some cases to confirm the existence of—national literatures that reflected and validated their unique experience of life. These literary works and the criticism they spawned challenged a humanistic and essentially Western, or Eurocentric, view of literature that emphasized the universality of human experience and that, in the case of the British Commonwealth nations, privileged English literature and English criticism. Their authors as well as other academic critics began to assert the importance of cultural context in the making of these literatures and to argue that colonial culture was different from rather than inferior to the mother culture. Some critics even suggested that Marxist theory, which examines issues of power and class, could provide a foundation for analysis of the relationship between the former colonial powers and their colonies, with the colonies as the oppressed class, and that the role of literature should also be considered from a Marxist perspective and thus as a vehicle of ideology. At the heart of postcolonial theory, then, is an analysis of the relationship between colonizer and colonized from the earliest days of exploration and colonization through an examination of texts, literary and otherwise, as expressions of the colonial enterprise.

In their efforts to understand this relationship, postcolonial critics have been particularly interested in the way in which literature constructs the colonizer's superiority and the colonized's inferiority and in attitudes of resistance on the part of the colonized. They have drawn on a number of postwar intellectual developments, in addition to Marxist theory, to find their answers. From the French psychoanalyst Jacques Lacan's views of identity formation, for instance, they have adapted his concept of others, individuals who resemble us but who are also undeniably different from us, and of the Other, the larger social order, both of which are integral to the construction of self, to explain how the "not me," or the colonized, becomes inferior to the "me," the colonizer. From feminist theory, they have connected the cultural construction of gender, which sees masculinity as superior to femininity, to language that sexualizes the landscape, or the colony, emphasizing its feminine characteristics, and thus its need to be possessed by male power, or the colonizer. From Antonio Gramsci, an Italian Marxist whose writings became available in the 1970s, they have borrowed a key concept, hegemony, or the set of ruling values and beliefs that dominate through consent rather than coercion, to understand the process of colonization itself. The range and scope of ideas that support postcolonial theory make it particularly appropriate to literary analysis in an age when literature has increasingly become multicultural and multiethnic. In fact, the theory has effectively transformed English literature into first Commonwealth literatures and now literatures in English, an acknowledgment, perhaps, of its relevance in the twenty-first century. While colonial empires may have disappeared since World War II, postcolonial critics acknowledge, neocolonial relations continue to exist, not only between the Western nations and their former colonies but also between immigrants from former colonies who live as ethnic minorities in the mother country and a nation's majority.

Postcolonial theory may seem to have little relevance to the study of American literature, for the United States, unlike Great Britain, never acquired a great colonial empire and was itself originally part of European imperialist agendas. Moreover, its attitude toward immigrants who shaped it and its citizens of non-European descent was always— and continues to be—assimilationist. Anyone who embraces the values and beliefs of the nation's founding documents may be an American. From the European "discovery" of the Americas, however, the history of the United States has been defined by cross-cultural encounters and cultural displacements that American writers from James Fenimore Cooper to Anzia Yezierska to Maxine Hong Kingston, Oscar Hijuelos, and Bharati Mukherjee, among others, have explored in more than 200 years of American literature. Postcolonial theory thus offers an appropriate lens through which to examine America's own expansionist project, the westward movement that constituted its policy of manifest destiny, as well as its melting-pot ideology, topics that have been inherent in most of Willa Cather's novels, including *Death Comes for the Archbishop.*

Cather's Southwest is home to a multicultural, multiethnic population of Laguna, Zuñi, Hopi, and Navajo tribes, Mexicans, and Americans, each of which she clearly differentiates from the others. Yet because they are seen through Europeanized eyes, they are essentially stereotypes. Her Mexicans, for instance, are passionate and sensual, especially in the practice of their faith, for their naive religiosity makes miracles and customs such as the bloody rites of the Penitentes crucial to their beliefs (*Later Novels* 363, 366–67). Fierce pride makes them generous and giving, even if they have little to give (*Later Novels* 434), but then the majority, as Father Vaillant tells Father Latour, care nothing for material possessions and "worldly advancement" (*Later Novels* 402). They are simple people with simple needs, relatively childlike to these European priests, and the native peoples, in their own way, are rather like them.

Dignified and reserved, almost courtly in manner, the Navajo and other tribal people ask little of others but to live freely and as they wish. His infant son, for example, may be dangerously ill, but Jacinto, Father Latour's native guide, follows traditional healing practices and would never accept the priest's advice about treatment (*Later Novels* 351). Their religious faith combines Christian and Native myth and ritual (*Later Novels* 360) and may be the source of their instinctive appreciation of the beautiful. Eusabio, for instance, the Navajo priest, continually surprises Father Latour when they travel together by his practice of stopping to gather flowers, and he erases from the land all traces of his presence whenever he and Father Latour break camp (*Later Novels* 419), a practice that the Catholic priest finds utterly foreign to the European practice of making a mark on the landscape. The native peoples are certainly not savages, but they do seem primitive by European standards of civilization. But then so, too, do Cather's Americans. Indeed, in *Death Comes for the Archbishop,* Americans and Americanization are seldom attractive prospects.

The American presence in Cather's Southwest is largely a military one, with its soldiers bent chiefly on subduing the native tribes and then winning their hearts and minds through kindness and generosity. Other representative Americans, including the murderous Buck Scales, whose name suggests his snake-like character, and the harmless but foolishly vain Doña Isabella, are similarly compromised. Even the frontiersman Kit Carson, who is initially sympathetic to the native peoples, eventually betrays them to American military authority. Glimpses of Americans in other regions of the country simply reinforce the image of crass materialism and insensitivity that the native peoples hold about them. Father Vaillant, for instance, is sent to Colorado to combat the rapacious greed, senseless violence, uproarious drunkenness, and rampant prostitution that have arrived with the prospectors for gold, and even the practical and industrious settlers of the Great Lakes region are faulted for their lack of sensibility by Father Latour, who deplores the drab brick churches that they call places of worship (*Later Novels* 423).

To the native peoples among whom these Americans live, they are "infidels" (*Later Novels* 291). Indeed, one old Mexican tells Father Latour that the Americans had destroyed their churches and stabled their horses in them (*Later Novels* 291). Yet these Americans are clearly on the ascendancy. They have the power and resources to tame the land, and they believe it is their manifest destiny to dominate the continent. Certainly that is the meaning of the annexation of the territory that brings Father Latour to New Mexico at the novel's beginning and the subsequent Gadsden Purchase of 1853. The United States, these historical events imply, is destined to extend from sea to shining sea, and everyone who inhabits the land must become American. In this process, the Church will even play its part. As Father Latour acknowledges in a letter to his brother shortly after he assumes his position, he conducts his business like an American trader, speaking and thinking and dressing the part but trading in souls, not in goods. Nevertheless, he tells his brother, "The Church can do more than the Fort to make these poor Mexicans 'good Americans.' And it is for the people's good" (*Later Novels* 297). With such certainty of their destiny and such crusading spirit, a sign, postcolonial critics would say, of a sense of their superiority to the native peoples, Americans lay claim to the land and assert their values and beliefs.

Cather's depiction of the native peoples, however sympathetic, essentially emphasizes their otherness and, by implication, their inferiority. To Father Latour, for instance, the tribal peoples are like ancient turtles or "crustaceans in their armor," seemingly "fixed" in time and place (*Later Novels* 339) and as if on the verge of extinction. Becoming American, therefore, is, according to Father Latour, the only hope they have of improving their condition (*Later Novels* 297), a belief that reinforces the melting-pot ideology of the United States.

This ideology, given first expression by a French immigrant, Hector St. John de Crèvecoeur in 1782, maintains that people of every nationality, of every religion, of every occupation and class who embrace the new ideas and the new way of life that America offers can be melded together to become someone new—an American. This transformation, which continues to be one of America's foundational myths, has gradually come to mean assimilation. Immigrants as well as native peoples absorbed by the process of manifest destiny must adapt to and adopt the culture and beliefs of the ruling class, which, in America, has been a white Anglo-Saxon Protestant majority. *Death Comes for the Archbishop* essentially affirms this process and the attitudes that uphold it. Indeed, the gradual subjugation of the tribal peoples; the quiet resignation of the Mexicans, aided, no doubt, by their religious faith; and the westward march of the "Americans" are the facts behind a seemingly innocent phrase such as "the march of history" (*Later Novels* 397) or "a man of the old order" (*Later Novels* 370).

Cather never questions the inevitability of these changes, although she clearly has some reservations about them. Yet her reservations have less to do with the triumph of the Americans than with the type of American who will triumph, and here again, Father Latour's Romanesque cathedral serves as the focus of her ideas. Behind that church lies the long tradition of Western civilization, of art and architecture and craftsmanship in the service of an ideal, a thing of beauty to honor and express a thing of beauty. When Father Latour plans his cathedral, he wants not to settle for the utilitarian structures that American pioneers were erecting along the Great Lakes but to transplant the best of Western tradition in the southwestern desert to inspire a people, and Cather clearly embraces his project. Yet the march of history that her novel records reveals a different sort of colonial relationship in the triumph of American over European culture. In 1880, Father Latour tells the young French priest who will eventually assume his position that "a period of incongruous American building" (*Later Novels* 440) began to redefine Santa Fe. At the bishop's death nearly nine years later, "half the plaza square was still adobe, and half was flimsy wooden buildings with double porches, scroll-work and jack-straw posts and banisters painted white" (*Later Novels* 440), all "quite wrong" (*Later Novels* 441) for the cathedral that overlooks the city. In anticipation of the twentieth century, America is clearly in the ascendancy and stands poised to assume a dominant position in relation to the colonial powers that once ruled its shores. Cather might have preferred the civilization that Father Latour had envisioned and for which he worked, but the march of history yields a different America.

It was this different America, a place of flappers and bathtub gin, of radicals and Klansmen, of boom and bust, in which Cather lived. It was this different America, amid the contradictions of postwar society, from which Cather looked to the past for hope and consolation. *Death Comes for the Archbishop* may record and even legitimize manifest destiny, but in the end, it celebrates the efforts of a man who endeavored to bring to life a vision of peace and harmony and the beauty of his achievement.

9

Shadows on the Rock
(1931)

Shadows on the Rock (1931), like its predecessor, *Death Comes for the Archbishop* (1927), is a deeply felt chronicle of a time and a place that give evidence of culture's civilizing influence. Set in late seventeenth-century Quebec, where hardy pioneers, dedicated missionaries, and bold adventurers had transplanted French civilization onto a sheltering rock high above the St. Lawrence River, *Shadows on the Rock* is the story of a city and its inhabitants and of the values, ideals, and beliefs that built and sustained life there. Far away from the culture that had shaped both their sense of self and their world, these early Quebecois battled the forces of nature, the tribal peoples, and their own human failings and shortcomings to transform the strange into the familiar. To examine this process, Willa Cather focuses on the quiet domestic life of one family, the philosopher-apothecary Euclide Auclair and his young daughter Cécile, rather than historic events and the exploits of great men, to announce its success. Yet what they create, she also makes clear, is not simply a reproduction but rather, under the influence of the new, an adaptation of the old. Indeed, in the figure of Cécile Auclair, Cather shapes a symbol of that new Canadian, a symbol that melds the best of two cultures into something vital and new. *Shadows on the Rock*, like *Death Comes for the Archbishop*, thus explores the impact of the Old World on the New and finds at the junction something beautiful and unique and utterly vital to human civilization, no matter where or when.

Framed by the annual departure of ships bound for France, *Shadows on the Rock* records a year in the life of one Quebecois family, the Auclairs, amidst the shadowy background of political and historical event. Eight years before the novel's contemporary setting of 1697, Euclide Auclair, an apothecary, had come to Canada with his wife and daughter as physician to his patron, the Count de Frontenac, governor of New France. Better suited to the bourgeois salons of Paris than the crude habitations of a northern frontier, Auclair lives now in resigned exile from his native land, awaiting the day that King Louis recalls the Count to France to secure his own desired return to his homeland. Until that day comes, Auclair enjoys the domestic comforts that his wife, prior to her death six years after their arrival, had re-created in Quebec and that his 12-year-old daughter Cécile now maintains. As the town's apothecary, Auclair ministers to the entire community, from its clergy to its tradesmen, its aristocrats to its *coureurs de bois,* or bold adventurers. Their stories merge with the legends of the saints and martyrs to form the backdrop to his and his daughter's lives, but it is Cécile on whom they have the greatest effect. Her ties to the Old World more tenuous than her father's and her appreciation for the New World greater than his, Cécile has no desire to abandon the only home she has ever known and the people she has come to love when her father tells her to begin preparations for their return to France. The death of Count de Frontenac resolves the Auclairs' conflicting desires, and a brief epilogue set 15 years later reveals the satisfying lives that these Canadians have forged on their rock. They are lives, Cather's novel makes clear, worthy of both their Old and their New World origins.

GENESIS AND CRITICAL RECEPTION

Cather composed *Shadows on the Rock* during a period of deep personal pain and upheaval. During the four years between the publication of *Death Comes for the Archbishop* and *Shadows on the Rock,* she and her companion, Edith Lewis, were forced from their Greenwich Village home to make way for the construction of the New York subway, her father died of a heart attack, and her mother suffered a debilitating stroke and, for the next three years, a slow, lingering death that Cather found difficult to watch when she traveled annually to California to help nurse her (Lee 289–90). Cather maintained her schedule of personal and professional travel during this time, summering on Grand Manan, the Maine island where she and Lewis had built a small cottage, sailing to France, and visiting for the first time the city of Quebec, the inspiration for *Shadows on the Rock.* That visit was the first of several subsequent trips during which Cather observed the city's seasonal changes and absorbed its unique atmosphere.

Quebec aroused in Cather some familiar emotions despite the fact that she did not have a long, intimate association with French Canada, as she had had with the American Midwest and Southwest, and that her subject took her farther back into historical time than had *Death Comes for the Archbishop*'s. Like the American Southwest, Quebec had been shaped by Roman Catholicism and pioneers, and its history connected it undeniably to European tradition, subjects that had already fueled Cather's imagination. In her memoir of Cather, Edith Lewis recorded her friend's "memory, recognition, surmise" at "the sense of its extraordinarily French character, isolated and kept intact through hundreds of years, as if by a miracle, on this great un-French continent" (153–54). In fact, she especially liked the French Canadians, she told the poet Louise Bogan in 1931, "because they have remained practically unchanged for over two hundred years" (Lee 293). In Quebec, Cather had clearly found another symbolic landscape, a place where tradition and change intersected to create a dynamic and satisfying new culture. Moreover, as Lewis noted, writing *Shadows on the Rock* had allowed Cather to use the remnants of the "world of Catholic feeling and tradition in which she had lived so happily for so long" (155) while writing *Death Comes for the Archbishop.* At a time of change in her own life, Cather could draw again from the historical past some meaning for the present. By the summer of 1929, she had begun work on the novel, conducting considerable research on her subject (Lee 290–91). Writing it, she later told her friend Elizabeth Shepley Sergeant, had provided her respite and a refuge from personal pain. It was "a kind of underground place, to which she could retire for a few hours of concentrated work" (240).

Despite its similarities in subject and focus to *Death Comes for the Archbishop, Shadows on the Rock* is far different in method. Where the first work focuses on the heroic work of great men, the second records the daily life of ordinary citizens. Where robust events fill the first work, quiet encounters recollected in tranquility dominate the second. Even the incidents most likely to thrill readers of *Shadows on the Rock,* such as the woodsman Antoine Frichette's harrowing tale of his unsuccessful efforts to save the life of his brother-in-law during the merciless Canadian winter and Father Hector Saint-Cyr's equally disturbing story of the martyrdom of Father Noël Chabanel, lack the sense of urgency in their telling that had quickened the pace of *Death Comes for the Archbishop.* These differences account in part for the mixed reviews that the novel received at its publication in 1931.

Writing in the *New York Times Book Review,* for instance, John Chamberlain complained that *Shadows on the Rock* lacked a single "memorable incident" and that "the salt, the sweat, the riot and the rigor of pioneering" conveyed in *Death Comes for the Archbishop* were "conspicuous by [their] absence" in the new novel (O'Connor 362). Similarly, the critic for *Time* magazine warned readers that "there is not so much as an Indian fight" in *Shadows on the Rock* "and even the deeds of pioneering derring do are all messangered actions" (O'Connor 365). Critic after critic remarked on the discursive quality of Cather's novel, her tendency to describe rather than dramatize events, and while they were almost unanimous in their praise of the poetic effect of her sharply rendered prose, the majority also tended to agree with Kenneth C. Kaufman, who wrote in *Southwest Review* that *Shadows on the Rock* was "something of a disappointment" (O'Connor 353).

One other source of critical dissatisfaction with *Shadows on the Rock* was its point of view. Cather had elected to filter the novel's action through the perspective of 12-year-old Cécile Auclair, whose lack of experience inevitably limited her understanding of events. Indeed, as Kaufman observed, "Through her eyes we see, as through a peep hole, a gigantic stage where Titans play their destined roles and come to heroic ends" (O'Connor 353). The effect, according to Carl Van Doren, in the *New York Herald Tribune Books,* was to create a "domesticated" novel (O'Connor 360). "Obliged by her method to forego heroism at first hand," Van Doren concluded, Cather "has had to run the risk of a certain lack of sinew, and her narrative does not have the force of that in *Death Comes for the Archbishop*" (O'Connor 360).

Judged on its merits, however, and not in comparison to *Death Comes for the Archbishop, Shadows on the Rock* did indeed have its champions, and the novel was a popular success. Perhaps Cather's readers, like her critics, admired the vivid prose that rendered Quebec and its inhabitants, according to Kaufman, "utterly convincing" (O'Connor 354). Perhaps they responded, as Van Doren did, to "the idyllic or pathetic touches which make up the flesh of the actual story," to the "quick glances into inarticulate hearts ... [that] almost take the place of heroism" (O'Connor 361). Perhaps they instinctively understood that *Shadows on the Rock,* as William E. Harris claimed in the *Boston Evening Transcript,* "represent[ed] a successful continuance of her earlier endeavors to write history in terms of timeless, authentic fiction" (O'Connor 357). Whatever the reason, *Shadows on the Rock* did not disappoint her readers.

PLOT DEVELOPMENT

Indeed, not even its lack of conventional plot, or series of related events that lead to a climax and devolve into its resolution, put readers off *Shadows on the Rock,* for the novel is so full of incident and embedded story and so tightly constrained by its temporal structure that it has a sense of movement when in fact very little happens beyond daily living. This strategy was, of course, deliberate. In a letter published in *The Saturday Review of Literature* in which she expressed appreciation for "the most understanding review" of her novel, Cather asserted that she was interested not in "Indian raids or the wild life in the forest" but in "an orderly little French household that went on trying to live decently." The subject of *Shadows on the Rock,* she claimed, was "the curious endurance of a kind of culture, narrow but definite, ... a kind of feeling about life and human life that I could not accept, wholly, but which I could not but admire." As such, it resisted action and even conclusion and thus defied conventional plot. "It is hard to state that feeling in language," she explained; "it was more like an old song, incomplete but uncorrupted, than a legend. The text was mainly anacoluthon, so to speak, but the meaning was clear" ("On *Shadows,*" *Stories, Poems, and Other Writings* 966).

In describing her work as anacoluthon, as something that shifts from one grammatical structure to another within a single sentence, rather than something ordered and complete, and in comparing it to a song, Cather had provided an explanation for her novel's structure. It would shift from one movement to another, or from verse to refrain, like a musical composition, to create its effect and to achieve unity. Indeed, she said, "I took the incomplete air and tried to give it what would correspond to a sympathetic musical setting; tried to develop it into a prose composition not too conclusive, not too definite." It would also, she continued, adding another structural comparison for her plot, give the effect of "a series of pictures remembered rather than experienced" ("On *Shadows,*" *Stories, Poems, and Other Writings* 966).

An old song, a series of pictures, however Cather conceived her novel, it was not in narrative terms.

Yet neither is *Shadows on the Rock* formless, for Cather uses chronological time and seasonal change to control many of the novel's narrative elements. She begins the novel in October 1697 with the annual departure of the ships for France and ends it a year later with the same event. For Euclide Auclair, those departures are like death, for with them go his hopes of returning to his native country. The impending death of Count de Frontenac, in fact, as the ships depart in October 1698, seems to seal the apothecary's fate. Yet Cather's tone is never as dark as the novel's frame would suggest. While the year that she chronicles certainly has its share of sad events and sad stories, they are without doubt overwhelmed by the unwavering optimism and genuine compassion of the energetic Cécile, the novel's point of view character. Cather, moreover, reinforces her heroine's perspective in the novel's epilogue, set in August 1713, 15 years later, where she reveals details of Cécile's happy life as a true Canadian and Auclair's resolution of homesickness into contentment. By compressing the novel's chronological time frame, Cather restricts incident and perspective to those associated in some way with her central characters, the Auclairs, and thus she controls both plot and tone, or the author's attitude toward her subject.

Cather also uses seasonal changes to determine the content of her chapters. Books One and Two, the events of which take place from October 1697 to the new year, and Books Four, Five, and Six, which chronicle events set between June and November 1698, feature the novel's most dramatic incidents, for Quebec and the Auclairs are not yet prisoners of "The Long Winter" that is the focus of Book Three. In addition to establishing the circumstances of her central characters, the Auclairs, in Books One and Two, for instance, Cather introduces other characters and records Quebecois life primarily through a series of visits that Cécile makes to the Reverend Mother Juschereau de Saint Ignace at the Hôtel Dieu; to the busy market where her father purchases his store of winter provisions; to the Count de Frontenac's chateau, where she appeals to the governor's charity for money to purchase shoes for her little protégé, the neglected child Jacques Gaux; to the cobbler Noël Pommier's shop; and to the cathedral, where she and Jacques encounter the retired Bishop Laval. Cécile moves freely between upper and lower Quebec, enjoying the favor of all, and many share a story with her, enhancing the books' sense of busy activity. Books Four and Five are equally full. The arrival of Quebec's summer permits Cécile to journey with the frontiersman Pierre Charron four miles downriver to the Île d' Orléans, where she experiences provincial country life with the Harnois family, and ushers in the arrival of the ships from France and the few days of "continual festival" (*Later Novels* 596) that follow the event. By fall, the flurry of the Auclairs' preparations for their projected return to France dominates all activity, and Count de Frontenac's death in Book Six provides a dramatic resolution to a significant chapter in the history of a city and of an individual.

Life, however, changes dramatically when Quebec's long winter sets in, and the pace and content of Cather's novel adapt correspondingly. While the season may keep her father overworked, it makes it difficult for Cécile to venture out too far or too often, and sickness even forces her to bed. Thus, most of the action takes place in the Auclairs' cozy salon, where father and daughter entertain a series of visitors including the woodsman Antoine Frichette and the missionary Father Hector Saint-Cyr. Action in this book takes the form primarily of recollections and stories vividly related but distanced, nevertheless, from their sources and thus lacking the urgency and verve of the events in the other books, evidence of Cather's use of plot elements to capture the reality of winter in the Canadian north.

Shadows on the Rock is without doubt a tightly structure novel, and Cather uses to her advantage its restricted time frame as well as its lack of conventional plot to focus on her true subject. If the novel can be said to have a climax, then it lies in Euclide's and Cécile's conflicting desires about returning to France, but the resolution of that conflict is never really in doubt: a 12-year-old girl lacks the power to overrule her father's decision. And while the death of Count de Frontenac will cause Euclide to change his mind, his is a quiet struggle, a resigned commitment to duty rather than a pitched battle with his heart. Little of historic import may happen in Cather's second historical novel, but as its title suggests, the plot of *Shadows on the Rock* gives life and color to the people who exist now as shadows only on the eternal rock of Quebec.

CHARACTER DEVELOPMENT

If a city can be said to have a character, then the Quebec of *Shadows on the Rock* owes its distinct qualities to the combination of its extreme weather, its dramatic geography, and the resolute industry and implacable forbearance of its French settlers. Indeed, Cather makes this point by devoting the novel's opening pages to a description of the "rock-set town" (*Later Novels* 466) rather than its inhabitants, but in doing so, she also magnifies their human achievement. "Kebec," the stronghold of a dream of "new France," is little more than a "fortified cliff... ,—a triangular headland wedged in by the joining of two rivers, and girdled about by the greater river as by an encircling arm" (*Later Novels* 465). On the opposite shore of the river, with its promise of "freedom" to the world beyond, lies the "black pine forest," a "dead, sealed world" threatening "annihilation" (*Later Novels* 467). This inhospitable headland the hardy settlers have "cunningly built over with churches, convents, fortifications, [and] gardens...; some high, some low, some thrust up on a spur, some nestling in a hollow, some sprawling unevenly along a declivity" (*Later Novels* 466). By sheer dint of will, politicians and ecclesiastics as well as ordinary citizens have taken possession of grey slabs and begun to transform them into the "proud rock" (*Later Novels* 467) of a city. Their achievement—not only of building a city, but also, Cather makes clear, of re-creating a world—is wondrous and reason enough to examine the lives of the people who contributed to it.

Great men, certainly, lie behind Quebec's existence, chief among them the Count de Frontenac, a historical figure who Cather captures not in the heroic glory of military victory but in the quiet nobility of approaching death. A brilliant soldier, the Count had served his king faithfully and well and even at the age of 70 was eager to accept reappointment as governor general of Canada (*Later Novels* 484). During the next eight years, he had subdued the Iroquois, "restored peace and order, secured the safety of the [fur] trade" (*Later Novels* 613), and held the territory for the glory of France. Yet the domineering man, "who got on admirably with his inferiors" (*Later Novels* 481), had never found much favor at Versailles, the site of the French court, and nine years later, his hopes that King Louis will recall him to France, so that he might die in his native land, are dashed when the ships from France fail to bring the king's reprieve. "Perhaps I offended His Majesty by trying to teach him geography" (*Later Novels* 614), he explains to his apothecary, Euclide Auclair, his only expression of regret for the king's indifference and ingratitude. But then the Count, who "had the bearing of a fencer," purposeful and direct, whose "carriage," in fact, "was his unconscious idea of himself" (*Later Novels* 614), had never been a man who complained, and when death comes, he accepts it with dignity and as he wishes—alone. A man who had governed a wilderness, on whose strength "even his enemies [had] relied" (*Later Novels* 614), the Count de Frontenac is Cather's symbol of the will to order, the determination to dominate essential to the city's life.

Quebec's religious community provides an alternate vision of peace and order and contributes equally to the quality of its life. The Count's chateau may stand at the edge of Quebec's rock cliff, but beside it are the convent and the church of the Récollet friars; near it are the convent of the Ursulines and the "massive foundation of the Jesuits, facing the Cathedral" (*Later Novels* 466). Towering above it, moreover, are the seminary of the old bishop, Monseigneur de Laval, and just beneath that the new palace of his successor, Monseigneur de Saint-Vallier. The practices and rituals of the Roman Catholic Church clearly lie at the heart of Quebec, all it is and becomes, and Cather reflects on the Church's influence by examining the qualities of its temporal leaders, two men who could not be more different.

The ascetic old Bishop Laval ruled his parishioners with an iron will for nearly four decades, and even in retirement, he awakes at four every morning to ring the church bells summoning the workers to early mass. A "stubborn, high-handed, tyrannical, quarrelsome old man" (*Later Novels* 511), whose presence alone is sufficient to quell the impudence of Antoinette Gaux (*Later Novels* 512), a symbol of the human wilds unleashed by the physical wilderness, Bishop Laval nevertheless holds the regard of the Quebecois, for he lives his convictions. All his wealth he has given to others and to his seminary for the continuation of its errand in the wilderness, and he lives now in poverty in the Priests' House, enduring the same hardships as his parishioners. Moreover, the stern and formidable cleric is not without compassion. Indeed, he holds a special place in his heart for Cécile Auclair, and the protection he offers the unfortunate waif Jacques Gaux one cold January night is proof that he has not lost the religious feeling that led him to his vocation (*Later Novels* 508–13).

The man Bishop Laval chose to succeed him, the aristocratic Monseigneur Jean Baptiste de la Croix de Chevrières de Saint-Vallier is, in contrast, vain, "imperious" (*Later Novels* 540), and "fickle as a woman" (*Later Novels* 541). He lives in splendor in a new Bishop's Palace and has done little more during his 12-year tenure (seven years of which he had spent in France) than build a residence befitting his self-importance and dismantle Bishop Laval's life's work (*Later Novels* 540). While few doubt his piety, Bishop Saint-Vallier has failed to endear himself to the parishioners, and every ship for France carries letters to the king complaining of "his arrogance and his rash impracticality" (*Later Novels*

542). King Louis responds by detaining him in France as much as possible, leaving the duties of the Church to the old bishop.

Yet after a 13-year absence, the record of which Cather includes in the novel's epilogue, Bishop Saint-Vallier returns to Quebec humbled and "wistful," longing to earn the affection that had been his predecessor's. While he may be, Auclair reflects, "a little theatrical in his humility, as he had been in his grandeur" (*Later Novels* 640), he has become the kind of man who in previous decades might have sought not only to claim a new world for his Church but also to convert the tribal peoples to his beliefs. Bishop Saint-Vallier's transformation is clearly important to Cather's characterization of her ecclesiastics, for it aligns him with her other noble representatives, such as Father Hector Saint-Cyr and Father Noël Chabanel as well as old Bishop Laval, of a civilization's sustaining faith. These men are not saints. Indeed, the petty quarrel between Bishops Laval and Saint-Vallier as well as each man's personal weaknesses makes them all too human. Yet Cather never loses sight of their difficult mission or of the heroic qualities that such men dedicated to achieving it. Those qualities are in fact the focus of her characterization of them.

In addition to politicians and clerics, France's *coureurs de bois,* its fur trappers and traders and fearless backwoodsmen, were integral to the foundation of the civilization, and Cather provides representatives of their class in Antoine Frichette and especially Pierre Charron, to whom she devotes an entire book, in order to reveal the qualities they embody. Frichette's tale of doomed heroism, for example, emphasizes the sacrifice, endurance, and stoicism necessary to survival in a hostile environment. His brief appearances in the novel, however, limit the scope of any real character development, and his tale thus serves as sketch to Cather's finished portrait of Charron, who "more than anyone else ... realized the romantic picture of the free Frenchman of the great forests which [the Auclairs] had formed at home on the bank of the Seine" (*Later Novels* 572).

Charron is a romantic conception not only to the Auclairs but also to Cather, who, as she does with some of Quebec's other unpleasant realities, skims the surface of his defects to focus instead on the qualities that make him the ideal of the new continent. He may, "like his comrades," squander half the profits of his year's work in the fur trade "on drink and women and new guns" (*Later Novels* 573), but at home in Montreal, "his behaviour was always exemplary, out of respect to his mother," to whom he also gives the other half of his earnings. Proud, vain, "relentless when he hated, and quickly prejudiced,"

Charron clings to "the old ideals of clan-loyalty" and would sacrifice all for a friend (*Later Novels* 572). Fluent in the native languages, he has earned the respect and trust of the tribal peoples (*Later Novels* 573) and lives at ease among them. Indeed, as he tells Cécile, he has shared their feast meals of dog boiled with blueberries and has also survived by eating *tripe de roche,* the moss that grows on rocks along the lake (*Later Novels* 583). People might expect a man who by his own admission would find it impossible to obey the property laws in his native France, where ownership has domesticated every field and forest, to be uncivilized, but with the Auclairs, and especially with Cécile during their adventure on the Île d' Orleans, he proves himself a charming courtier. Everything about Charron supports Cather's assertion that he combines "the good manners of the Old World, the dash and daring of the New" (*Later Novels* 572), and he thereby exemplifies a new breed of hero. It is clearly this breed of frontiersman rather than the cruder, less sophisticated version, such as Frichette, that she prefers, so his marriage to Cécile, reported in the novel's epilogue, is both fitting and natural.

Pierre Charron, however, as well as the Count de Frontenac and the feuding bishops, resides in the background of *Shadows on the Rock*. In the foreground lie the Auclairs, two ordinary Quebecois citizens. Neither bold adventurers nor dedicated dreamers, they represent for Cather the heart of Quebec. Moreover, their comfortable and tidy salon reflects the civilized virtues that they and all the other townspeople, who are glad of any opportunity to visit the apothecary's shop and thereby catch a glimpse of it (*Later Novels* 480), value and are determined to preserve and perpetuate. In the habits of mind and being of these simple people, Cather locates the source of their achievement and a city's strength.

The apothecary Euclide Auclair is certainly an unlikely immigrant, by his own reckoning, "not of the proper stuff for a colonist" (*Later Novels* 467), but perhaps his very unsuitability makes him the perfect cultural preservationist. A man who regards dinner "as the thing that kept him a civilized man and a Frenchman" (*Later Novels* 444), Auclair is cosmopolitan to his soul. He is also a "creature of habit" (*Later Novels* 484), capable of tolerating any hardship as long as he knows the security of the familiar. Indeed, had it not been for his relationship with the Count (*Later Novels* 480), Auclair would have lived his life in perfect contentment along the banks of the Seine. (Eight years later, he will still feel "a helpless exile in a strange land" [*Later Novels* 630] when he realizes that he has missed his long-desired opportunity to return to France.) So when he agrees to accompany his patron to Quebec, he and his wife, who shares his view of civilized living and cannot "imagine life" without "her household goods" (*Later Novels* 478), transport and transplant not only their possessions but also their traditions (not least in their daughter Cécile).

Intellectual curiosity makes Auclair worthy of the name Euclide, for like the ancient Greek philosopher and mathematician, he is "not afraid of new ideas." Yet innate conservatism makes him cautious, so Auclair, true to form, also refuses to dismiss traditional beliefs simply because "they had gone out of fashion" (*Later Novels* 482). To the end, for instance, he supports the king, a traditional symbol of order and continuity, at one point assigning injustice of the sort that leads to the execution of the unfortunate knife grinder Bichet not to the monarch but to laws that protect property rather than people (*Later Novels* 523) and eventually relieved that his grandsons will escape the "probable evils of a long regency" (*Later Novels* 641) at the king's death. Traditionalism is Auclair's defining quality. From it he draws his strength as well as his concepts of honor and fidelity. It gives meaning to his life and, because he instills it within his daughter, to hers as well. Cécile Auclair, however, who barely remembers her native country and so knows its traditions only as they have been adapted to a new world, is far more flexible than her father. Indeed, in the combination of her heartfelt appreciation of Canada and her French traditionalism lies the source of its real Canadians.

Cécile is another romantic conception for Cather, an ideal of devotion, goodness, faith, and sheer love, yet the girl's youth makes credible her perfection. Before her death, Madame Auclair had worked diligently to train her daughter in proper French customs and traditions—"the sense of 'our way'" (*Later Novels* 479), and Cécile has remained loyal to her mother's hope. Devoted to her father, she takes great care in preparing his dinner each day and in maintaining a clean, well-ordered household. Few scenes in the novel are, in fact, more poignant than the one in which the earnest adolescent, worried that the parsley will freeze in the bitterness of winter, rouses herself from sleep to cover the kitchen herb (*Later Novels* 480). Generous and warmhearted, Cécile, following her mother's death, continues to provide an evening meal for old Blinker, the misshapen man who tends the baker's fires. She also becomes a surrogate mother to six-year-old Jacques Gaux, who has been virtually abandoned by his birth mother, Antoinette, the daughter of one of the "King's Girls" sent to Canada 30 years before to marry disbanded French soldiers and a woman who now has earned the nickname La Grenouille for her seduction of hungry sailors with the promise of fresh frogs (*Later Novels* 495–96). Cécile cares for his physical well-being and his spiritual life, nurturing the neglected child on the saints' stories so long a part of her life and so important to her worldview. Nearly inseparable, they are Cather's secular Madonna and child, proof of the abiding love that animates the best part of humanity.

An intelligent girl who reads Plutarch or the fables of La Fontaine to her father in the evenings (*Later Novels* 474), Cécile is also attuned to the beautiful. She likes few things so much as the Count's glass fruit and rich tapestries (*Later Novels* 501), but she takes equal pleasure from Quebec's natural wonders, relishing, for instance, a sled ride through the city's "constantly changing colour" (*Later Novels* 528). This quality distinguishes Cécile from her father and makes her the country's future. Indeed, as much as she reveres tradition and enjoys the solid bourgeois comforts that devolve from it, Cécile respects her adopted homeland and "liked to think they had things of their own in Canada" (*Later Novels* 529). In the weeks following her father's disclosure of their approaching return to France, she feels as if she is being wrenched from everything dear to her life (*Later Novels* 530–31, 612) and roams the city as if to preserve its special qualities forever in her heart and mind.

Cécile is far too much a concept than a character in *Shadows on the Rock*. Her perspective is naive, and she is literal minded. She believes, for instance, that the Kingdom of Heaven looks exactly like the representation of a feudal French castle reproduced as the cathedral's high altar (*Later Novels* 505). She is not particularly self-aware. Her only real self-discovery, in fact, occurs when she visits the Harnois family on the Île d' Orléans and, in her repulsion by the filth and disorder in which they live, realizes that her homemaking habits are no longer expressions of honor and respect for her parents but rather part of her nature. In them, she observes, "one made life" (*Later Novels* 589). Yet she fulfills utterly her purpose in *Shadows on the Rock*. Cécile represents an attitude toward life, and by making her the novel's point-of-view character, Cather makes readers sympathetic to it.

THEMATIC ISSUES

Cécile's attitude toward life is without doubt the primary theme, or central point, of *Shadows on the Rock,* and she expresses it through housekeeping, which thereby becomes the novel's central metaphor, or implied comparison, for an ordered and stable society. Early in the novel, Cather details the Auclairs' domestic environment, from their red velvet sofa to their walnut dining table, from their Lyon carpet to their store of fine linens, feather beds, and down pillows, from their candelabra to their china shepherd boy (*Later Novels* 478). In a crude foreign outpost on the ragged edge of civilization, such items might seem frivolous or pretentious. Certainly none is essential to life, yet that is exactly the case for the Auclairs. Indeed, they have transported these items from France "to make the new life as much as possible as the old" (*Later Novels* 478). They are the symbols of civilized life. To maintain such a life distinguishes the human from the savage (*Later Novels* 479).

Housekeeping to Cécile, as it was to her mother, is a moral imperative. People who live amid filth and disorder are "disgusting" (*Later Novels* 479) and "repulsive" (*Later Novels* 586). The truth of this judgment she experiences when she visits the Harnois family, whose four daughters tumble into a dirty bed with their legs splashed with mud and bloody from mosquito bites, dry their faces with a common towel, and chatter vulgarly about animal behavior. Cécile, who acknowledges their kindness to her, tries hard not to judge them harshly, but when, under cover of darkness, she spreads her clean handkerchief over the rumpled bolster before placing her head on it, she silently condemns them. This truth lies as well behind her genuine distress at the chaos that develops in the Auclair household because her father, believing in his imminent return to France, fails to make his customary preparations for winter. Without their store of wood doves preserved in fat, winter vegetables, and wild rice, Cécile is "deeply mortified" (*Later Novels* 632) when Pierre Charron unexpectedly arrives to comfort her father at the Count's death. After all, she, like her mother before her, grows green salad in the warmth of their cellar until long past Christmas, believing that only "careless people" must survive winter on a diet of "smoked eels and frozen fish" (*Later Novels* 493). Quality of life, Cather makes clear in these examples, defines a people and its civilization, and through Cécile she celebrates the beauty of French culture, particularly in a time of change. Its emphasis on order and stability makes possible the dignity and grace with which they confront the unknown.

So, too, does religious faith, which is integral to Cécile's worldview, and here, Cather reworks a thematic strand that had been so important to her previous novel, *Death Comes for the Archbishop*. Nurtured on stories of the saints' lives, not only the martyrs' but also the missionaries', Cécile lives in awe of these examples of courage and sacrifice, but the labors of Quebec's nuns and priests as well as the recluse Jeanne Le Ber are equally inspiring to her. Indeed, she can hear again and again the story of the angels' visit to the pious woman, for like all miracles, Cather's narrator observes, it is the "actual flowering of desire" (*Later Novels* 551). Religious faith is a living thing for Cécile. From All Souls' Day to St. Nicholas' Day to Christmas to Epiphany through all the other holy days of the calendar, Christianity testifies to a well-ordered universe and the benevolence of its Creator and makes her life secure. Cather actually credits it with laying the foundation of everything that Quebec is and will become: "When an adventurer," the narrator asserts, "carries his gods with him into a remote and savage country, the colony he founds will ... have graces, traditions, riches of the mind and spirit" (*Later Novels* 526).

Cather's exploration of the French civilization that develops in Quebec is related as well to the secondary theme of change in *Shadows on the Rock*. From the moment Euclide Auclair agrees to accompany the Count de Frontenac to Quebec, his life is never the same. When all he craved lay along the banks of the Seine, Auclair and his family found themselves in a foreign land amid a civilization in flux. Auclair's instinct, in which his wife aided him, was to re-create the world he had known and still loved. Unlike Bishop Saint-Vallier, who enjoys change simply for its novelty (*Later Novels* 541), Auclair, as he confesses to the ecclesiastic, is an "old-fashioned" man, and he does not equate change with progress (*Later Novels* 539). Indeed, it can merely disturb the established order of existence to create turmoil and uncertainty.

Any doubt of this perspective Cather dispels in the novel's epilogue, when Bishop Saint-Vallier and Auclair discuss once again the subject of change. Returning to Quebec after another of his extended absences from the city, the Bishop reports to Auclair the political machinations in the royal court, caused, most certainly, by the approaching death of King Louis, and bemoans the death of an age, in France as well as England. The problem, he tells Auclair, is that its replacement is "still hidden." In political terms, it could be the Duc de Barry, who will protect the young Dauphin until he is old enough to ascend the throne and, perhaps, resume his grandfather's powerful legacy; it could be the Duc d' Orléans, the suspected poisoner of the Dauphin's parents and an "arch-atheist," a man, in other words, bent on destroying the old order (*Later Novels* 639). Everything about the new order, in other words, is merely speculative and thus a source of doubt and discomfort. In ironic reversal for a man who had once been the agent of change, Bishop Saint-Vallier now responds to these uncertainties by reassuring Auclair, "You have done well to remain here where nothing changes" (*Later Novels* 639), a judgment with which the aging apothecary concurs in the novel's final paragraph.

Yet change has, of course, occurred in Quebec, for it is an inevitability. Indeed, the Count de Frontenac's death symbolizes the passing of the old order in the New World, just as Pierre Charron's immediate journey to reassure the Auclairs in its aftermath signifies the arrival of the new. Cather's thematic interest lies in the nature of that new order. Because Charron is one of those adventurers who "carries his gods with him" (*Later Novels* 526), it is inevitably based on the culture and traditions of the Old World. Its defining characteristics remain essentially unchanged, Cather makes clear, because they are neither tired nor irrelevant. Yet this new order is not entirely of the old. Charron, one of its embodiments, brings a new "authority" to it, a "power" derived "from knowledge of the country and its people" and, most important, from "passion" (*Later Novels* 633), from true and deep feeling for his adopted homeland. This proud and daring man is the symbol of New France. Like Father Hector Saint-Cyr, he has given himself "heart and soul" (*Later Novels* 559) to his new life, and his marriage to the novel's other embodiment of New France, Cécile, promises generations of real Canadians. In the closing paragraphs of *Shadows on the Rock,* Cather thus makes clear that, like Auclair, she is a traditionalist and offers a vision of continuity in the midst of change, of an Old World animated by a New.

Embedded stories fill *Shadows on the Rock,* providing details of lives that then seem anything but ordinary as well as raising another thematic issue, the nature of narrative, that may be minor to the novel but that gets to the heart of the novelist's art. Cécile Auclair, the novel's imaginative center, may not create tales, but she absorbs them. Indeed, few things give her more pleasure than the saints' stories or heroic tales of adventure and escape in the Canadian wilderness. The past lives for her in narrative, providing an experience of another time, another place, another life to the reader or listener that is reason enough for its existence but that also reveals truth. Cather makes this point early in the novel when, during a visit to Mother Juschereau at the Hôtel Dieu, Cécile asks her for a story of Mother Catherine de Saint-Augustin, who surmounted every obstacle to fulfill her vocation in Quebec. As Mother Juschereau concludes her tale, her avid listener stops her midsentence to beg her not to explain its meaning (*Later*

Novels 489). A true story, a good story, Cécile's request implies, needs no explanation. Its meaning unfolds in action and in its interplay with the sympathetic imagination. Cécile's response to stories makes clear the power of narrative to reveal truth and to shape lives. She has learned the nature of sacrifice, the power of faith, and the resolve in courage from stories and has modeled her own behavior on the behavior of others whose stories inspire her to action. For Cather, narrative is a means by which to understand and order life. *Shadows on the Rock* is her contribution to that effort.

A DECONSTRUCTIONIST INTERPRETATION

From the perspective of a deconstructionist, however, a literary critic who denies the possibility of ever really knowing the world because language is a fundamentally unstable and unreliable medium of communication and thus can never yield a coherent interpretation, *Shadows on the Rock* is thematically far less conventional than it seems. While its form, for example, is the historical novel, it depicts very little historical event, effectively undermining any real notion of the relationship between continuity and change. Similarly, the presence of female characters who are far more complex than stereotyped versions of ideal womanhood challenges the novel's positive presentation of domesticity. Indeed, it is this inconsistency, especially given Cécile Auclair's privileged position in the novel, to which a deconstructionist critic might point to argue that in *Shadows on the Rock* Willa Cather resists her own traditionalism.

Such a perspective depends, of course, on the theoretical base supporting deconstruction, a literary theory that owes its name and energy to the precepts and examples of the French philosopher Jacques Derrida, whose works have been available in English translation since the 1960s. Derrida argues that all thought is necessarily inscribed in language and that language itself is fraught with intractable paradoxes, or self-contradictions. These paradoxes may be ignored or repressed, but we can neither escape from nor solve them. Such a view extends the linguistic theories of Ferdinand de Saussure, who established that the special symbol systems of natural languages are based on differences, and challenges the Western tradition of rationalist thought and its essentialist notion of certainty of meaning. For the deconstructionist, in other words, the signifier and the signified are fluid rather than fixed, and the presence of one calls forth the absence of the other. Culture, for instance, posits nature just as soul calls forth body, and neither is privileged over the other. Thus, language can never be limited to meaning, and ultimate meaning is always deferred. As David H. Richter notes, "To the extent that ... polarities [such as divine vs. human, man vs. woman, and culture vs. nature] are at the heart of Western culture, deconstruction attempts to expose the illusions upon which authority in Western culture is established" (946).

In extending the linguistic model to describe other systems, Derrida replaces concepts of thing, substance, event, and absolute with concepts of relation, ratio, construct, and relativity. According to this view, "any meaning or identity (including our own) is provisional and relative, because it is never exhaustive, it can always be traced further back to a prior network of differences, and further back again almost to infinity or the 'zero degree' of sense" (Appignanesi and Garratt 79). To convey his view that meaning includes both identity (what it is) and differences (what it is not), Derrida coined the term "difference," which includes difference, differing, deferring, deference, and deferral. Deconstruction is, then, a "strategy for revealing the underlayers of meanings 'in' a text that were suppressed or assumed in order for it to take its actual form" (Appignanesi and Garratt 80). It is an activity intended to generate skepticism about most of the doctrines we accept as truth.

Like the structuralism it challenges and even attempts to supplant, deconstruction is not solely or even primarily a mode of literary criticism. In fact, some deconstructionists suggest that the application of Derrida's method to literary texts in support of new interpretations is itself paradoxical because his revolutionary contribution was to apply to philosophical texts the same sort of linguistic ambiguity and fluidity characteristic of literature. Nevertheless, deconstruction has had tremendous impact on the study of literature in the postmodern era, especially since the 1970s. Prior to that time, literary criticism had been dominated by the New Criticism, which treated poetry as a complex mode of discourse, complete in and of itself, that sought to convey a truth. New Critics discovered that truth through analysis of paradox, ambiguity, and other formal elements of the work.

Deconstructionists, in contrast, posit a world of multiple, even contradictory, meanings. For them, literary texts contain elements that contradict their own assertions and even their authors' intentions, and so they analyze paradox and ambiguity to disclose the way in which texts deconstruct themselves. Deconstructionists, in other words, analyze "the inconsistency between a text's grammar and its rhetoric, between its message and its activity, between what a text means and the way it goes about meaning it" (Richter 950). It is the contradictory messages of *Shadows on the Rock* that make a deconstructionist reading particularly appropriate.

In its treatment of masculinity and femininity, *Shadows on the Rock* is utterly conventional and grounded in patriarchy, or male domination. Its male characters are primarily explorers and adventurers, politicians and prelates, men of action and of the world. Its female characters, in contrast, generally fulfill their traditional domestic role in either the home or the convent, where they nurture life and lend a civilizing influence to existence. These differences have long been considered the natural order in Western culture, a perspective that Cather essentially endorses when Father Hector Saint-Cyr, who overcomes his doubts and fears to become "twice the man I was before" and a positive example of the missionary spirit, gestures to Cécile after telling his story and asserts to her father, "From the beginning women understand devotion, it is a natural grace with them; they have only to learn where to direct it. Men have to learn everything" (*Later Novels* 559). She reinforces this perspective of woman's innate characteristics in her treatment of Cécile, whose commitment to domesticity essentially defines her.

In *Shadows on the Rock,* Cather clearly privileges woman's civilizing influence, one important aspect of which is mothering. Indeed, the majority of the novel's mothers, both secular and sacred, embody the traditional ideal of womanhood. Cécile has learned all the domestic arts from her mother, who encouraged her as well to develop that innate female quality that makes housekeeping a moral imperative, distinguishing the savage from the civilized (*Later Novels* 479). At Madame Auclair's death, the child Cécile easily assumes her mother's role in their home, even continuing her charity to Old Blinker, and then secures her position as embodiment of domesticity by becoming surrogate mother to Jacques Gaux, a four-year-old child neglected by his own mother. Cécile provides for Jacques's physical and spiritual needs, securing shoes and knitting stockings for the boy as well as telling him the stories that have filled her life with meaning. Indeed, his notion of her as a person, derived from watching her drink from a silver cup engraved with her name, contributes to the development of his own sense of self (*Later Novels* 519). Cather idealizes Cécile's maternal instincts, transforming her and Jacques into Madonna and child and thereby investing motherhood with ineffable value.

Cécile's role as surrogate mother, however, as well as her own status as motherless daughter, exposes an inconsistency and inner contradiction within Cather's text that, for the deconstructionist critic, effectively compromise this vision of ideal womanhood. Antoinette Gaux, Jacques's birth mother, neglects her son in pursuit of her own needs and desires. Mothering to her is anything but a natural instinct or a civilizing grace. While the community judges Antoinette harshly and Bishop Laval's disapproval is capable of making her feel some measure of shame for her failings (*Later Novels* 512), she makes no real effort at reform and assumes the freedom generally accorded to men as her right as well. It is as if she learned early, as the daughter of one of the King's Girls transported to New France to marry his soldiers, the nature of her value but refuses to accept it (*Later Novels* 520). This bad mother in effect resists biological determination.

Another female character who resists biology is the recluse Jeanne Le Ber, and because she, unlike Antoinette, holds such a positive place in Cather's novel, her resistance, perhaps surprisingly, is even more a challenge to convention and ideals. Like many young women, Jeanne Le Ber, the only daughter of a wealthy Montreal merchant, receives a convent education and then returns to her family, who introduces her to society in expectation of her suitable marriage. Her devoted father delights in dressing Jeanne in the finest French fabrics. He also offers a substantial dowry to attract her many suitors, among whom is her childhood friend Pierre Charron (*Later Novels* 547). This source of her father's pride, however, and emblem of his position refuses his idea of her destiny. She asserts her will and takes a vow of seclusion, immuring herself first in the family home, which becomes "the tomb of his hopes" (*Later Novels* 548), and then in a tiny cell behind the high altar of a chapel she had built with her dowry (*Later Novels* 549). There she intends to live out her days in utter devotion to her faith.

Cather presents Jeanne Le Ber's story from multiple and contradictory perspectives. To Cécile, her story is "a joy" (*Later Novels* 550). She cannot hear it often enough, nor can she resist telling it again and again to Jacques. To the French Canadians, Jeanne, to whom it is said angels have appeared, is part of a miracle. The embodiment of desire, she offers an "incomparable gift" (*Later Novels* 551), the promise of the actual, to people pursuing a dream. Pierre Charron, in contrast, who loved and lost her to her ideal, offers a bitter antidote to the popular impression, telling Auclair about the night he had spied on Jeanne at prayer and heard a voice made "hoarse" and "hollow" with "such resignation and despair" that he was left sobbing for their losses (*Later Novels* 579–80). Cather's language, moreover, adds to the story's complexity. Words such as "tomb" (*Later Novels* 548), "immured," and "entombment" (*Later Novels* 549) transform Jeanne's life into a death and make her choice fearsome and unnatural, like Charron's story, contradicting any favorable response to her tale. These contradictions leave readers without a cohesive viewpoint of and a coherent statement about Jeanne Le Ber's significance to the novel, yet within the context of other anomalies that cohere around Cather's treatment of the ideal of womanhood, it makes a contribution.

Jeanne Le Ber, unlike the conventional representatives of the ideal of womanhood in *Shadows on the Rock,* retains her indomitable will and remains a powerful force throughout her life chiefly by resisting that ideal. Indeed, not only does she reject marriage and motherhood, but she also resists their socially accepted alternative—becoming a bride of Christ. Instead, she becomes a recluse, suffering for humanity, like Christ. "*I will be that lamp,*" she determines (*Later Novels* 547), lighting the path to salvation, and become it she does. Her example is thus as inspiring as any man's. Madame Auclair, the absent mother, is, in contrast, little more than a concept, and that concept, embodied in Cécile, who has disappeared by the novel's end to become the anonymous mother of future generations of Canadians, is eventually subsumed in patriarchy, or male domination.

Despite the privileged position that Cather accords to domesticity in *Shadows on the Rock,* the examples of Jeanne Le Ber and, to a lesser extent, Antoinette Gaux seriously challenge that traditional ideal. They are a type of domestic outlaw, defying stereotypes to live on their own terms. Their presence in a novel so unremittingly positive in its portrayal of domesticity is incongruous, and for the deconstructionist critic, such incongruities unsettle the author's discourse. In Cather's case, they reveal some disquieting reservations about women's innate characteristics and their traditional role that make *Shadows on the Rock* a far more modern novel than its subject and form suggest.

Yet the force of Cécile Auclair and all that she represents is hard to deny. Her faith, her goodness, her instinct for beauty, and her capacity for wonder make her an endearing young heroine, just the sort not only to appreciate a new world but also to contribute to it. What she offers are timeless traditions and civilizing habits, the foundation of order and security, revitalized by a wilderness. In the midst of change, in the face of the unknown, Cécile responds to life with such certainty of the future that her example offers a way forward to all. Of all the shadows on the rock, it is Cécile's that lives again most fully because it is her attitude toward life that Cather ultimately endorses.

10

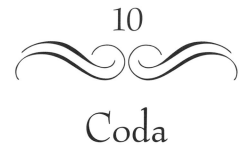

Coda

When Willa Cather died in 1947, at the age of 73, she had long reached the point in her life when she could find little to recommend the modern world. During her lifetime, society had changed immeasurably and irrevocably, and the woman for whom "the world had broke in two" a quarter century before disliked many of its characteristics—the cheap commercialism, the dehumanizing mechanization, the crushing conventionality. Reinforced by her own criticism of the age, critics once tended to focus on Cather's traditionalism and to find in it an unremitting, almost reactionary, nostalgia and a cloying sentimentality. Today, however, recognition of Cather's subtle ironies and disturbing inclusivity, among other distinguishing characteristics, has largely displaced such a view. While Cather's best fiction may be nostalgic in tone and may celebrate distant civilizations, it is anything but sentimental. Indeed, it portrays with stark reality the human struggle to realize an ideal. Working within and against tradition, Cather was in fact as much a critic of her era as many of her contemporary writers. What she offered her readers were models of human endeavor that testified to the possibility of heroic achievement.

Working within and against tradition, Cather also became an individual talent, for her work has certain qualities that resist definition and easy classification. Her friend and fellow writer Dorothy Canfield Fisher, for instance, once offered in an essay published in the *New*

York Herald Tribune "a hypothesis about Willa Cather's work: that the one real subject of all her books is the effect a new country— our new country—has on people transplanted to it from the old traditions of a stable, complex civilization" (Woodress, *Willa Cather: Her Life and Art* 247). While this hypothesis certainly expresses a great deal of truth about Cather's fiction, it does not state the whole truth. Indeed, Cather's vision is too complex for one defining statement, her art too unique to be categorized. These qualities are, by Cather's own reckoning, the marks of a "first-rate writer," whose work, Cather observed, can "only be experienced," for "it is just the thing in him which escapes analysis that makes him first-rate" ("Katherine Mansfield," *Stories, Poems, and Other Writings* 877).

Cather offered these words in appreciation of the British novelist Katherine Mansfield. She could not have known that one day they would apply to her as well.

Selected Bibliography

All citations of Willa Cather's writings refer to the following three-volume Library of America editions unless otherwise stated:

Early Novels and Stories. Selected and with notes by Sharon O'Brien. New York: Library of America, 1987.
Later Novels. Selected and with notes by Sharon O'Brien. New York: Library of America, 1990.
Stories, Poems, and Other Writings. Selected and with notes by Sharon O'Brien. New York: Library of America, 1992.

LITERARY WORKS BY WILLA CATHER

April Twilights. New York: Richard G. Badger, 1903.
The Troll Garden. New York: McClure, Phillips & Co., 1905.
Alexander's Bridge. New York: Houghton Mifflin, 1912.
O Pioneers!. New York: Houghton Mifflin, 1913.
The Song of the Lark. New York: Houghton Mifflin, 1915; rpt. 1937.
My Ántonia. New York: Houghton Mifflin, 1918.
Youth and the Bright Medusa. New York: Alfred A Knopf, 1920.
One of Ours. New York: Alfred A. Knopf, 1922.
April Twilights and Other Poems. New York: Alfred A. Knopf, 1923.
A Lost Lady. New York: Alfred A. Knopf, 1923.
The Professor's House. New York: Alfred A. Knopf, 1925.
My Mortal Enemy. New York: Alfred A. Knopf, 1926.

Death Comes for the Archbishop. New York: Alfred A. Knopf, 1927.
Shadows on the Rock. New York: Alfred A. Knopf, 1931.
Obscure Destinies. New York: Alfred A. Knopf, 1932.
Lucy Gayheart. New York: Alfred A. Knopf, 1935.
Sapphira and the Slave Girl. New York: Alfred A. Knopf, 1940.
The Old Beauty and Others. New York: Alfred A. Knopf, 1948.
Collected Stories. New York: Random House, 1992.

NONFICTION BY WILLA CATHER

The Kingdom of Art: Willa Cather's First Principles and Critical Statements, 1893–1896. Selected and edited by Bernice Slote. Lincoln: University of Nebraska Press, 1966.
Not Under Forty. 1936. Lincoln: University of Nebraska Press, 1988.
Willa Cather in Person: Interviews, Speeches, and Letters. Edited by L. Brent Bohlke. Lincoln: University of Nebraska Press, 1986.
The World and the Parish: Willa Cather's Articles and Reviews, 1893–1902. Selected and edited by William Curtin. 2 vols. Lincoln: University of Nebraska Press, 1970.

BIBLIOGRAPHIES AND CHECKLISTS

Arnold, Marilyn. *Willa Cather: A Reference Guide*. Boston: G. K. Hall, 1986.
March, John. *A Reader's Companion to the Fiction of Willa Cather*. Ed. Marilyn Arnold with Debra Lynn Thornton. Westport, CT: Greenwood, 1993.
Meyering, Sheryl L. *A Reader's Guide to the Short Stories of Willa Cather*. New York: G. K. Hall, 1994.
O'Connor, Margaret Ann, ed. *Willa Cather. The Contemporary Reviews*. Cambridge: Cambridge University Press, 2001.

BIOGRAPHICAL WORKS AND MEMOIRS

Bennett, Mildred. *The World of Willa Cather*. Rev. ed. Lincoln: University of Nebraska Press, 1961.
Brown, E. K. *Willa Cather: A Critical Biography*. Completed by Leon Edel. Lincoln: University of Nebraska Press, 1953.
Lee, Hermione. *Willa Cather: Double Lives*. New York: Random House, 1989.
Lewis, Edith. *Willa Cather Living: A Personal Record*. Foreword by Marilyn Arnold. Athens: Ohio University Press, 1989.
O'Brien, Sharon. *Willa Cather: The Emerging Voice*. New York: Oxford University Press, 1987.
Robinson, Phyllis. *Willa: The Life of Willa Cather*. Garden City, NY: Doubleday, 1983.

Sergeant, Elizabeth Shepley. *Willa Cather: A Memoir*. Athens: Ohio University Press, 1953.

Stout, Janis P. *Willa Cather: The Writer and Her World*. Charlottesville: University Press of Virginia, 2000.

Woodress, James. *Willa Cather: A Literary Life*. Lincoln: University of Nebraska Press, 1987.

———. *Willa Cather: Her Life and Art*. Pegasus American Authors. New York: Western Publishing, 1970.

CRITICAL STUDIES OF CATHER'S WORKS

Acocella, Joan. *Willa Cather and the Politics of Criticism*. New York: Vintage Books, 2002.

Anders, John P. *Willa Cather's Sexual Aesthetics and the Male Homosexual Tradition*. Lincoln: University of Nebraska Press, 1999.

Ammons, Elizabeth. *Conflicting Stories: American Women Writers at the Turn into the Twentieth Century*. New York: Oxford University Press, 1992.

Byatt, A. S. "Willa Cather." In *The Passions of the Mind: Selected Writings*. New York: Random House, 1991. 197–216.

Daiches, David. *Willa Cather: A Critical Introduction*. Ithaca, NY: Cornell University Press, 1951.

Fetterley, Judith. "Willa Cather and the Fiction of Female Development." In *Anxious Power: Reading, Writing, and Ambivalence in Narrative by Women*. Edited by Carol J. Singley and Susan Elizabeth Sweeney. Albany: State University of New York Press, 1993. 221–34.

Fryer, Judith. *Felicitous Space: The Imaginative Structures of Edith Wharton and Willa Cather*. Chapel Hill: University of North Carolina Press, 1986.

Giannone, Richard. *Music in Willa Cather's Fiction*. Lincoln: University of Nebraska Press, 1968.

———. "Music, Silence, and the Spirituality of Willa Cather." *Renascence: Essays on Values in Literature* 57 (2005): 123–49.

Goldberg, Jonathan. *Willa Cather and Others*. Durham, NC: Duke University Press, 2001.

Harvey, Sally Peltier. *Redefining the American Dream: The Novels of Willa Cather*. Rutherford, NJ: Fairleigh Dickinson University Press, 1995.

Kaye, Frances W. *Isolation and Masquerade: Willa Cather's Women*. American University Studies, series XXIV, American Literature, vol. 30. New York: Peter Lang, 1993.

Lindemann, Marilee, ed. *The Cambridge Companion to Willa Cather*. Cambridge: Cambridge University Press, 2005.

Lindemann, Marilee. *Willa Cather: Queering America*. New York: Columbia University Press, 1999.

McDonald, Joyce. *The Stuff of Our Forebears: Willa Cather's Southern Heritage*. Tuscaloosa: University of Alabama Press, 1998.

Moers, Ellen. *Literary Women*. New York: Oxford University Press, 1985.

Murphy, John J., ed. *Critical Essays on Willa Cather*. Boston: G. K. Hall, 1984.

Murphy, John J., Linda Hunter Adams, and Paul Rawlins, eds. *Willa Cather: Family, Community, and History*. Provo, UT: Brigham Young University Humanities Publishing Center, 1990.

Nelson, Robert J. *Willa Cather and France: In Search of the Lost Language*. Urbana: University of Illinois Press, 1988.

Nettles, Elsa. *Language and Gender in American Fiction: Howells, James, Wharton, and Cather*. Charlottesville: University Press of Virginia, 1997.

O'Brien, Sharon. "Mothers, Daughters, and the 'Art Necessity': Willa Cather and the Creative Process." In *American Novelists Revisited: Essays in Feminist Criticism*. Edited by Fritz Fleishmann. Boston: G. K. Hall, 1982. 265–98.

Randall, John H., III. *The Landscape and the Looking Glass: Willa Cather's Search for Value*. Boston: Houghton Mifflin, 1960.

Reynolds, Guy. *Willa Cather in Context: Progress, Race, Empire*. New York: St. Martin's, 1996.

Romines, Ann. *The Home Plot: Women, Writing, and Domestic Ritual*. Amherst: University of Massachusetts Press, 1992.

———, ed. *Willa Cather's Southern Connections: New Essays on Cather and the South*. Charlottesville: University Press of Virginia, 2000.

Rose, Phyllis. "Modernism: The Case of Willa Cather." In *Modernism Reconsidered*. Edited by Robert Kiely. Harvard English Studies 11. Cambridge, MA: Harvard University Press, 1983. 123–45.

Rosowski, Susan J. *The Voyage Perilous: Willa Cather's Romanticism*. Lincoln: University of Nebraska Press, 1986.

Russ, Joanna. "To Write 'Like a Woman': Transformations of Identity in the Work of Willa Cather." In *Historical, Literary, and Erotic Aspects of Lesbianism*. Edited by Monika Kehoe. New York: Harrington Park Press, 1986. 77–87.

Ryder, Mary Ruth. *Willa Cather and Classical Myth: The Search for a New Parnassus*. Lewiston, NY: Mellen, 1990.

Schroeter, James, ed. *Willa Cather and Her Critics*. Ithaca, NY: Cornell University Press, 1967.

Sedgwick, Eve Kosofsky. "Across Gender, Across Sexuality: Willa Cather and Others." *South Atlantic Quarterly* 88 (1989): 53–72.

Shaw, Patrick. *Willa Cather and the Art of Conflict: Re-Visioning Her Creative Imagination*. Troy, NY: Whitson, 1992.

Skaggs, Merrill Maguire. *After the World Broke in Two: The Later Novels of Willa Cather*. Charlottesville: University Press of Virginia, 1990.

Slote, Bernice, and Virginia Faulkner, eds. *The Art of Willa Cather*. Lincoln: University of Nebraska Press, 1974.

Stouck, David. *Willa Cather's Imagination*. Lincoln: University of Nebraska Press, 1975.

Stout, Janis, P., ed. *Willa Cather and Material Culture: Real World Writing, Writing the Real World*. Tuscaloosa: University of Alabama Press, 2004.

Swift, John N., and Joseph R. Urgo, eds. *Willa Cather and the American Southwest*. Lincoln: University of Nebraska Press, 2002.

Trout, Steven. *Memorial Fictions: Willa Cather and the First World War*. Lincoln: University of Nebraska Press, 2002.

Urgo, Joseph. "The Iconic Willa Cather." *Modernism/Modernity* 9 (2002): 327–33.

————. *Willa Cather and the Myth of the American Imagination*. Denton: University of North Texas Press, 1995.

————. *Willa Cather and the Myth of American Migration*. Urbana: University of Illinois Press, 1995.

Wagenknecht, Edward. *Willa Cather*. New York: Continuum, 1994.

Wasserman, Loretta. *Willa Cather: A Study of the Short Fiction*. Twayne's Studies in Short Fiction Series, No. 19. Boston: G. K. Hall, 1991.

Woodress, James. "Willa Cather: American Experience and European Tradition." In *The Art of Willa Cather*. Edited by Bernice Slote and Virginia Faulkner. Lincoln: University of Nebraska Press, 1974. 43–62.

ALEXANDER'S BRIDGE (1912)

REVIEWS

"Explaining Her Novel: *Alexander's Bridge* Has Nothing to Do with Whist." [New York] *Sun* 25 May 1912.

Mencken, H. L. "A Visit to a Short Story Factory." *Smart Set* 38 (December 1912): 156–57.

New York Times Book Review 12 May 1912: 295.

CRITICISM

Ammons, Elizabeth. "The Engineer as Cultural Hero and Willa Cather's First Novel, *Alexander's Bridge*." *American Quarterly* 38 (1986): 746–60.

Brunauer, Dalma It. "*Alexander's Bridge*: Novel and Archetype." *Journal of Evolutionary Psychology* 10 (1989): 295–99.

Lee, Hermione. "Cather's Bridge: Anglo-American Crossings in Willa Cather." In *Forked Tongues? Comparing Twentieth-Century British and American Literature*. Edited by Ann Massa and Alistair Stead. London: Longman, 1994. 38–56.

Wasserman, Loretta. "*Alexander's Bridge*: 'The Other' First Novel." *Cather Studies* 4 (1999): 294–306.

O PIONEERS! (1913)

REVIEWS

"A Novel without a Hero." *New York Times Book Review* 14 September 1913: 466.

Dell, Floyd. "A Good Novel." *Chicago Evening Post* 25 July 1913: 9.

E. U.S. "O Pioneers! A New Heroine and a New Country Appear." *Boston Evening Transcript* 16 July 1913: 18.

New York Times Book Review 30 November 1913: 664.

Wood, Gardner W. "Books of the Day." *McClure's Magazine* 41 (July 1913): 199.

CRITICISM

Fischer, Mike. "Pastoralism and Its Discontents: Willa Cather and the Burden of Imperialism." *Mosaic* 23 (1990): 31–44.

Gustafson, Neil. "Getting Back to Cather's Text: The Shared Dream in O Pioneers!" *Western American Literature* 30 (1995): 151–62.

Moseley, Ann. "Mythic Reality: Structure and Theme in Cather's O Pioneers!" In *Under the Sun: Myth and Realism in Western American Literature.* Edited by Barbara Howard Meldrum. Troy, NY: Whitson, 1985.

Motley, Warren. "The Unfinished Self: Willa Cather's O Pioneers! and the Psychic Cost of a Woman's Success." *Women's Studies* 12 (1986): 149–65.

Paniccia Carden, Mary. "Creative Fertility and the National Romance in Willa Cather's O Pioneers! and My Ántonia." *Modern Fiction Studies* 45 (1999): 275–302.

Ryan, Melissa. "The Enclosure of America: Civilization and Confinement in Willa Cather's O Pioneers!" *American Literature* 75 (2003): 275–303.

Seaton, James. "The Beauty of Middle-Class Virtue: Willa Cather's O Pioneers!" In *The Moral of the Story: Literature and Public Ethics.* Edited by Henry T. Edmonson III. Lanham, MD: Lexington, 2000. 193–202.

THE SONG OF THE LARK (1915)

REVIEWS

Boynton, H. W. "The Great Novel Is Only a Dream but a Chapter in It Is Willa Sibert Cather's *The Song of the Lark.*" *New York Evening Post, The Literary Review* 13 November 1915.

———. "Varieties of Realism." *The Nation* 101 (14 October 1915): 461–62.

Ford, James L. "Miss Cather's Story of a Prima Donna from the Western Desert." *New York Herald Tribune* 9 October 1915: 8.

Hale, Edward E. *Dial* 59 (25 November 1915): 496–97.

Mencken, Henry Louis. "Cinderella the Nth." *Smart Set* 48 (January 1916): 306–8. *New York Times Book Review* 31 October 1915: 420.

CRITICISM

Ahearn, Amy. "Full-Blooded Writing and Journalistic Fictions: Naturalism, the Female Artist and Willa Cather's *The Song of the Lark.*" *American Literary Realism* 33 (2001): 143–56.

Aronoff, Eric. "'Coming into Possession': Imperial Movement, Culture and Composition in Willa Cather's *The Song of the Lark* and *The Professor's House*." *Willa Cather Newsletter & Review* 48 (2004): 14–18.

Dubek, Laura. "Rewriting Male Scripts: Willa Cather and *The Song of the Lark*." *Women's Studies* 23 (1994): 293–306.

Hallgarth, Susan A. "The Women Who Would Be an Artist in *The Song of the Lark* and *The Professor's House*." In *Willa Cather: Family, Community, and History*. Edited by John J. Murphy, Linda Hunter Adams, and Paul Rawlins. Provo, UT: Brigham Young University Humanities Publishing Center, 1990. 169–73.

Shively, Steven B. "'A Full, Perfect, and Sufficient Sacrifice': Eucharistic Imagery in Cather's *The Song of the Lark*." *Literature and Belief* 14 (1994): 73–86.

MY ÁNTONIA (1918)

REVIEWS

Mencken, H. L. "Mainly Fiction." *Smart Set* 58 (March 1919): 140–41.

———. "Sunrise on the Prairie: VII." *Smart Set* 58 (February 1919): 143–44.

New York Times Book Review 6 October 1918: 429.

"Two Portraits." *The Nation* 107 (2 November 1918): 522–23.

CRITICISM

Adams, Timothy Dow. "My Gay *Ántonia*: The Politics of Willa Cather's Lesbianism." In *Historical, Literary, and Erotic Aspects of Lesbianism*. Edited by Monika Kehoe. New York: Harrington Park Press, 1986. 89–98.

Fetterley, Judith. "*My Ántonia*, Jim Burden and the Dilemma of the Lesbian Writer. " In *Gender Studies: New Directions in Feminist Criticism*. Edited by Judith Spector. Bowling Green, OH: Bowling Green State University Popular Press, 1986. 43–59.

Gelfant, Blanche H. "The Forgotten Reaping Hook: Sex in My *Ántonia*." *American Literature* 43 (1971): 60–82. Rpt. in *Critical Essays on Willa Cather*. Edited by John J. Murphy. Boston: G. K. Hall, 1984. 147–64.

Goggans, Jan. "Social (Re)Visioning in the Fields of My *Ántonia*." *Cather Studies* 5 (2003): 153–72.

Hoffman, Karen A. "Identity Crossings and the Autobiographical Act in Willa Cather's My *Ántonia*." *Arizona Quarterly* 58 (2002): 25–50.

Holmes, Catherine D. "Jim Burden's Lost Worlds: Exile in My *Ántonia*." *Twentieth Century Literature* 45 (1999): 336–46.

Lambert, Deborah G. "The Defeat of a Hero: Autonomy and Sexuality in My *Ántonia*." *American Literature* 53 (1982). Rpt. in *Willa Cather's* My *Ántonia*. Edited by Harold Bloom. Philadelphia: Chelsea House, 1987. 119–31.

Lucenti, Lisa Marie. "Willa Cather's My Ántonia: Haunting the Houses of Memory." *Twentieth Century Literature* 46 (2000): 193–213.

McElhiney, Annette Bennington. "Willa Cather's Use of a Tripartite Point of View in My Ántonia." *The CEA Critic* 56 (1993): 65–76.

Prchal, Tim. "The Bohemian Paradox: My Ántonia and Popular Images of Czech Immigrants." *MELUS* 29 (2004): 3–25.

Shively, Steven B. "My Ántonia and the Parables of Sacrifice." *Literature and Belief* 22 (2002): 51–62.

Woolley, Paula. "'Fire and Wit': Storytelling and the America Artist in Cather's My Ántonia." *Cather Studies* 3 (1996): 134–81.

THE PROFESSOR'S HOUSE (1925)

REVIEWS

Butcher, Fanny. "Willa Cather Tells Purpose of New Novel." *Chicago Tribune* 12 September 1925: 9.

Canby, Henry Seidel. "A Novel of the Soul." *Saturday Review of Literature* 2 (26 September 1925): 151.

Gibbs, A. Hamilton. "Contamination of Rewards: Willa Cather's Portrait of a Professor to Whom Success Was Extinction." *New York Evening Post, The Literary Review* 5 September 1925: 1.

Sherman, Stuart P. "Willa Cather." *New York Herald Tribune Books* 13 September 1925: 1–3.

"Willa Cather's *The Professor's House* among New Novels." *New York Times Book Review* 6 September 1925: 8.

CRITICISM

Charles, Sister Peter Damian. "*The Professor's House*: An Abode of Love and Death." *Colby Literary Quarterly* 8 (1968): 70–82.

Grumbach, Doris. "A Study of the Small Room in *The Professor's House*." *Women's Studies* 11 (1984): 327–45.

Hilgart, John. "Death Comes for the Aesthete: Commodity Culture and the Artifact in Cather's *The Professor's House*." *Studies in the Novel* 30 (1998): 377–404.

Karush, Deborah. "Bringing Outland Inland in *The Professor's House*: Willa Cather's Domestication of Empire." *Cather Studies* 4 (1999): 144–71.

Kot, Paula. "Speculation, Tourism, and *The Professor's House*." *Twentieth Century Literature* 48 (2002): 393–426.

Leddy, Michael. "'Distant and Correct': The Double Life and *The Professor's House*." *Cather Studies* 3 (1996): 182–96.

Lucenti, Lisa Marie. "Willa Cather's *The Professor's House*: Sleeping with the Dead." *Texas Studies in Literature and Language* 41 (1999): 236–61.

Mosley, Ann. "Spatial Structures and Forms in *The Professor's House*." *Cather Studies* 3 (1996): 197–211.

Murphy, John J. "Holy Cities, Poor Savages, and the Science Culture: Positioning in *The Professor's House*." In *Willa Cather and the American Southwest*. Edited by John N. Swift and Joseph R. Urgo. Lincoln: University of Nebraska Press, 2002. 55–68.

Schwind, Jean. "This Is a Frame-Up: Mother Eve in *The Professor's House*." *Cather Studies* 2 (1993): 72–91.

Stout, Janis P. "Autobiography as Journey in *The Professor's House*." *Studies in American Fiction* 19 (1991): 203–15.

Wallace, Honor McKitrick. "'An Orgy of Acquisition': The Female Consumer, Infidelity, and Commodity Culture in *A Lost Lady* and *The Professor's House*." In *Willa Cather and Material Culture: Real World Writing, Writing the Real World*. Edited by Janis P. Stout. Tuscaloosa: University of Alabama Press, 2004. 144–55.

Wilson, Sarah. "'Fragmentary and Inconclusive' Violence: National History and Literary Form in *The Professor's House*." *American Literature* 75 (2003): 571–99.

DEATH COMES FOR THE ARCHBISHOP (1927)

REVIEWS

Ballou, Robert O. "The Story of the West Which Willa Cather Sees." *Chicago Daily News* 7 September 1927: 14.

Butcher, Fanny. "Willa Cather's New Novel Is Simply, Beautifully Told." *Chicago Daily Tribune* 3 September 1927: 8.

Dodd, Lee Wilson. "A Hymn to Spiritual Beauty." *Saturday Review of Literature* 4 (10 September 1927): 101.

Krutch, Joseph Wood. "The Pathos of Distance." *The Nation* 125 (12 October 1927): 390.

Lovett, Robert Morss. "A Death in the Desert." *New Republic* 52 (26 October 1927): 266–67.

Stuart, Henry Longan. "A Vivid Page of History in Miss Cather's New Novel." *New York Times Book Review* 4 September 1927: 2.

West, Rebecca. "Miss Cather's Business as an Artist." *New York Herald Tribune Books* 11 September 1927: 1, 5–6.

CRITICISM

Birns, Nicholas. "Building the Cathedral: Imagination, Christianity, and Progress in Willa Cather's *Death Comes for the Archbishop*." *Religion and the Arts* 3 (1999): 1–19.

Kuhlken, Pam Fox. "Hallowed Ground: Landscape as Hagiography in Willa Cather's *Death Comes for the Archbishop*." *Christianity and Literature* 52 (2003): 367–85.

Reynolds, Guy. "The Ideology of Cather's Catholic Progressivism: *Death Comes for the Archbishop*." *Cather Studies* 3 (1996): 1–30.

Skaggs, Merrill Maguire. "*Death Comes for the Archbishop*: Willa Cather's Varieties of Religious Experience." *Literature and Belief* 22 (2002): 101–21.

———. "Willa Cather's *Death Comes for the Archbishop* and William Faulkner's *The Sound and the Fury*." *Faulkner Journal* 13 (1997–1998): 89–99.

Smith, Patricia Clark. "Achaeans, Americanos, Prelates and Monsters: Willa Cather's *Death Comes for the Archbishop* as a New World Odyssey." In *Padre Martinez: New Perspectives from Taos*. Edited by E. A. Mares. Taos, NM: Millicent Rogers Museum, 1998. 101–24.

Wilson, Sarah. "Material Objects as Sites of Cultural Mediation in *Death Comes for the Archbishop*." In *Willa Cather and Material Culture: Real World Writing, Writing the Real World*. Edited by Janis P. Stout. Tuscaloosa: University of Alabama Press, 2004. 171–87.

SHADOWS ON THE ROCK (1931)

REVIEWS

Chamberlain, John. "Willa Cather's Tale of Canada." *New York Times Book Review* 2 August 1931: 1.

C[oates], R[obert] M. "The Art of Willa Cather." *New Yorker* 7 (15 August 1931): 49–50.

Cross, Wilbur. "Men and Images." *Saturday Review of Literature* 8 (22 August 1931): 67–68.

Harris, William E. "Willa Cather and *Shadows on the Rock*." *Boston Evening Transcript* 1 August 1931: 8.

Hawkins, Ethel Wallace. "The Atlantic Bookshelf." *Atlantic Monthly* 148 (August 1931): 8, 10.

"Home-Grown Parnassian." *Time* 18 (3 August 1931): 47–48.

Kaufman, Kenneth C. *Southwest Review* 16 (Summer 1931): xi–xiii.

Robbins, Frances Lamont. "Three Novels by Women." *Outlook and Independent* 158 (5 August 1931): 440.

Van Doren, Carl. "Willa Cather's New Chronicle of Virtue." *New York Herald Tribune Books* 2 August 1931: 1.

CRITICISM

Funda, Evelyn I. "New World Epiphany Stories: Transformation and Community-Building in *Shadows on the Rock*." *Literature and Belief* 22 (2002): 169–201.

Moseley, Ann. "'The Hero Within': Heroic Archetypes in *Shadows on the Rock*." *Cather Studies* 4 (1999): 97–117.

Murphy, John J. "Willa Cather's City of God: *Shadows on the Rock*." *Literature and Belief* 15(1995): 119–35.

Rosowski, Susan J. "Willa Cather's Magnificat: Matriarchal Christianity in *Shadows on the Rock*." *Literature and Belief* 8 (1988): 66–75.

Skaggs, Merrill Maguire. "A Good Girl in Her Place: Cather's *Shadows on the Rock*." *Religion and Literature* 17 (1985): 27–36.

RELATED SECONDARY SOURCES

Appignanesi, Richard, and Chris Garratt. *Introducing Postmodernism*. New York: Totem Books, 1995.

Berger, Arthur Asa. *Cultural Criticism: A Primer of Key Concepts*. Foundations of Popular Culture, 4. Thousand Oaks, CA: Sage Publications. 1995.

Fitzgerald, F. Scott. *A Life in Letters*. Edited by Matthew J. Bruccoli. New York: Simon & Schuster, 1994; Touchstone Edition, 1995.

Lynn, Kenneth. *Hemingway*. New York: Simon & Schuster, 1987.

Marx. Leo. *The Machine in the Garden: Technology and the Pastoral Ideal in America*. 1964; rpt. London: Oxford University Press, 1973.

Richter, David H., ed. *The Critical Tradition: Classic Texts and Contemporary Trends*. New York: St. Martin's Press, 1989.

Showalter, Elaine. "The Feminist Critical Revolution." In *The New Feminist Criticism: Essays on Women, Literature, and Theory*. Edited by Elaine Showalter. London: Virago Press, 1986. 3–17.

———. "Toward a Feminist Poetics." In *The New Feminist Criticism: Essays on Women, Literature, and Theory*. Edited by Elaine Showalter. London: Virago Press, 1986. 125–43.

Singal, Daniel Joseph. "Towards a Definition of American Modernism." *American Quarterly* 39 (1987): 7–26.

Smith-Rosenberg, Carroll. "The New Woman as Androgyne: Social Disorder and Gender Crisis, 1870–1936." In *Disorderly Conduct: Visions of Gender in Victorian America*. New York: Alfred A. Knopf, 1985; rpt. Oxford University Press, 1986. 245–96.

Index

About the Author

Linda De Roche is Professor of English and American Studies at Wesley College in Dover, Delaware. A specialist in American literature and a former Fulbright scholar, she has published *Student Companion to F. Scott Fitzgerald* (Greenwood 2000) and studies of Mary Higgins Clark and Erich Segal for Greenwood's Student Companions to Popular Contemporary Writers Series as well as articles on Gail Godwin and Fitzgerald.

Recent Titles in
Student Companions to Classic Writers